# ANGULAR
# AND
# DEEP LEARNING
## *Pocket Primer*

# ANGULAR
# AND
# DEEP LEARNING
## *Pocket Primer*

### Oswald Campesato

## MERCURY LEARNING AND INFORMATION
*Dulles, Virginia*
*Boston, Massachusetts*
*New Delhi*

Publisher: David Pallai
Mercury Learning and Information
22841 Quicksilver Drive
Dulles, VA 20166
info@merclearning.com
www.merclearning.com
(800) 232-0223

O. Campesato. *Angular and Deep Learning Pocket Primer.*
ISBN: 978-1-68392-473-9

The publisher recognizes and respects all marks used by companies, manufacturers, and developers as a means to distinguish their products. All brand names and product names mentioned in this book are trademarks or service marks of their respective companies. Any omission or misuse (of any kind) of service marks or trademarks, etc. is not an attempt to infringe on the property of others.

Library of Congress Control Number: 2020946795

202122 321 Printed on acid-free paper in the United States of America.

Our titles are available for adoption, license, or bulk purchase by institutions, corporations, etc. For additional information, please contact the Customer Service Dept. at (800) 232-0223(toll free).

Digital versions of our titles are available at: www.academiccourseware.com and other electronic vendors. *Companion files are available from the publisher by writing to info@merclearning.com.*

*I'd like to dedicate this book to my parents –
may this bring joy and happiness into their lives.*

# CONTENTS

# PREFACE

## What is The Goal?

The goal of this book is to introduce Web developers to deep learning and incorporate that knowledge in Angular 10 applications. This book is intended to be a fast-paced introduction to some basic features of deep learning and an overview of several popular deep learning classifiers and code samples.

This book will also save you the time required to search for code samples, which is a potentially time-consuming process. In any case, if you're not sure whether or not you can absorb the material in this book, glance through the code samples to get a feel for the level of complexity.

At the risk of stating the obvious, please keep in mind the following point: *you will not become an expert in deep learning or Angular 10 by reading this book.*

## What Will I Learn from This Book?

The first three chapters contain a short tour of basic Angular functionality, such as UI components and forms in Angular applications. The fourth chapter introduces you to concepts that you will encounter in deep learning, such as perceptrons, hyperparameters, activation functions, loss functions, and optimizers. Then you will learn about MLPs (Multi Layer Perceptrons) and CNNs (Convolutional Neural Networks). The fifth chapter discusses RNNs (Recurrent Neural Networks), LSTMs (Long Short-Term Memory), GRUs (Gated Recurrent Units), autoencoders, and GANs (Generative Adversarial Networks).

The sixth chapter introduces some preliminary TensorFlow concepts and a short introduction to TensorFlow.js (i.e., TensorFlow in modern browsers), followed by an example of Angular with TensorFlow.js and machine learning. The final portion of this chapter contains an example of Angular with TensorFlow.js and deep learning that involves the MNIST dataset. The appendices contain an introduction to Keras and TensorFlow 2, along with some basic code samples.

Another point: although Jupyter is popular, all the code samples in this book are Python scripts. However, you can quickly learn about the useful features Jupyter through various online tutorials. In addition, it's worth looking at Google Colaboratory that is entirely online and is based on Jupyter notebooks, along with free GPU usage.

## How Much Keras Knowledge is Needed for this Book?

Some exposure to Keras is helpful, and you can read the appendix if Keras is new to you. The Keras-related code samples involve the XOR function, the MNIST dataset, CNNs, and RNNs. In most cases the code samples involve some understanding of activation functions, optimizers, and loss functions, all of which are discussed in Chapter 5.

Please keep in mind that Keras is well-integrated into TensorFlow 2 (in the tf.keras namespace), and it provides a layer of abstraction over "pure" TensorFlow that will enable you to develop prototypes more quickly.

## Do I Need to Learn the Theory Portions of this Book?

Once again, the answer depends on the extent to which you plan to become involved in Deep Learning. In addition to creating a model, you will use various algorithms to see which ones provide the level of accuracy (or some other metric) that you need for your project. If you fall short, the theoretical aspects of Deep Learning can help you perform a "forensic" analysis of your model and your data, and ideally assist in determining how to improve your model.

## How were the Code Samples Created?

The code samples in this book were created and tested using Python 3 and Keras that's built into TensorFlow 2 on a MacBook Pro. Regarding their content: the code samples are derived primarily from the author for his Deep Learning and Keras graduate course. In some cases, there are code samples that incorporate short sections of code from discussions in online forums. The key point to remember is that the code samples follow the "Four Cs": they must be Clear, Concise, Complete, and Correct to the extent that it's possible to do so, given the size of this book.

## Launching the Code Samples: Please Read

Since the complete code samples requires more than 10GB of disk space, which is greater than the capacity of a DVD, all the `node_modules` sub-directories have been deleted. Hence, you need to run the following command from the top-level directory of each Angular application:

```
npm install
```

The version numbers for the Angular CLI and NodeJS are displayed in the section "Installing the Angular CLI" in Chapter 1, and they are displayed below for your convenience (note the version numbers for Angular and Node):

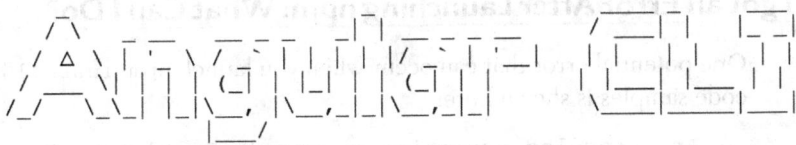

```
Angular CLI: 10.1.0-next.5
Node: 12.0.0
OS: darwin x64

Angular:
...
Ivy Workspace:

Package                            Version
----------------------------------------------------------
@angular-devkit/architect          0.1001.0-next.5
@angular-devkit/core               10.1.0-next.5
@angular-devkit/schematics         10.1.0-next.5
@schematics/angular                10.1.0-next.5
@schematics/update                 0.1001.0-next.5
rxjs                               6.6.2
```

You might have different versions of the Angular CLI and Node, and if they are close to the version numbers displayed above, they will probably work as well.

Another point to keep in mind: several code samples in Chapter 3 were created with an additional manual invocation of npm, which means that the file package.json is slightly different in those directories. Therefore, do not copy package.json from one code sample to other code samples.

In the event that you do overwrite package.json with another copy of this file, the code samples that involve the extra command line invocation will have the following comment in app.component.ts, which is shown in bold to make sure that you notice this comment:

**// remember: npm install jquery --save**

If the file app.component.ts does not have this type of comment line, then you only need to invoke npm install once from the command line.

## I got an Error After Launching npm: What Can I Do?

One potential error that can occur when you launch npm install in the code samples is shown here:

```
An unhandled exception occurred: Could not find mod-
ule "@angular-devkit/build-angular.
```

The first step involves removing the file package-lock.json:

```
rm package-lock.json
```

The second step is to install the package (introduced in Angular 6) listed in the preceding error message as a dependency, which involves the following command:

```
npm install --save-dev @angular-devkit/build-angular
```

The third step involves the standard npm invocation:

```
npm install
```

There are other errors that can occur for various reasons (such as different versions of the Angular CLI), and in those situations perform an Internet search and there's a good chance that someone else has encountered the same error, along with a solution for that error.

## What are the Technical Prerequisites for This Book?

For the deep learning portion of this book, some familiarity with basic Python is helpful, and also an understanding of how to launch Python code from the command line (in a Unix-like environment for Mac users). In addition, a general familiarity with basic linear algebra (vectors and matrices), probability/statistics (mean, median, standard deviation) and rudimentary concepts in calculus (such as derivatives) will sometimes be helpful for the material in this book.

Regarding the Angular aspect of this book, you need some familiarity with TypeScript as well as RxJS and Observables. Since RxJS is a JavaScript-based implementation of FRP (Functional Reactive Programming), some knowledge of the latter would be especially useful.

One other prerequisite is important for understanding the code samples in the second half of this book: some familiarity with neural networks, which includes the concept of hidden layers and activation functions (even if you don't fully understand them).

## What are the Non-Technical Prerequisites for This Book?

Although the answer to this question is more difficult to quantify, it's very important to have strong desire to learn about deep learning, along with the motivation and discipline to read and understand the code samples. Even simple machine language APIs can be a challenge to understand them the first time you encounter them, so be prepared to read the code samples several times.

Since you are probably a developer, you also know how to get additional help using online resources, such as documentation when you don't understand a specific detail, or stackoverflow when you encounter an error in your code.

## How do I Set up a Command Shell?

If you are a Mac user, there are three ways to do so. The first method is to use Finder to navigate to Applications > Utilities and then double click on the Utilities application. Next, if you already have a command shell available, you can launch a new command shell by typing the following command:

```
open /Applications/Utilities/Terminal.app
```

A second method for Mac users is to open a new command shell on a MacBook from a command shell that is already visible simply by clicking command+n in that command shell, and your Mac will launch another command shell.

If you are a PC user, you can install Cygwin (open source *https://cygwin.com/*) that simulates bash commands or use another toolkit such as MKS (a commercial product). Please read the online documentation that describes the download and installation process. Note that custom aliases are not automatically set if they are defined in a file other than the main start-up file (such as .bash_login).

## Companion Files

All the code samples and figures in this book may be obtained by writing to the publisher at info@merclearning.com.

## What are the "Next Steps" After Finishing This Book?

The answer to this question varies widely, mainly because the answer depends heavily on your objectives. If you are interested primarily in Angular, then you can learn more advanced Angular features that you can incorporate in new Angular applications.

If you are primarily interested in deep learning, there are many resources available, and you can perform an Internet search for those resources. The aspects of deep learning for you to learn depend on who you are: the needs of a deep learning engineer, data scientist, manager, student, or software developer are all different.

O. Campesato
October 2020

# QUICK INTRODUCTION TO ANGULAR

This chapter provides a fast introduction to Angular-based applications. While many of the code samples are straightforward, please keep in mind that you need to invest additional time and effort to acquire a deeper understanding of Angular. Although some of fine-grained details are discussed, you need to consult the online documentation to gain a thorough understanding of the features of Angular.

The purpose of the code samples in this book is to illustrate some fundamental features of Angular, and later you will learn about deep learning concepts that will enable you to incorporate deep learning in Angular applications.

Another important factor is your learning style: you might prefer to read the details regarding the "scaffolding" for Angular applications before you delve into the first code sample. However, it's perfectly acceptable to skim the introductory portion of this chapter, quickly "get into the weeds" with the Angular sample code, and afterward review the initial portion again.

The first part of this chapter discusses the design goals of Angular and various features, such as components, modules, and one-way data binding. The second part of this chapter discusses the Angular CLI, which is a command-line tool for generating Angular applications.

**NOTE** *The Angular applications in this book are based on Angular 10, using the ng command line utility for creating Angular applications.*

There are several points to keep in mind before you read this book. First, the code samples highlight basic coding techniques in Angular applications. Hence, you will not find highly detailed descriptions of Angular concepts, design goals, and architecture that are available in 600-page books. However, you can fill in some of those gaps via online articles.

You can learn Angular concepts in the various applications without having previous experience with Angular, but some knowledge of Angular would be helpful.

This chapter contains Angular applications for generating SVG-based graphics and D3-based animation effects. Due to space constraints, this chapter does not contain an introduction to SVG or D3. Fortunately, there are many online tutorials that provide detailed information regarding the features of SVG and D3. If you are not interested in either of these technologies, feel free to skip the associated code samples with no loss of continuity (and you can always return to them later).

## What You Need to Understand for Angular Applications

Two important technologies in Angular are TypeScript and RxJS. In very casual terms, TypeScript might remind you of combining JavaScript with a classical object-oriented approach. If you are already familiar with Java, you will probably be more comfortable with TypeScript than JavaScript.

RxJS is JavaScript-based FRP (Functional Reactive Programming) that supports many intermediate operators, such as `filter()`, `map()`, `take()`, and many other useful operators. The following subsections contain some additional detail regarding TypeScript and RxJS.

### Learn TypeScript

Knowledge of TypeScript is highly recommended, along with a basic proficiency in NodeJS (i.e., the npm utility) and ES6. The Angular applications have been created with node v6.14.7 and npm 12.0.0, but it's likely that slightly lower versions will work as well. Determine the version on your machine with the following commands in a terminal:

```
node -v
npm -v
```

If necessary, navigate to the NodeJS home page to download a more recent version of the node executable. If you have not worked with Node, you can find many online tutorials that explain how to use basic npm commands.

The code samples also involve basic concepts about ES6 and TypeScript, and their respective home pages contain plenty of information to help you get started. In particular, learn about classes and template strings. As you will see in subsequent chapters, Angular applications rely heavily on dynamic templates, which frequently involve interpolation (via the "{{}}" syntax) of variables. In addition, the following website provides an online "playground," along with links for documentation and code samples about TypeScript:

*https://www.typescriptlang.org/play/*

Angular takes advantage of ES6 features, such as components and classes, as well as features that are part of TypeScript, such as annotations and its type system. TypeScript is preferred over ES6 because TypeScript supports all the features of ES6, and TypeScript provides an optional type inferencing system that can catch many errors for you.

## Learn RxJS and Observables

If you have worked with ES6, then you probably know about functions such as the `filter()` function (which is handy for Angular `Pipes`), and also the `map()` function (often used with `Observables` and HTTP requests in earlier versions of Angular). Other functions, such as `merge()` and `flatten()`, can also be useful, and you can learn about them and other functions on an as-needed basis.

In RxJS, these functions are called "intermediate operators," and you will frequently encounter them in RxJS `Observables`. In highly simplified terms, you can define an `Observable` involving one or more intermediate operators, and then invoke the `Observable` via a so-called "terminal operator."

Different languages can support different methods as terminal operators, and in the case of RxJS, the `subscribe()` method is a terminal operator. RxJS `Observables` are more powerful than `Promises`, and knowledge of the latter will simplify your transition to RxJS `Observables`. After you learn the basic features of RxJS, the following (more advanced) article contains very good information regarding the RxJS `unsubscribe()` method:

*https://blog.bitsrc.io/6-ways-to-unsubscribe-from-observables-in-angular-ab912819a78f*

## Promises versus Observables

Chapters 2 and 3 have examples of Angular applications that involve `Observables`. Although you can find online code samples that use `Promises`,

Angular with TypeScript favors Observables. While this book does not provide tutorial-like information regarding Observables (or Promises), you can learn about the advantages of Observables over Promises here:

*https://www.syncfusion.com/blogs/post/angular-promises-versus-observables.aspx*

There are many other online tutorials available regarding Observables, and if necessary, you can read them on an as-needed basis in parallel with the code samples in the next two chapters. Fortunately, the code samples involve only a few features of Observables, so you do not need to become highly proficient with Observables for this book.

You can develop Angular applications in Electron, Webstorm, and Visual Studio Code. Check their respective websites for pricing and feature support.

## A High-Level View of Angular

Angular was designed as a platform that supports Angular applications in a browser and provides support for server-side rendering and Angular applications on mobile devices. Rendering Angular applications in browsers is the focus of the chapters in this book. Angular Universal (aka server-side rendering) is not discussed in this book, but in essence, server-side rendering creates the "first view" of an Angular application on a server instead of a browser. Since browsers do not need to construct this view, they can render a view more quickly and create a faster perceived load time. Angular applications on mobile devices are also outside the scope of this book.

Angular supports the most recent versions of Chrome and Firefox, as well as the two most recent versions of Edge, iOS, and Safari. The full list of supported browsers by the Angular framework is here:

*https://angular.io/guide/browser-support*

### A Short List of Features

Angular has a component-based architecture, where components are organized in a tree-like structure (the same is true of Angular modules). Angular also supports powerful technologies that you will learn in order to become proficient in writing Angular applications. Some of the important features of Angular are listed here:

- one-way data binding
- "tree shaking"

- change detection
- style encapsulation

The first two features are briefly discussed below and you should consult the online documentation regarding style encapsulation.

### One-way Data Binding in Angular

Angular provides declarative one-way binding as the default behavior (but you can switch to two-way binding if you wish to do so). One-way binding acts as a unidirectional change propagation that provides an improvement in performance as well as a reduction in code complexity. Angular also supports stateful, reactive, and immutable models. The meaning of the previous statement will become clearer as you work with Angular applications.

Angular applications involve defining a top-level ("root") module that references a `Component` that in turn specifies an HTML element (via a mandatory `selector` property) that is the "parent" element of the `Component`. The definition of the `Component` involves a so-called "decorator" that contains a `selector` property and also a `template` property (or a `templateUrl` property).

The `template` property contains a mixture of HTML and custom mark-up that you can place in a separate file and then reference that file via the `templateUrl` property. In addition, the `Component` is immediately followed by a TypeScript class definition that contains "backing code" that is associated with component-related variables that appear in the `template` property. These details will become much clearer after you have worked with some Angular applications.

**NOTE**  *The `templateUrl` property and `styleUrls` property refer to files whereas the `template` property and `styles` property refer to inline code.*

### New Features in Angular 10

Angular 10 introduces new features and also deprecates some earlier features. It provides improved performance and a reduced application size. Some of the main differentiating features in Angular 10 are listed here:

- New Date Range Picker
- The Ivy Renderer
- Language Service
- Localization
- TypeScript 3.9
- The --strict Option

In brief, the new date range picker is available in Angular Material, along with some relatively minor changes to other features. The Ivy renderer provides the improvements in terms of increased performance and reduced application size.

Angular 10 was released in June 2020 and supports TypeScript 3.9. Since TypeScript 4.0 was released in August 2020, perhaps this version (or an even new version) will be supported in Angular 11. In case you're interested, you can learn about TypeScript 4.0 here:

*https://devblogs.microsoft.com/typescript/announcing-typescript-4-0/*

One other important change in Angular 10 is its support for the --strict option for the ng command line utility that performs stricter type checking in your custom code. For instance, the following snippet compiles successfully without the --strict option:

```
employees = [];
```

However, if you create an Angular application with the --strict option, then the following code snippet is required because the previous snippet is invalid:

```
employees : any;
```

These (and other) differences are noted in the Angular 10 applications in this chapter that were created with the --strict option. Keep in mind that the Angular 10 applications in all other chapters were created without the --strict option.

## The node and npm Utilities for Angular 10

If you do not have the node utility (which also contains the npm utility) on your machine, download the distribution from this link:

*https://www.npmjs.com/get-npm*

**Important:** Angular 10 requires a version of the node executable whose version number is in the following range (which is specified in package.json):

```
"node": ">=10.9.0 <13.0.0"
```

All the Angular applications in this book were created with the following version of the npm and node utilities (the version of ng is displayed later in this chapter):

```
$ npm --version
6.14.7
```

```
$ node --version
v12.0.0
```

After this book goes to print, it's possible that higher versions of node and npm will be compatible with Angular 10 applications: the range of version numbers for node are available in the file package.json.

## A High-Level View of Angular Applications

Angular applications consist of a combination of built-in components and custom components (the latter are written by you), each of which is typically defined in a separate TypeScript file (with a ts extension). Each component uses one or more import statements to include its dependencies.

There are various types of dependencies available in Angular, such as directives and pipes. A *custom directive* is essentially the contents of a TypeScript file that defines a component. Thus, a custom directive consists of import statements, a Component decorator, and an exported TypeScript class.

Angular provides *built-in directives*, such as *ngIf (for "if" logic) and *ngFor (for loops). These two directives are also called "structural directives" because they modify the content of an HTML page. Angular *built-in pipes* include date and numeric (currency, decimal, number, and percent) formats, whereas *custom pipes* are defined by you.

In addition, TypeScript classes use a *decorator* (which is a built-in function) that provides metadata to a class, its members, or its method arguments. Decorators are easy to identify because they always have an @ prefix. Angular provides a number of built-in decorators, such as @Component and @NgModule.

This concludes the high-level introduction to Angular features. The next portion of this chapter introduces the Angular CLI, which is used throughout this book to create Angular applications.

## The Angular CLI

The ng utility is an Angular command-line utility for creating (via ng new) Angular applications and for launching (via ng serve) Angular applications. The Angular CLI is the official Angular application generator from Google. The ng utility generates complete Angular applications, which includes test-related code, and (by default) launches npm install to install the required files in `node_modules`. A concise set of examples for the Angular CLI is here:

`cli.angular.io`

The Angular CLI generates a configuration file called `package.json` to manage the "core" dependencies and their version numbers. After generating an Angular application, navigate to the `node_modules` subdirectory, and you will see an assortment of Angular subdirectories that contain files that are required for Angular applications.

## Installing the Angular CLI

If you do not have the `ng` utility already installed on your machine, you can download the latest version of Angular here:

*https://github.com/angular/angular/releases*

If you already have the `ng` utility installed on your machine, you can perform an upgrade to Angular 10 from an earlier release of Angular as follows:

`ng update @angular/cli @angular/core`

The `ng` utility has many useful options, and you can find detailed information regarding the `ng` utility here:

*https://angular.io/cli*

If you encounter issues during the creation of Angular 10 applications, you might also need to uninstall an older version of the CLI and install the latest version of the CLI. You can uninstall an older version with this command:

```
sudo npm uninstall -g angular-cli
npm cache clean
```

Next, install the new CLI with this command (note the new package name):

```
[sudo] npm install -g @angular/cli
```

The preceding command installs the `ng` executable, whose location you can find via the following command:

```
which ng
```

If the preceding command displays a blank line, that means that the directory that contains the ng executable is not included in the PATH environment variable. In this case, type the following command in a command shell:

```
export PATH=/Users/owner/.npm-global/bin:$PATH
```

Note that preceding command is valid for Mac OS X, Linux, bash, ksh, zsh, and any other Unix shells that are derived from the Bourne shell. If you are using Windows or a BSD-like shell, search online to find the correct syntax for the preceding command for your system.

Now display the versions of the various components of the CLI by invoking the following command in a command shell:

```
ng -version
```

As this book goes to print, the output of the preceding command is something similar to what is shown below (version numbers might be slightly different for you):

```
Angular CLI: 10.1.0-next.5
Node: 12.0.0
OS: darwin x64

Angular:
...
Ivy Workspace:

Package                         Version
-----------------------------------------------------
@angular-devkit/architect       0.1001.0-next.5
@angular-devkit/core            10.1.0-next.5
@angular-devkit/schematics      10.1.0-next.5
@schematics/angular             10.1.0-next.5
@schematics/update              0.1001.0-next.5
rxjs                            6.6.2
```

## Features of the Angular CLI (optional)

Although this section contains useful information, you don't need these details in order to create an Angular application (which you already did in the previous section). After you have created some basic Angular applications and you want to incorporate additional functionality, you can return to this section and read about the Angular CLI options.

In order to see the various options of the ng executable, type the following command from a command shell (make sure that your PATH environment variable has been set correctly, as discussed in a previous section):

```
$ ng help
```

Available Commands:

- add: Adds support for an external library to your project
- analytics: Configures the gathering of Angular CLI usage metrics. See *https://angular.io/cli/usage-analytics-gathering*
- build (b): Compiles an Angular app into an output directory named dist/ at the given output path. Must be executed from within a workspace directory.
- deploy: Invokes the deploy builder for a specified project or for the default project in the workspace
- config: Retrieves or sets Angular configuration values in the **angular.json** file for the workspace
- doc (d): Opens the official Angular documentation (angular.io) in a browser, and searches for a given keyword
- e2e (e): Builds and serves an Angular app, then runs end-to-end tests using Protractor
- generate (g): Generates and/or modifies files based on a schematic
- help: Lists available commands and their short descriptions
- lint (l): Runs linting tools on Angular app code in a given project folder
- new (n): Creates a new workspace and an initial Angular app
- run: Runs an Architect target with an optional custom builder configuration defined in your project
- serve (s): Builds and serves your app, rebuilding on file changes
- test (t): Runs unit tests in a project
- update: Updates your application and its dependencies
- Sio/version(v): Outputs Angular CLI version
- xi18n (i18n-extract): Extracts i18n messages from source code

For more detailed help, type `ng [command name] -help`.

The `ng g` option is equivalent to the `ng generate` option, which enables you to generate an Angular custom `Component`, an Angular `Pipe` (discussed in Chapter 5), and so forth. The `ng x18n` option extracts `i18n` messages from source code. The next section shows you an example of generating an Angular custom `Component` in an application, and the contents of the files that are automatically generated for you.

The default prefix is `app` for components (e.g., `<app-root></app-root>`), but you can specify a different prefix with this invocation:

```
ng new app-root-name -prefix abc
```

**NOTE** *Angular applications created via ng always contain the src/app directory.*

Information about upgrading the Angular CLI is here:

*https://github.com/angular/angular-cli*

Documentation for the Angular CLI is here:

*http://cli.angular.io*

Now that you have an understanding of some of the features of the `ng` utility, let's create our first Angular application, which is the topic of the next section.

## A Hello World Angular Application

As you will discover, it's possible to create many basic Angular applications with a small amount of custom code. When you are ready to create medium-sized applications, you can take advantage of the component-based nature of Angular applications in order to incrementally add new components (and modules).

Now let's create a new project called `HelloWorld` by navigating to a suitable directory on your machine and then invoking the following command:

```
ng new HelloWorld
```

In addition, Angular 10 supports the `--strict` option when creating Angular applications, an example of which is here:

```
ng new --strict HelloWorld
```

The preceding command results in stricter type checking in Angular 10 applications, which you will see later in this chapter. If you encounter difficulties when you specify the preceding command-line option, you can revert to the older style of creating Angular applications.

NOTE *Only the first three Angular 10 applications in this chapter specify the* --strict *switch when creating them via the ng utility.*

The Angular CLI provides everything except for your custom code. Second, the Angular CLI enables you to generate new components, routers, and so forth, which are possible with starter applications. Third, the Angular CLI is based purely on TypeScript, and the generated application includes the JSON files tsconfig.json, tslint.json, typedoc.json, and typings.json.

You will see the following type of output in the command shell where you launched the preceding command:

```
? Would you like to add Angular routing? No
? Which stylesheet format would you like to use? CSS
CREATE HelloWorld/README.md (1035 bytes)
CREATE HelloWorld/.editorconfig (274 bytes)
CREATE HelloWorld/.gitignore (631 bytes)
CREATE HelloWorld/angular.json (3686 bytes)
CREATE HelloWorld/package.json (1331 bytes)
CREATE HelloWorld/tsconfig.json (697 bytes)
CREATE HelloWorld/tslint.json (3205 bytes)
CREATE HelloWorld/.browserslistrc (853 bytes)
CREATE HelloWorld/karma.conf.js (1022 bytes)
CREATE HelloWorld/tsconfig.app.json (287 bytes)
CREATE HelloWorld/tsconfig.spec.json (333 bytes)
CREATE HelloWorld/src/favicon.ico (948 bytes)
CREATE HelloWorld/src/index.html (296 bytes)
CREATE HelloWorld/src/main.ts (372 bytes)
CREATE HelloWorld/src/polyfills.ts (2835 bytes)
CREATE HelloWorld/src/styles.css (80 bytes)
CREATE HelloWorld/src/test.ts (753 bytes)
CREATE HelloWorld/src/assets/.gitkeep (0 bytes)
CREATE HelloWorld/src/environments/environment.prod.ts
(51 bytes)
CREATE HelloWorld/src/environments/environment.ts
(662 bytes)
```

```
CREATE HelloWorld/src/app/app.module.ts (314 bytes)
CREATE HelloWorld/src/app/app.component.css (0 bytes)
CREATE HelloWorld/src/app/app.component.html (25725 bytes)
CREATE HelloWorld/src/app/app.component.spec.ts (952 bytes)
CREATE HelloWorld/src/app/app.component.ts (214 bytes)
CREATE HelloWorld/src/app/package.json (817 bytes)
CREATE HelloWorld/e2e/protractor.conf.js (869 bytes)
CREATE HelloWorld/e2e/tsconfig.json (294 bytes)
CREATE HelloWorld/e2e/src/app.e2e-spec.ts (643 bytes)
CREATE HelloWorld/e2e/src/app.po.ts (301 bytes)
Installing packaI...
✓ Packages installed successfully.
  Successfully initialized git.
```

Now launch the HelloWorld application by navigating into the src sub-directory of the HelloWorld application and then launching the ng command, as shown here:

**cd HelloWorld/src**
**ng serve**
```
Compiling @angular/core : es2015 as esm2015
Compiling @angular/common : es2015 as esm2015
Compiling @angular/platform-browser : es2015 as esm2015
Compiling @angular/platform-browser-dynamic : es2015 as
esm2015

chunk {main} main.js, main.js.map (main) 57.1 kB [initial]
[rendered]
chunk {polyfills} polyfills.js, polyfills.js.map (poly-
fills) 141 kB [initial] [rendered]
chunk {runtime} runtime.js, runtime.js.map (runtime)
6.15 kB [entry] [rendered]
chunk {styles} styles.js, styles.js.map (styles) 12.5 kB
[initial] [rendered]
chunk {vendor} vendor.js, vendor.js.map (vendor) 2.37 MB
[initial] [rendered]
Date: 2020-08-13T23:10:47-037Z - Hash: acec74a5d422175-701e
- Time: 21053ms
** Angular Live Development Server is listening on local-
host:4200, open your browser on http://localhost:4200/ **
: Compiled successfully.

Date: 2020-08-13T23:10:48-965Z - Hash: acec74a5d422175c701e
```

```
5 unchanged chunks
```

```
Time: 1425ms
: Compiled successfully.
```

Launch a new browser session, navigate to localhost:4200, and you will see the same contents as shown in Figure 1.1.

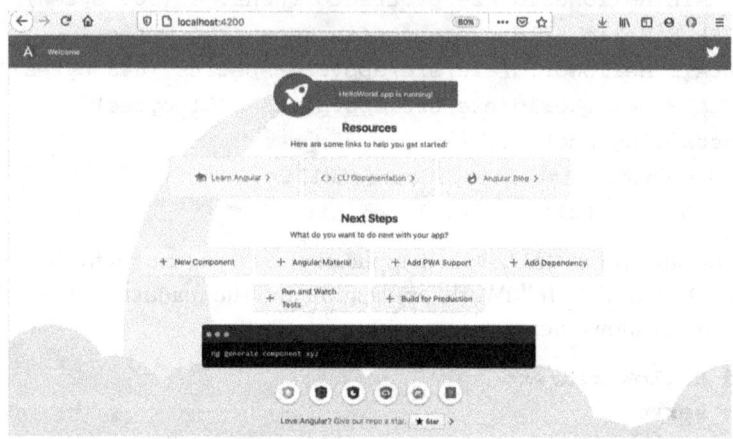

**FIGURE 1.1**   A "Hello World" Angular application

## The Anatomy of an Angular Application

The ng command that you launched in the previous section created an Angular application that contains more than 35,000 files, most of which are in the node_modules subdirectory. Fortunately, you only need to focus on a handful of files when you need to create your own Angular applications.

Here is the list of files and directories in the root directory of the HelloWorld Angular application:

```
node_modules
package-lock.json
README.md
angular.json
e2e
karma.conf.js
package.json
src
```

```
tsconfig.app.json
tsconfig.json
tsconfig.spec.json
tslint.json
```

The most relevant files are package.json and angular.json, and the most important directory for creating custom code is the src directory (all of these are shown in bold in the preceding list). In general, you do not need to modify either of these files. As you will see later in this chapter, you need to perform an extra step from the command line when you work with D3-based graphics.

## The Main Files in the src/app Subdirectory (Overview)

The src subdirectory contains a combination of subdirectories and files, as shown here:

```
app
assets
environments
favicon.ico
index.html
main.ts
polyfills.ts
styles.css
test.ts
```

Notice that the preceding list contains the TypeScript file main.ts, which will be discussed later in this chapter.

Next, the src/app subdirectory contains your custom code and the src/assets subdirectory contains other assets, such as JSON files. Later, you will see an example of an Angular application that reads the content of authors.json, which is located in the src/assets subdirectory.

The following list displays the contents of the src/app subdirectory:

```
app.component.css
app.component.html
app.component.spec.ts
app.component.ts
app.module.ts
package.json
```

Unless it's noted differently, you can delete the contents of app. component.html for every code sample in this book. The file app.

`component.ts` contains TypeScript code that is specific to your Angular application, and the file `app.module.ts` specifies any dependencies in your Angular application, which can include Angular modules as well as custom modules (you'll see examples in Chapter 3).

The three TypeScript files `main.ts`, `app.component.ts`, and `app.module.ts` are the bootstrap file, the main module, and the main component class, respectively, for Angular applications.

Here is the condensed explanation about the purpose of these three files: Angular uses `main.ts` as the initial "entry point" to bootstrap the Angular module `AppModule` (defined in `app.module.ts`), which in turn references the main component `AppComponent` (defined in `app.component.ts`), as well as any other custom components (and modules) that you have imported into `AppModule`.

## The Contents of the Three Main Files

The preceding section briefly described the sequence in which files are processed in Angular applications. The code samples this book involve custom code in the TypeScript file `app.component.ts` and sometimes involve updating the contents of the file `app.module.ts`, but there is no need to modify the file `main.ts`. The following sections display the contents of these three files and include a brief description of their contents.

### The main.ts Bootstrap File

Listing 1.1 shows the content of `main.ts` in the `src` subdirectory (not the `src/app` subdirectory) that imports and bootstraps the top-level Angular module `AppModule`. Angular applications have a component-based architecture, which might seem more complex than alternate frameworks. However, this architecture enables teams of developers to work in parallel on different parts of a complex application.

*LISTING 1.1: main.ts*

```
import { enableProdMode } from '@angular/core';
import {    platformBrowserDynamic    }    from    '@angular/
platform-browser-dynamic';

import { AppModule }    from './app/app.module';
import { environment }    from './environments/environment';
```

```
if (environment.production) {
  enableProdMode();
}


platformBrowserDynamic().bootstrapModule(AppModule)
   .catch(err => console.error(err));
```

The first line of code in Listing 1.1 is an import statement that is needed for the conditional logic later in the code listing. The second import statement appears in many Angular code samples, and it's necessary for launching Angular applications on desktops and laptops.

The third import statement involves the top-level module of Angular applications, which in turn contains all the custom components and services that are included in this Angular module. The fourth import statement contains environment-related information that is used in the next conditional logic snippet: if the current application is in production mode, the enableProdMode() function is executed.

The final line of code is the actual bootstrapping process that involves rendering the code in app.component.ts in a browser.

## The app.component.ts File

Listing 1.2 shows the content of app.component.ts, which illustrates the typical properties of an Angular application.

### LISTING 1.2: app.component.ts

```
import { Component } from '@angular/core';

@Component({
  selector:      'app-root',
  templateUrl:   './app.component.html',
  styleUrls:     ['./app.component.css']
})
export class AppComponent {
  title = 'HelloWorld';
}
```

Listing 1.2 starts with an import statement for the Angular @Component decorator in order to define metadata for the class AppComponent. At a minimum, the metadata involves two properties: selector and either template or templateUrl. Except for routing-related components, both of these properties are required in custom components. In this example, the `selector` property specifies the custom element `app-root` (which you can change) that is in the HTML Web page `index.html`.

The `templateURL` property specifies a file that contains HTML markup that is inserted in the custom element `app-root`. An alternative is the `template` property that contains the HTML markup that is inserted in the custom element `app-root`. The final line of code in Listing 1.2 is an `export` statement that makes the `AppComponent` class available for import in other TypeScript files, such as `app.module.ts`, which is shown in Listing 1.3 in the next section.

Although the property `templateUrl` specifies an HTML Web page with mark-up, the Angular code samples in this book use the `template` property to define the layout of the HTML web page for Angular applications (that's why the HTML Web page `app.component.html` in the code samples in this book is empty).

## The app.module.ts File

Listing 1.3 shows the content of `app.module.ts`, which displays the dependencies of various modules in an Angular application.

*LISTING 1.3: app.module.ts*

```
import { BrowserModule } from '@angular/platform-browser';
import { NgModule }      from '@angular/core';
import { AppComponent }  from './app.component';

@NgModule({
  declarations: [
    AppComponent
  ],
  imports: [
    BrowserModule
  ],
  providers: [],
  bootstrap: [AppComponent]
})
export class AppModule { }
```

Listing 1.3 contains `import` statements that import `BrowserModule` and `NgModule`. The third `import` statement imports the class `AppComponent` that is the top-level component illustrated in Listing 1.2 in the previous section.

*Angular dependencies always contain the "@" symbol whereas custom dependencies specify a relative path to TypeScript files.*

Next, the @NgModule decorator contains an object with various properties (discussed in the next section). These properties specify the metadata for the class AppModule that is exported in the final line of code in Listing 1.3. The metadata in AppModule involves the following array-based properties of values: imports, providers, declarations, exports, and bootstrap.

In Listing 1.3, the array properties declarations, imports, and bootstrap are non-null, whereas the providers property is an empty array. This metadata is required in order for Angular to "bootstrap" the code in AppComponent, which in turn contains the details of what is rendered (e.g., an <h1> element) and where it is rendered (e.g., the app-root element in index.html).

Now let's take a look at the contents of the HTML Web page index.html, which contains the main Web page for our Angular application.

## The index.html Web Page

Listing 1.4 shows the contents of index.html for a new Angular application that is generated from the command line via the ng utility.

### LISTING 1.4: index.html

```
<!doctype html>
<html lang="en">
<head>
  <meta charset="utf-8">
  <title>HelloWorld</title>
  <base href="/">

  <meta name="viewport" content="width=device-width,
initial-scale=1">
  <link rel="icon" type="image/x-icon" href="favicon.ico">
</head>
<body>
  <app-root></app-root>
```

```
</body>
</html>
```

Listing 1.4 is minimalistic: only the custom `<app-root>` element (which is specified in the `selector` property in `app.component.ts`) gives you an indication that this Web page is part of an Angular application.

**NOTE** *The Angular CLI automatically inserts JavaScript dependencies in index. html during the "build" of the project.*

Before we delve into the TypeScript files in an Angular application, let's take a quick detour to understand how `import` statements work in Angular applications. Feel free to skip the next section if you are already familiar with `import` and `export` statements in Angular.

## Exporting and Importing Packages and Classes (optional)

Every TypeScript class that is imported in a TypeScript file must be exported in the TypeScript file where that class is defined. You will see many examples of `import` and `export` statements: in fact, this is true of every Angular application in this book.

There are two common types of `import` statements: one type involves importing packages from Angular modules, and the other type involves importing custom classes (written by you). Here is the syntax for both types:

```
import {some-package-name} from 'some-angular-module';
import {some-class }       from 'my-custom-class';
```

Here is an example of both types of `import` statements:

```
import { NgModule }     from '@angular/core';
import {EmpComponent}   from './emp.component';
```

In the preceding code snippet, the `NgModule` package is imported from the `@angular/core` module that is located in the `node_modules` directory. The `EmpComponent` class is a custom class that is defined and exported in the TypeScript file `emp.component.ts`.

In the second `import` statement, the "`./`" prefix is required whenever a custom class is imported from a TypeScript file: notice the omission of the "`.ts`" suffix.

## Working with Components in Angular

As you have already learned, an Angular application is a tree of nested components, where the top-level component is the application. The components define the UI elements, screens, and routes. In general, organize Angular applications by placing each custom component in a TypeScript file and then import that same TypeScript file in the "main" file (which is often named `app.component.ts`) that contains the top-level component.

### The MetaData in Components

Angular components are often a combination of an `@Component` decorator and a class definition that can optionally contain a constructor. A simple example of an `@Component` decorator is here:

```
import { Component }  from '@angular/core';
import {EmpComponent} from './emp/emp.component';


@Component({
    selector:   'app-container',
    template:   '<tasks>{{message}}</tasks>',
    directives: [EmpComponent]
})
```

The preceding `@Component` decorator contains several properties, some of which are mandatory and others that are optional. Let's look at both types in the preceding code block.

The `selector` property is mandatory, and it specifies the HTML element (whether it's an existing element or a custom element) that serves as the "root" of an Angular application.

Next, the `template` property (or a `templateUrl` property) is mandatory, and it contains a mixture of markup, interpolated variables, and TypeScript code. One important detail: the template property requires "backticks" when its definition spans multiple lines. The `directives` property is an optional property that specifies an array of components that are treated as nested components. In this example, the `directives` property specifies the component `EmpComponent`, which is also imported (via an `import` statement) near the beginning of the code block. Notice that the `import` statement does not contain a "@" symbol, which means that `EmpComponent` is a custom component defined in the file `emp/emp.component.ts`.

### Stateful versus Stateless Components in Angular

In high-level terms, a *stateful* component retains information that is relevant to other parts of the same Angular application. Stateless components do not maintain the application state, nor do they request or fetch data: they are data passed via property bindings from another component (such as its parent).

The code samples in this book can be a combination of stateful components, stateless components, and sometimes also "value objects." which are instances of custom classes that "model" different entities (such as an employee, customer, student, and so forth).

There is an example of a presentational component in Chapter 2. A good article that delves into stateful and stateless components is here:

*https://toddmotto.com/stateful-stateless-components#stateful*

## Syntax, Attributes, and Properties in Angular

Angular introduced the square brackets "[]" notation for attributes and properties, as well as round parentheses "()" notation for functions that handle events. This syntax is actually valid HTML5 syntax. Here is an example of a code snippet that specifies an attribute and a function:

```
<foo [bar]= "x+1" (baz)="doSomething()">Hello World</foo>
```

An example that specifies a property and a function is here:

```
<button [disabled]="!inputIsValid" (click)="authenti-
cate()">Login </button>
```

An example of a data-related element with a custom element is here:

```
<my-chart [data]="myData" (drag)="handleDrag()"></
my-chart>
```

The new syntax in the preceding code snippet eliminates the need for many built-in directives.

### Attributes versus Properties in Angular

Keep in mind the following distinction: a property can specify a complex model, whereas an attribute can only specify a string. For example, in Angular 1.x you can write the following:

```
<my-directive foo="{{something}}"></my-directive>
```

The corresponding code in Angular (which does not require interpolation) is here:

```
<my-directive [foo]="something"></my-directive>
```

Before delving into code samples that show you how to create graphics and animation effects, let's look at the Angular lifecycle methods.

## Angular Lifecycle Methods

Angular applications have lifecycle methods that are executed in a pre-defined sequence. Hence, you can place custom code in those methods in order to handle various events (such as application start, run, and so forth). The "Lifecycle Hook" interfaces are defined in the @angular/core library, and they are listed here:

- OnInit
- OnDestroy
- DoCheck
- OnChanges
- AfterContentInit
- AfterContentChecked
- AfterViewInit
- AfterViewChecked

Each interface has a single method whose name is the interface name prefixed with ng. For example, the OnInit interface has a method named ngOnInit. Angular invokes these lifecycle methods in the following order:

- ngOnChanges: called when an input or output binding value changes
- ngOnInit: after the first ngOnChanges
- ngDoCheck: developer's custom change detection
- ngAfterContentInit: after the component content is initialized
- ngAfterContentChecked: after every check of the component's content
- ngAfterViewInit: after the component's view(s) are initialized
- ngAfterViewChecked: after every check of a component's view(s)
- ngOnDestroy: just before the directive is destroyed

Since Angular invokes the constructor of a component when that component is created, the constructor is a convenient location to initialize the state for that component. However, child components must be initialized before accessing any properties or data that is defined in those child components. In this scenario, place custom code in the `ngOnInit` lifecycle method to access data from child components.

The complete set of Angular lifecycle events is here:

*https://angular.io/docs/ts/latest/guide/lifecycle-hooks.html*

## A Simple Example of Angular Lifecycle Methods

Copy the directory `LifeCycle` from the companion files into a convenient location. Listing 1.5 shows the content of `app.component.ts`, which illustrates the sequence in which some Angular lifecycle methods are invoked.

**LISTING 1.5: *app.component.ts***

```
import {Component} from '@angular/core';

@Component({
  selector: 'app-root',
  template: '<h2>Angular Lifecycle Methods</h2>',
})
export class AppComponent{
  ngOnInit() {
    // invoked after child components are initialized
    console.log("ngOnInit");
  }
  ngOnDestroy() {
    // invoked when a component is destroyed
    console.log("ngOnDestroy");
  }
  ngDoCheck() {
    // custom change detection
    console.log("ngDoCheck");
  }
  // => without the --strict option: ngOnChanges(changes)
  ngOnChanges(changes:any) {
    console.log("ngOnChanges");
    // Invoked after bindings have been checked
    // but only if one of the bindings has changed.
    //
```

```
      // changes is an object of the format:
      // {
      //    'prop': PropertyUpdate
      // }
    }
    ngAfterContentInit() {
      // Component content has been initialized
      console.log("ngAfterContentInit");
    }
    ngAfterContentChecked() {
      // Component content has been checked
      console.log("ngAfterContentChecked");
    }
    ngAfterViewInit() {
      // Component views are initialized
      console.log("ngAfterViewInit");
    }
    ngAfterViewChecked() {
      // Component views have been checked
      console.log("ngAfterViewChecked");
    }
}
```

Listing 1.5 contains all the Angular lifecycle methods, and each method contains `console.log()` so that you can see the order in which the methods are executed.

Launch the application by navigating to the `src` subdirectory of the `LifeCycle` application, and invoke the following command:

`ng serve`

Navigate to `localhost:4200` in a Chrome session and open Chrome Inspector, after which you will see the following output in the `Console` tab:

```
ngOnInit
ngDoCheck
ngAfterContentInit
ngAfterContentChecked
ngAfterViewInit
ngAfterViewChecked
ngDoCheck
```

```
ngAfterContentChecked
ngAfterViewChecked
```

The preceding lifecycle methods are useful if you need to execute some custom code in a specific method. The next section shows you how to add CSS3 animation effects in Angular applications.

## CSS3 Animation Effects in Angular

This section enhances the code sample in an earlier section by adding a CSS3 animation effect. If you are unfamiliar with CSS3, there are many online tutorials available. If you have no interest in Angular applications with custom CSS3 code, feel free to skip this section.

Now copy the directory SimpleCSS3Anim from the companion files into a convenient location. Listing 1.6 shows the content of app.component. ts, which illustrates how to change the color of list items whenever users hover over each list item with their mouse.

*LISTING 1.6: app.component.ts*

```
import {Component} from '@angular/core';

@Component({
    selector: 'app-root',
    template: '
      <h2>Employee Information</h2>
      <ul>
        <li *ngFor="let emp of employees">
          {{emp.fname}} {{emp.lname}} lives in {{emp.city}}
        </li>
      </ul>
    ',
    styles:  ['
      @keyframes hoveritem {
          0%   {background-color: red;}
          25%  {background-color: #880;}
          50%  {background-color: #ccf;}
          100% {background-color: #f0f;}
      }
```

```
    li:hover {
        width: 50%;
        animation-name: hoveritem;
        animation-duration: 4s;
    }
  ']
})
export class AppComponent {
  // => without the --strict option: employees = [];
  employees : any;

  constructor() {
    this.employees = [
  {"fname":"Jane","lname":"Jones","city":"San Francisco"},
    {"fname":"John","lname":"Smith","city":"New York"},
    {"fname":"Dave","lname":"Stone","city":"Seattle"},
    {"fname":"Sara","lname":"Edson","city":"Chicago"}
  ];
  }
}
```

Listing 1.6 contains the `styles` property, which contains a `@keyframes` definition for creating an animation effect involving color changes. The `styles` property contains an `li:hover` selector that references the `@keyframes` definition and specifies a time duration of 4 seconds for the animation effect. The colors are specified in the `@keyframes` definition. If you have worked with CSS3 animation effects, then `@keyframes` is probably very familiar to you.

Launch the Angular application and navigate to `localhost:4200` in a browser session. When the list of names is displayed, move your mouse slowly over each name and watch how they change color. The text display is shown below, but you need to launch the application to see the color-related transformations:

**Employee Information**
- Jane Jones lives in San Francisco
- John Smith lives in New York
- Dave Stone lives in Seattle
- Sara Edson lives in Chicago

Instead of using CSS3 to perform animation effects, you can also do so via Angular functionality, which is illustrated in the next section.

## Animation Effects via the "Angular Way"

This section enhances the code in the previous section by creating an animation effect by means of Angular-specific functionality instead of CSS3-based functionality. This section also requires an understanding of how to instantiate a custom TypeScript class, which in this section is the custom Emp class that is defined in Listing 1.7.

Now copy the directory SimpleAnimation from the companion files into a convenient location. Listing 1.8 shows the content of app.component. ts, which illustrates how to move the position of the <li> elements whenever users hover over them with their mouse.

**LISTING 1.7: app.component.ts**

```
// part #1: new import statement
import { Component, Input } from '@angular/core';

import {trigger, state, style, transition, animate} from '@
angular/animations';

// part #2: new Emp class
class Emp {
   constructor(public fname: string,
              public lname: string,
              public city:  string,
              public state = 'inactive') {
   }

   toggleState() {
       this.state = (this.state==='active' ? 'inactive' :
'active');
      console.log(this.fname+" "+"new state = "+this.state);
   }
}
@Component({
   selector: 'app-root',
   // part #3: new animations property
   animations: [
```

```
      trigger('empState', [
        state('inactive', style({
          backgroundColor: '#eee',
          transform: 'scale(1)'
        })),
        state('active',   style({
          backgroundColor: '#cfd8dc',
          transform: 'scale(1.1)'
        })),
          transition('inactive => active', animate('100ms
ease-in')),
          transition('active => inactive', animate('100ms
ease-out'))
      ])
    ],
    template: '
      <h2>Employee Information</h2>
      <ul>
        <li *ngFor="let emp of employees"
                [@empState]="emp.state"
                (mousemove)="emp.toggleState()">
          {{emp.fname}} {{emp.lname}} lives in {{emp.city}}
        </li>
      </ul>
      '
})
export class AppComponent {
  // => without the --strict option: employees = [];
  employees : any;

  constructor() {
    // part #5: array of Emp objects
    this.employees = [
      new Emp("Jane","Jones","San Francisco"),
      new Emp("John","Smith","New York"),
      new Emp("Dave","Stone","Seattle"),
      new Emp("Sara","Edson","Chicago")
    ];
  }
}
```

Listing 1.7 consists of five modifications to the code in Listing 1.6. Specifically, the section labeled "part #1" is a new `import` statement that replaces the original `import` statement. The section labeled "part #2" is the newly added `Emp` class that holds data for each employee.

The section labeled "part #3" is the new `transitions` property that defines the behavior when an animation event is triggered (which occurs during a `mousemove` event "over" an `<li>` element). The portion in bold (which is not labeled, but is "part #4") in the `ngFor` element essentially binds the `mousemove` event to the `toggleState()` method in the `Emp` class. Finally, the section labeled "part #5" is an array of `Emp` objects that replaces the original array in which each employee is represented as a JSON string.

Listing 1.8 shows the content of `app.module.ts`, which contains two additional code snippets (shown in bold) that you must add to the default contents of this file.

### LISTING 1.8: app.module.ts

```
import { BrowserModule } from '@angular/platform-browser';
import { NgModule } from '@angular/core';
import { BrowserAnimationsModule } from '@angular/
platform-browser/animations';

import { AppComponent } from './app.component';

@NgModule({
  declarations: [
    AppComponent
  ],
  imports: [
    BrowserModule,
    BrowserAnimationsModule
  ],
  providers: [],
  bootstrap: [AppComponent]
})
export class AppModule { }
```

If you do not include the two code snippets (shown in bold) in Listing 1.8, you will see the following error message in the console of the browser session where you launch this application:

```
ERROR: Found the synthetic property @empState. Please include
either "BrowserAnimationsModule" or "NoopAnimationsModule"
in your application.
```

**NOTE** *The two code snippets that are shown in bold in Listing 1.8 are required for Angular 10 applications, but they are not required for Angular 8 applications.*

Launch this Angular application from the command line via ng serve, navigate to localhost:4200, and then move your mouse over each person's name and observe the "fading" effect. The output in your browser will look like this:

### Employee Information

- Jane Jones lives in San Francisco
- John Smith lives in New York
- Dave Stone lives in Seattle
- Sara Edson lives in Chicago

Although this example is simple, you can extend this code with your own custom modifications to create other CSS3-based animation effects.

Now open the Inspector option in your browser (Chrome or Firefox) and you will see the following type of output:

```
Dave new state = active
Dave new state = inactive
John new state = active
John new state = inactive
Jane new state = inactive
Jane new state = active
Jane new state = inactive
Jane new state = active
Jane new state = inactive
John new state = active
Dave new state = active
Dave new state = inactive
Sara new state = active
Sara new state = inactive
```

## A Basic SVG Example in Angular

This section shows you how to specify a custom component that contains SVG code for rendering an SVG element. This example serves as the foundation for the SVG code in the next section, which involves dynamically creating and appending an SVG element to the DOM.

Copy the directory SVGEllipse from the companion files into a convenient location. Listing 1.9 shows the content of app.component.ts, which references an Angular custom component to render an SVG ellipse.

### LISTING 1.9: app.component.ts

```
import {Component} from '@angular/core';

@Component({
    selector: 'app-root',
    template: '<div><my-svg></my-svg></div>'
})
export class AppComponent {}
```

Listing 1.9 is very straightforward: the code defines a component whose template property contains a custom <my-svg> element inside a <div> element.

Listing 1.10 shows the content of MyEllipse.ts, which contains the SVG code for rendering three overlapping ellipses in SVG.

### LISTING 1.10: MyEllipse.ts

```
import {Component} from '@angular/core';

@Component({
    selector: 'my-svg',
    template: `
      <svg width="500" height="300">
        <ellipse cx="100" cy="100"
                 rx="50" ry="30"
                 fill="red"/>
        <ellipse cx="180" cy="100"
                 rx="80" ry="40"
                 fill="blue"/>
        <ellipse cx="140" cy="140"
                 rx="80" ry="40"
                 fill="yellow"/>
      </svg>
    `
})
export class MyEllipse{}
```

Listing 1.10 is also straightforward: the `template` property contains the code for an SVG `<svg>` element with `width` and `height` attributes, which in turn contains a nested SVG `<ellipse>` element with hard-coded values for the required attributes `cx`, `cy`, `rx`, `ry`, and `fill`.

Listing 1.11 shows the content of `app.module.ts` with the new code shown in bold.

### LISTING 1.11: app.module.ts

```
import {Component}          from '@angular/core';
import { NgModule }         from '@angular/core';
import { BrowserModule }  from '@angular/platform-browser';
import { AppComponent }    from './app.component';
import { MyEllipse }        from './MyEllipse;


@NgModule({
   imports:        [ BrowserModule ],
   declarations:  [ AppComponent, MyEllipse ],
   bootstrap:      [ AppComponent ]
})
export class AppModule { }
```

Listing 1.11 contains generic code that you are familiar with from previous examples in this chapter, as well as a new `import` statement (shown in bold) involving the `MyEllipse` class. The other modification in Listing 1.11 is the inclusion of the `MyEllipse1` class (shown in bold) in the `declarations` array.

Launch the Angular application in the usual fashion. In the browser session, you will see three colored ellipses in SVG, as shown in Figure 1.2.

The following links explain how to create SVG gradients and then how to create SVG Gradient Effects in Angular applications:

**FIGURE 1.2** Rendering ellipses in SVG in an Angular application

- *https://developer.mozilla.org/en-US/docs/Web/SVG/Tutorial/Gradients*
- *https://medium.com/@OlegVaraksin/how-to-proper-use-svg-gradients-in-angularjs-2-3241672e4de2#.oah0e9z1k*

## Detecting Mouse Positions in Angular Applications

This section shows you how to detect a mouse position inside an SVG <svg> element. Copy the directory SVGMouseMove from the companion files into a convenient location. Listing 1.12 shows the content of app. component.ts, which illustrates how to detect a mousemove event and display the coordinates of the current mouse position.

*LISTING 1.12: app.component.ts*

```
import {Component} from '@angular/core';


@Component({
    selector: 'app-root',
    template: `<svg id="svg" width="600px" height="400px"
})
class AppComponent {}
```

Listing 1.12 contains a template property that consists of a <div> element that contains a nested <mouse-move> element, where the latter is the value of the selector property in the custom component MouseMove that is defined in the custom TypeScript file mousemove.ts. In essence, the component AppComponent "delegates" the handling of mousemove events to the MouseMove component, which defines the mouseMove() function in order to handle such events.

Listing 1.13 shows the content of mousemove.ts, which illustrates how to detect a mousemove event and to display the coordinates of the current mouse position.

*LISTING 1.13: mousemove.ts*

```
import {Component} from '@angular/core';
@Component({
  selector: 'mouse-move',
  template: `<svg id="svg" width="600px" height="400px"
                (mousemove)="mouseMove($event)">
              </svg>

})
export class MouseMove{
    // => without the --strict option: mouseMove(event)
    mouseMove(event:any) {
      console.log("Position x: "+event.clientX+" y: "+event.
clientY);
```

```
    }
}
```

Listing 1.13 contains the `mouseMove()` method, whose lone argument event is an object that contains information (such as its location) about the mouse event. The `mouseMove()` method contains a `console.log()` statement that simply displays the x-coordinate and the y-coordinate of the location of the mouse click event.

Make sure that you update the contents of `app.module.ts` to include the MouseMove class, as shown in Listing 1.14.

### LISTING 1.14: app.module.ts

```
import { NgModule }        from '@angular/core';
import { BrowserModule } from '@angular/platform-browser';
import { AppComponent }  from './app.component';
import { MouseMove }        from './mousemove';
@NgModule({
  imports:        [ BrowserModule ],
  declarations: [ AppComponent, MouseMove ],
  bootstrap:      [ AppComponent ]
})
export class AppModule { }
```

Listing 1.14 imports the MouseMove class and adds this class to the declarations property (both of which are shown in bold).

Now launch this Angular application. In a new browser session, navigate to `View -> Developer -> JavaScript Console` (for a Chrome browser) to display the console. As you move your mouse around the screen, you will see the following type of output displayed in the console:

```
Position x: 506 y: 254 mousemove.ts:12:13
Position x: 505 y: 255 mousemove.ts:12:13
Position x: 505 y: 258 mousemove.ts:12:13
Position x: 504 y: 259 mousemove.ts:12:13
Position x: 503 y: 261 mousemove.ts:12:13
Position x: 502 y: 262 mousemove.ts:12:13
Position x: 501 y: 263 mousemove.ts:12:13
Position x: 505 y: 263 mousemove.ts:12:13
Position x: 510 y: 262 mousemove.ts:12:13
Position x: 515 y: 261 mousemove.ts:12:13
Position x: 520 y: 260 mousemove.ts:12:13
Position x: 526 y: 259 mousemove.ts:12:13
```

The next section combines SVG graphs with mouse movements to render a set of "follow the mouse" SVG ellipses.

## Angular and Follow-the-Mouse in SVG

The code sample in this section relies on mouse-related events to create dynamic graphics effects. Copy the directory SVGFollowMe from the companion files into a convenient location.

Listing 1.15 shows the content of app.component.ts, which illustrates how to reference a custom Angular component that renders an SVG <ellipse> element at the current mouse position.

### LISTING 1.15: app.component.ts

```
import {Component} from '@angular/core';
@Component({
    selector: 'app-root',
    template: '<div><mouse-move></mouse-move></div>'
})
export class AppComponent {}
```

As you can see, the template property in Listing 1.15 specifies a <div> element that contains a custom <mouse-move> element.

Listing 1.16 shows the content of MouseMove.ts, which illustrates how to reference a custom Angular component that renders an SVG <ellipse> element at the current mouse position.

### LISTING 1.16: MouseMove.ts

```
import {Component} from '@angular/core';

@Component({
  selector: 'mouse-move',
  template: `<svg id="svg" width="600" height="400"
                (mousemove)="mouseMove($event)">
             </svg>
`
})
export class MouseMove {
    radiusX = "25";
    radiusY = "50";
```

```
// mouseMove(event:any) {
  var svgns = "http://www.w3.org/2000/svg";
  var svg   = document.getElementById("svg");
  var colors = ["#ff0000", "#88ff00", "#3333ff"];

  var sum = Math.floor(event.clientX+event.clientY);

  var ellipse = document.createElementNS(svgns,
"ellipse");
  ellipse.setAttribute("cx", event.clientX);
  ellipse.setAttribute("cy", event.clientY);
  ellipse.setAttribute("rx", this.radiusX);
  ellipse.setAttribute("ry", this.radiusY);
  ellipse.setAttribute("fill", colors[sum % colors.
length]);
  svg.appendChild(ellipse);
  }
}
```

Listing 1.16 contains a `template` property that defines an SVG `<svg>` element. The `(mousemove)` event handler is executed whenever users move their mouse, which in turn executes the custom method `mouseMove()`.

Notice that the `mouseMove` method accepts an `event` argument, which is an object that provides the coordinates of the location of each `mousemove` event. The coordinates of the current point are specified by `event.clientX` and `event.clientY`, which are the x-coordinate and the y-coordinate, respectively, of the current mouse position.

The next code block in the `mouseMove` method dynamically creates an SVG `<ellipse>` method, sets the values of the five required attributes (see the previous section for the details), and then appends the newly created SVG `<ellipse>` method to the DOM. This functionality creates the "follow the mouse" effect when you launch the Angular application code in this section.

Note that the final line of code in the `mouseMove` method appends an SVG `<ellipse>` element *directly* to the DOM, which is better to avoid if it's possible to do so.

Listing 1.17 shows the content of `app.module.ts`. The new contents of `app.component.ts` are shown in bold.

*LISTING 1.17: app.module.ts*

```
import { BrowserModule } from '@angular/platform-browser';
import { NgModule }      from '@angular/core';
import { AppComponent } from './app.component';
import { MouseMove }       from './MouseMove';

@NgModule({
  declarations: [ AppComponent, MouseMove ],
  imports: [
    BrowserModule
  ],
  providers: [],
  bootstrap: [AppComponent]
})
export class AppModule { }
```

The code in Listing 1.17 follows a familiar pattern: start with the "baseline" code, add an `import` statement that references an exported TypeScript class (which is `MouseMove` in this example) and also add that same TypeScript class to the `declarations` array.

Launch the Angular application in the usual manner, and then slowly move your mouse to see different colored SVG ellipses rendered near your mouse. Figure 1.3 shows a sample of the output that can be generated in this application.

**FIGURE 1.3** Ellipses in a "Follow-the-Mouse" in SVG in an Angular Application

In case you are looking for ideas for enhancing this code sample, modify the code in `MouseMove.ts` so that new SVG ellipses are "centered" underneath your mouse.

## Angular and SVG Charts

This section creates a child component and also uses mouse-related events in order to create dynamic graphics effects. The graphics effects are very rudimentary; however, they provide a starting point from which you can add custom enhancements.

Now copy the directory SVGCharts from the companion files into a convenient location. Listing 1.18 shows the content of app.component.ts, whose template code specifies a <div> element that contains a custom <mycharts> element (as a child element) in which the SVG-based charts are rendered.

*When you launch this application, you will see a blank screen. However, each time you click inside the screen, you will see a different bar chart, scatter chart, and line graph.*

**LISTING 1.18: app.component.ts**

```
import { Component } from '@angular/core';

@Component({
  selector: 'app-root',
  template: '<div><mycharts></mycharts></div>'
})
export class AppComponent { }
```

Listing 1.18 shows the content of app.component.ts, whose template property specifies a custom <mycharts> element as a child of a <div> element. The charts and graphs in this code sample are rendered inside the <mycharts> element.

Listing 1.19 shows the content of app.module.ts, which specifies the custom component MyGraphics that contains the SVG-based code.

**LISTING 1.19: app.module.ts**

```
import { BrowserModule } from '@angular/platform-browser';
import { NgModule }      from '@angular/core';
import { AppComponent }  from './app.component';
import { MyGraphics }    from './MyGraphics';

@NgModule({
  declarations: [
    AppComponent,
    MyGraphics
  ],
  imports: [
    BrowserModule
  ],
  providers: [],
  bootstrap: [AppComponent]
```

```
})
export class AppModule { }
```

Listing 1.19 contains a code snippet to import the `MyGraphics` class and updates the `declarations` property to include the `MyGraphics` class. The remaining code in Listing 1.19 is the same as the code in previous code samples.

Listing 1.20 shows the content of `MyGraphics.ts`, which contains the SVG-based code for rendering a line graph, scatter plot, and a bar chart.

### LISTING 1.20: MyGraphics.ts

```
import { BrowserModule } from '@angular/platform-browser';
import {Component} from '@angular/core';

@Component({
 selector: 'mycharts',
 template: `<svg id="svg" width="600" height="600"
           (click)="drawCharts($event)">
          </svg>
`
})
export class MyGraphics {
    public scatterWidth:number  = 400;
    public scatterHeight:number = 400;
    public scatterCount:number  = 40;
    public offsetX:number       = 0;
    public offsetY:number       = 0;
    public clickCount:number    = 0;
    public radius:number        = 5;
    public barCount:number      = 15;
    public barWidth:number      = 30;
    public barHeight:number     = 50;
    public maxBarHeight:number  = 200;
    public barHeights:any       = [];
    public polyPts:any          = "";

 public colors = ["#ff0000","#00ff00","#ffc800","#0000ff"];
 public svgns = "http://www.w3.org/2000/svg";

 private generateBarHeights() {
    for(let i=0; i<this.barCount; i++) {
```

```
                this.barHeights[i]  =  ""+Math.random()*this.
maxBarHeight;
      }
   }

   drawCharts(event) {
      this.generateBarHeights();
      this.drawBarChart();
      this.drawScatterPlot();
      this.drawLineGraph();
      this.clickCount += 1;
   }

   private drawBarChart() {
     var svg = document.getElementById("svg");
    var gElem = document.createElementNS(this.svgns, "g");
     svg.appendChild(gElem);

     for(let i=0; i<this.barCount; i++) {
         var rect = document.createElementNS(this.svgns,
"rect");
        rect.setAttribute("x",        ""+i*this.barWidth);
           rect.setAttribute("y",          ""+(200-this.
barHeights[i]));
         rect.setAttribute("width",   ""+this.barWidth);
        rect.setAttribute("height", ""+this.barHeights[i]);

           rect.setAttribute("fill",  this.colors[i%this.
colors.length]);
          gElem.appendChild(rect);
      }
     svg.appendChild(gElem);
    }

   private drawLineGraph() {
     var svg = document.getElementById("svg");
     var gElem = document.createElementNS(this.svgns, "g");
     svg.appendChild(gElem);

     // construct a line graph
     for ( let i = 0; i < this.barCount; i++) {
```

```
        this.polyPts += (i*this.barWidth).toString() + "," +
                        (600-this.barHeights[i]) + " ";
    }


        var polyline = document.createElementNS(this.svgns,
    "polyline");
        polyline.setAttribute("points", ""+this.polyPts);
        polyline.setAttribute("style",
                    "fill:none;stroke:blue;stroke-width:3");
        gElem.appendChild(polyline);
        svg.appendChild(gElem);
    }


    private drawScatterPlot() {
        var svg = document.getElementById("svg");
        var gElem = document.createElementNS(this.svgns, "g");
        svg.appendChild(gElem);

        // construct circles
        for(let i=0; i<this.scatterCount; i++) {
            var circle = document.createElementNS(this.svgns,
    "circle");
            this.offsetX = this.scatterWidth*Math.random();
            this.offsetY = 200*Math.random();
            circle.setAttribute("cx", ""+this.offsetX);
            circle.setAttribute("cy", ""+(200+this.offsetY));
            circle.setAttribute("r",  ""+this.radius);

            circle.setAttribute("fill", this.colors[i%this.
    colors.length]);
            gElem.appendChild(circle);
        }
        svg.appendChild(gElem);
    }
}
```

Listing 1.20 starts with the usual import statements, followed by a template property that specifies an SVG <svg> element whose width and width attributes are both 600 pixels (and you can specify different values if you need to do so). Notice that the SVG <svg> element also specifies an Angular (click) attribute, as shown here:

```
template: `<svg id="svg" width="600" height="600"
```

```
        (click)="drawCharts($event)">
      </svg>
```

When users click anywhere inside the SVG <svg> element, the draw-
Charts() method is executed, whose contents are reproduced here:

```
drawCharts(event) {
    this.generateBarHeights();
    this.drawBarChart();
    this.drawScatterPlot();
    this.drawLineGraph();
    this.clickCount += 1;
}
```

Notice that the drawCharts() method also receives an event argument,
which is actually an object that contains information about the location of the
mouse event. This method invokes five other methods, starting with the gen-
erateBarHeights() method that populates the barHeights array with a
set of random numbers that represent the height of each bar element in the
bar chart.

Next, the drawCharts() method invokes the drawBarChart() method,
which starts by obtaining a reference to the existing <svg> element (specified in the template property), creating a new SVG <g> element called
gElem, and then appending the newly created SVG <g> element to the
SVG <svg> element, as shown here:

```
var svg = document.getElementById("svg");
var gElem = document.createElementNS(this.svgns, "g");
svg.appendChild(gElem);
```

Although it's not absolutely necessary, it's a good idea to place the bar
chart inside an <g> element as a way to "modularize" the graphics (the
same thing is done for the scatter plot and the line graph).

The next code block consists of a for loop that creates an SVG <rect>
element, populates its attributes appropriately, and then appends the
SVG <rect> element to the existing SVG <g> element, as shown here:

```
for(let i=0; i<this.barCount; i++) {
    var rect = document.createElementNS(this.svgns, "rect");
    rect.setAttribute("x",        ""+i*this.barWidth);
    rect.setAttribute("y",        ""+(200-this.barHeights[i]));
    rect.setAttribute("width",    ""+this.barWidth);
```

```
rect.setAttribute("height", ""+this.barHeights[i]);

    rect.setAttribute("fill", this.colors[i%this.colors.
length]);
    gElem.appendChild(rect);
}
svg.appendChild(gElem);
```

Next, the `drawCharts()` method invokes the `drawScatterPlot()` method, that also starts with the same code block as `drawBarChart()` that pertains to the SVG `<svg>` element. This method also contains a `for` loop that creates a set of SVG `<circle>` elements, populates their attributes appropriately, and then appends them to the third `<g>` element.

Finally, the `drawCharts()` method invokes the `drawLineGraph()` method, which also starts with the same code block as `drawBarChart()` that pertains to the SVG `<svg>` element. This method contains a `for` loop that updates the string `polyPts` with the x-coordinate and y-coordinate of the top-level vertex of each bar element, as shown here:

```
for ( let i = 0; i < this.barCount; i++) {
   this.polyPts += (i*this.barWidth).toString() + "," +
                    (600-this.
barHeights[i]) + " ";
}
```

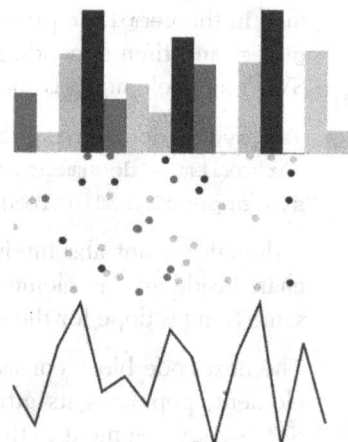

The next portion of the `drawLin-eGraph()` method creates a new SVG `<polyline>` element, sets its points attribute equal to the content of `polyPts`, and then appends the SVG `<polyline>` element to the SVG `<svg>` element.

Launch this Angular application. Then, in the new browser session, click anywhere on the screen to see a rudimentary bar chart, scatter plot, and line graph, as shown in Figure 1.4.

**FIGURE 1.4** An SVG bar chart, scatter plot, and line graph in an Angular Application

## D3 Animation and Angular

The previous two sections provided examples of Angular applications with SVG, and this section shows you how to create D3 animation effects with Angular. Note that the code sample in this section also appends the SVG elements directly to the DOM.

D3 is an open source toolkit that provides a JavaScript-based layer of abstraction over SVG. Fortunately, the attributes of every SVG element have the same name in D3 (so your work is cut in half).

Copy the directory D3Anim from the companion files into a convenient location. Listing 1.21 shows the content of app.component.ts, which illustrates how to use D3 to render basic SVG graphics in an Angular application.

***LISTING 1.21: app.component.ts***

```
import { Component, ViewChild, ElementRef } from '@angular/
core';
import * as d3 from 'd3';

// remember: npm install d3 --save

@Component({
  selector: 'app-root',
  template: '<app-root><mysvg></mysvg></app-root>',
  styleUrls: ['./app.component.css']
})
export class AppComponent {
  constructor() {
    var width = 800, height = 500, duration=2000;
    var radius = 30, moveCount = 0, index = 0;
    var circleColors = ["red", "yellow", "green", "blue"];

    var svg = d3.select("body")
                .append("svg")
                .attr("width",  width)
                .attr("height", height);
```

```
svg.on("mousemove", function() {
  index = (++moveCount) % circleColors.length;

    var circle = svg.append("circle")
                  .attr("cx", (width-100)*Math.random())
                 .attr("cy", (height-100)*Math.random())
                    .attr("r",  radius)
                    .attr("fill", circleColors[index])
                    .transition()
                    .duration(duration)
                    .attr("transform", function() {
                       return "scale(0.5, 0.5)";
                      //return "rotate(-20)";
                    })
   });
 }
}
```

Listing 1.21 starts with two import statements, followed by a comment block that summarizes the key points for using D3.js in Angular applications. The template property contains a <div> element that is available in the ngAfterContentInit method, which in turn simply invokes the createSVG() method that populates an SVG <svg> element with four 2D shapes: a circle, an ellipse, a rectangle, and a line segment.

Note the @ViewChild decorator that defines the variable mysvg that has type ElementRef. This variable "links" the <div> element in the template property with the variable svgElement that is defined in the createSVG() method:

```
let svgElement = this.mysvg.nativeElement;
```

Notice how the various SVG elements are dynamically created and how their mandatory attributes (which depend on the SVG element in question) are assigned values via the attr() method, as shown here (and in the preceding code block, as well):

```
// append a circle
svg.append("circle")
    .attr("cx", cx)
    .attr("cy", cy)
    .attr("r",  radius1)
    .attr("fill", colors[0]);
```

After you learn the mandatory attribute names for SVG elements, you can use the preceding syntax to create and append such elements to the DOM.

Listing 1.22 shows the content of `app.module.ts` with the new code in bold.

### LISTING 1.22: app.module.ts

```
import { BrowserModule } from '@angular/platform-browser';
import { NgModule } from '@angular/core';
import { AppComponent } from './app.component';
import { NO_ERRORS_SCHEMA } from '@angular/core';

@NgModule({
  declarations: [
    AppComponent
  ],
  imports: [
    BrowserModule
  ],
  providers: [],
  schemas: [NO_ERRORS_SCHEMA],
  bootstrap: [AppComponent]
})
export class AppModule { }
```

Listing 1.22 contains code that is already familiar to you, along with the following new `import` statement:

```
import { NO_ERRORS_SCHEMA } from '@angular/core';
```

The preceding code snippet allows us add any element that is created in the D3-based code without generating an error message. Notice that the schemas property in Listing 1.22 must also be updated to include NO_ERRORS_SCHEMA.

Launch this Angular application. Then, in the new browser session, click anywhere on the screen to see a "cascade" of animated circles.

Launch the Angular application in the usual manner, and then slowly move your mouse to see different colored SVG ellipses rendered near your mouse. Figure 1.5 shows a sample of the output that can be generated in this application.

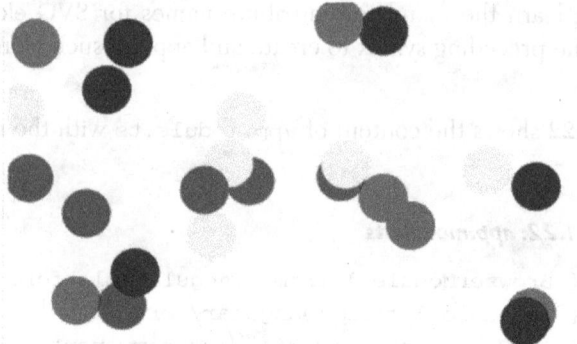

**FIGURE 1.5** Rendering circles with D3 in an Angular application

You can also find many similar code samples involving SVG and Angular (with older beta-version Angular code) here:

*https://github.com/ocampesato/angular2-svg-graphics*

## D3 and SVG Animation in Angular

The following code block illustrates how to add D3-based animation effects to the SVG <circle> element in the D3Angular Angular application:

```
svg.on("mousemove", function() {
  index = (++moveCount) % circleColors.length;
  var circle = svg.append("circle")
                  .attr("cx", (width-100)*Math.random())
                  .attr("cy", (height-100)*Math.random())
                  .attr("r",  radius)
                  .attr("fill", circleColors[index])
                  .transition()
                    .duration(duration)
                    .attr("transform", function() {
                      return "scale(0.5, 0.5)";
                    //return "rotate(-20)";
                    })
});
```

The code inside the preceding event handler is executed during each mousemove event, accompanied by the dynamic creation of an SVG <ellipse> element. The new functionality involves the transition()

method and the `duration()` method, and it also sets the `transform` attribute, all of which is shown in bold in the preceding code block.

The `transform` attribute is set to a `scale()` value, which sets the width and height to `50%` of their initial value during an interval of 2 seconds (which equals `2000` milliseconds), thereby creating an animation effect.

## Summary

This chapter started with a description overview of Angular and its hierar-chical component-based structure. Next, you learned about the Angular CLI utility `ng` and how to create an Angular "Hello world" application with the `ng` utility.

You also learned about the TypeScript files `app.component.ts` and `app.module.ts` that contain the TypeScript code for Angular applications. Finally, you learned about creating Angular applications for rendering SVG-based ellipses and charts, followed by D3-based animation effects.

# UI CONTROLS, USER INPUT, AND PIPES

This chapter contains Angular applications with an assortment of UI Controls, along with code samples that involve user input. Note that the Angular applications in this chapter render UI Controls using standard HTML syntax instead of using functionality that is specific to Angular. In addition, the last section in this chapter contains links to toolkits that provide Angular UI components.

The first part of this chapter contains a simple example of displaying a hard-coded list of strings, followed by an Angular application that supports click events on a button. The second part of this chapter shows how to manage lists of items, which includes displaying, adding, and deleting items from a list. You will also learn about `Controls` and `ControlGroups`.

The third section contains two examples of displaying a list of user names: the first retrieves user names that are stored as strings in a JavaScript array, and the second retrieves user names that are stored in object literals in a JavaScript array. The third section goes a step further: you learn how to define a custom user component that contains user-related information (also contained in a JavaScript array). Later in this chapter, we make an `HTTP GET` request to retrieve data (such as user-related information) to populate a list of items.

The fourth part of this chapter discusses Angular Pipes. There is an Angular application that uses `async` pipes, which can eliminate the need for defining instance variables and reduce the likelihood of memory leaks in Angular applications.

Now let's create a simple Angular application that displays a hard-coded list of strings via the ngFor directive, as discussed in the next section.

## The ngFor Directive in Angular

The code sample in this section displays a hard-coded list of strings via the *ngFor directive. This simple code sample is a starting point from which you can create more complex Angular applications.

Copy the directory SimpleList from the companion files into a convenient location. Listing 2.1 shows the content of app.component.ts, which illustrates how to display a list of items using the *ngFor directive in Angular.

### LISTING 2.1: app.component.ts

```
import {Component} from '@angular/core';

@Component({
  selector: 'app-root',
  template: `<div *ngFor="let item of items">
              {{item}}
            </div>`
})
export class AppComponent {
  items : any;

  constructor() {
    this.items = ['one','two','three','four'];
  }
}
```

Listing 2.1 contains a Component annotation that in turn contains the standard selector property. Next, the template property consists of a <div> element that contains the ngFor directive that iterates through the items array and also displays each item in that array. Notice that the items array is initialized as an empty array in the AppComponent class, and then its value is set to an array consisting of four strings in the constructor method.

Launch the application in this section and you will see the following output in a browser session:

one
two

three
four

The next section contains a code sample involving a `<button>` element, which is probably one of the most common UI controls in HTML Web pages. The file `app.component.ts` contains the required custom code, and the file `app.component.ts` contains auto-generated code that does not require any modification.

## Displaying a Button in Angular

Copy the directory `ButtonClick` from the companion files into a convenient location. The file `app.component.ts` in this section contains all the custom code for this Angular application. Listing 2.2 shows the content of `app.component.ts`, which illustrates how to render a `<button>` element and respond to click events by displaying the number of times that users have clicked the `<button>` element during the current session.

### LISTING 2.2: app.component.ts

```
import { Component } from '@angular/core';

@Component({
    selector: 'app-root',
    template: `<div>
                <button (click)="clickMe()">ClickMe</button>
                 <p>Click count is now {{clickCount}}</p>
               </div>`,
    styles: [` button {
                   color: red;
               }`
             ]
})
export class AppComponent {
    clickCount = 0;

    clickMe() {
        ++this.clickCount;
        console.log("click count: "+this.clickCount);
    }
}
```

Listing 2.2 starts with an `import` statement followed by the required `selector` property. Next, the `template` property contains a `<button>` element that responds to click events and a `<p>` element whose contents are updated whenever users click on the `<button>` element. The value of the term `(click)` is the `clickMe()` function (defined in the `AppComponent` class) that increments and then displays the value of the `clickCount` variable.

In addition, the `styles` property specifies a value of `red` for the `<button>` element. The `styles` property is an example of component style, which means that the styles only apply to the template of the given component. In effect, Angular applies CSS locally instead of globally by generating unique attributes that are visible when you click on the `Elements` tab in Chrome Inspector.

More detailed information regarding component styles in Angular is here:

*https://angular.io/docs/ts/latest/guide/component-styles.html*

The next portion of Listing 2.2 is the definition of the `AppComponent` class that contains the `clickCount` variable that is incremented in the `clickMe()` function. Now launch the Angular application whose output is displayed in Figure 2.1 (after it has been clicked three times).

**ClickMe**

**Click count is now 3**

FIGURE 2.1  A `<button>` element that responds to click events

Since the file `app.module.ts` contains auto-generated code that does not require any modification, there is no need to display its contents because they have already been discussed in Chapter 1.

## Element versus Property

In Listing 2.2, the `selector` property matched the element `<app-root></app-root>` in the HTML page `index.html`:

```
selector: 'app-root'
```

However, you can also specify a property instead of an element. For example, suppose that `index.html` contains the following element:

```
<div app-root>Loading. . .</div>
```

In this scenario, you also need to modify the `selector` property as follows (and notice the square brackets):

```
selector: '[app-root]'
```

The next section contains an Angular application keeps track of the radio button that users have clicked. After that we'll see how to use a <button> element in order to add new user names to a list of users.

Once again, the file `app.module.ts` contains auto-generated code that does not require any modification, so there is no need to display its contents because they have already been discussed in Chapter 1.

## Angular and Radio Buttons

Copy the directory `RadioButtons` from the companion files into a convenient location. Listing 2.3 shows the content of `app.component.ts`, which illustrates how to render a set of radio buttons and also keep track of the one that users have clicked.

***LISTING 2.3: app.component.ts***

```
import {Component} from '@angular/core';

@Component({
  selector: 'app-root',
  template: `
   <h2>{{radioTitle}}</h2>
   <label *ngFor="let item of radioItems">
      <input type="radio" name="options"
             (click)="model.options = item"
             [checked]="item === model.options">
    {{item}}
   </label>
   <p><button (click)="model.options='option1'">Set Option
#1</button>
   `
})
export class AppComponent {
  radioTitle = "Radio Buttons in Angular";
  radioItems = ['option1','option2','option3','option4'];
  model = { options: 'option3' };
}
```

Listing 2.3 defines the AppComponent component whose template property contains three parts: a <label> element, an <input> element, and a <button> element. The <label> element contains an ngFor directive that displays a set of radio buttons by iterating through the radioItems array that is defined in the AppComponent class.

By default, the first radio button is highlighted. However, when users click on the <button> element, the (click) attribute of the <input> element sets the *current* item to the value of model. options, and then the [checked] attribute of the <input> element sets the *checked* item to the current value of model.options. The <input> element in Listing 2.3 contains functionality that is more compact than using JavaScript to achieve the same results.

Now launch the Angular application to see the output that is displayed in Figure 2.2.

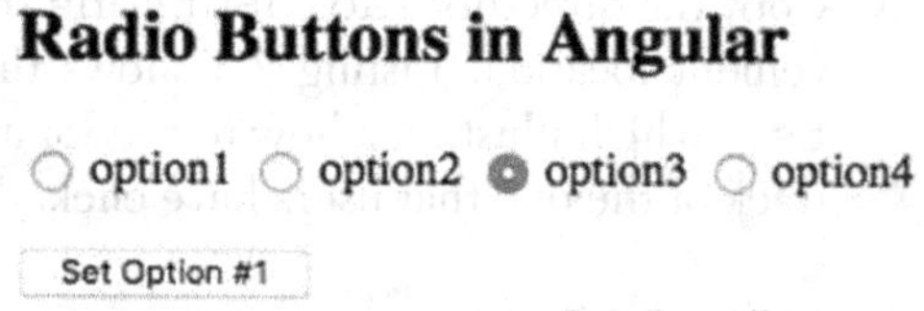

The file app.module. ts contains auto-generated code that does not require any modification, so we'll skip the discussion of its contents.

## Radio Buttons in Angular

○ option1  ○ option2  ◉ option3  ○ option4

Set Option #1

**FIGURE 2.2** A set of radio buttons that respond to click events

## Adding Items to a List in Angular

The code sample in this section shows how to update a list of strings whenever users click on a button. Copy the directory AddListButton from the companion files into a convenient location. Listing 2.4 shows the content of app.component.ts, which illustrates how to append strings to an array of items whenever users click on a button.

**LISTING 2.4: app.component.ts**

```
import {Component} from '@angular/core';

@Component({
    selector: 'app-root',
    template: `
        <div>
            <input #fname>
```

```
          <button (click)="clickMe(fname.value)">ClickMe</
button>
        <ul>
         <li *ngFor="let user of users">
           {{user}}
         </li>
        </ul>
        </div>`
})
export class AppComponent {
   users = ["Jane", "Dave", "Tom"];

   clickMe(user) {
     console.log("new user = "+user);
     this.users.push(user);
/*
     // prevent empty user or duplicates
     if(user is non-null) {
       if(user is duplicate) {
        // display alert message
       } else {
        // display alert message
       }
     } else {
       // display alert message
     }
*/
   }
}
```

Listing 2.4 contains code that is similar to Listing 2.3 that displays a list of strings. In addition, the template property in Listing 2.4 contains an <input> element so that users can enter text. When users click on the <button> element, the clickMe() method is invoked with fname. value as a parameter, which is a reference to the text in the <input> element.

Notice the use of the #fname syntax as an identifier for an element, which in this case is an <input> element. Thus, the text that users enter in the <input> element is referenced via fname.value. The following code snippet provides this functionality:

```
<input #fname>
<button (click)="clickMe(fname.value)">ClickMe</button>
```

The `clickMe()` method in the `AppComponent` component contains a `console.log()` statement to display the user-entered text (which is optional) and then appends the new text to the array `user`. The final section in Listing 2.4 consists of a commented-out block of pseudocode that prevents users from entering an empty string or a duplicate string. This code block involves "pure" JavaScript, and the actual code is left as an exercise for you.

Now, launch the Angular application and you will see the output that is displayed in Figure 2.3 when you enter the string "Sara" and click the button element.

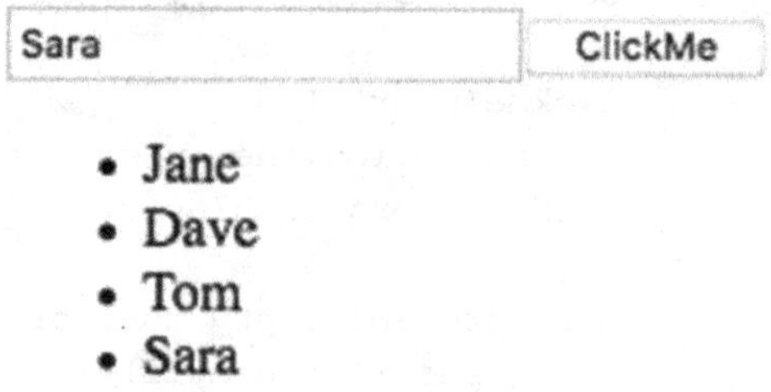

In addition, the file `app.module.ts` contains auto-generated code that does not require any modification.

| Sara | ClickMe |

- Jane
- Dave
- Tom
- Sara

**FIGURE 2.3**  Adding a text string to a list

## Deleting Items from a List in Angular

This section enhances the code in the previous section by adding a new `<button>` element next to each list item. Now copy the directory `DelListButton` from the companion files into a convenient location. Listing 2.5 shows the content of `app.component.ts`, which illustrates how to delete individual elements from an array of items whenever users click on a button that is adjacent to each array item.

**LISTING 2.5: app.component.ts**

```
import {Component} from '@angular/core';

@Component({
    selector: 'app-root',
    template: `
    <div>
        <input #fname>
```

```
        <button (click)="clickMe(fname.value)">ClickMe</
button>
        <ul>
          <li *ngFor="let user of users">
            <button (click)="deleteMe(user)">Delete</button>
            {{user}}
          </li>
        </ul>
      </div>`
})
export class AppComponent {
   users = ["Jane", "Dave", "Tom"];

   deleteMe(user) {
      console.log("delete user = "+user);
      var index = this.users.indexOf(user);

      if(index >=0 ) {
         this.users.splice(index, 1);
      }
   }
   clickMe(user) {
      console.log("new user = "+user);
      this.users.push(user);
   /*
      // prevent empty user or duplicates
      if(user is non-null) {
        if(user is duplicate) {
          // display alert message
        } else {
          // display alert message
        }
      } else {
        // display alert message
      }
   */
   }
}
```

Listing 2.5 contains an ngFor directive that displays a list of "pairs" of items, where each "pair" consists of a <button> element followed by a user that is defined in the users array.

When users click on any <button> element, the "associated" user is passed as a parameter to the deleteMe() method, which simply deletes that user from the users array in the AppComponent class. The content of deleteMe() is written in standard JavaScript code for removing an item from an array. You can replace the block of pseudocode in Listing 2.5 with the same code that you added in Listing 2.4 that prevents users from entering an empty string or a duplicate string.

The file app.module.ts contains auto-generated code that does not require any modification, so there is no need to discuss its familiar content.

## Angular Directives and Child Components

The code sample in this section shows you how to create a child component in Angular that you can reference in an Angular application. Copy the directory ChildComponent from the companion files into a convenient location. Listing 2.6 shows the content of app.component.ts, which illustrates how to import a custom component (written by you) in an Angular application.

### LISTING 2.6: app.component.ts

```
import {Component}    from '@angular/core';

@Component({
    selector: 'app-root',
    template: `<div>Goodbye<child-comp></child-comp>World!</div>`
})
export class AppComponent {}
```

Listing 2.6 contains a template property that consists of a <div> element that contains a nested <child-comp> element, where the latter is the value of the selector property in the child component ChildComponent.

Notice that Listing 2.6 does *not* import the ChildComponent class: this class is imported in app.module.ts in Listing 2.8 (shown later).

Listing 2.7 shows the content of child.component.ts in the app subdirectory.

*LISTING 2.7: child.component.ts*

```
import {Component} from '@angular/core';

@Component({
    selector: 'child-comp',
    template: `<div>Hello World from ChildComponent!</div>`
})
export class ChildComponent{}
```

Listing 2.7 is straightforward: the `template` property specifies a text string that is displayed inside the `<child-comp>` element that is nested inside the `<div>` element in Listing 2.7.

<table>
<tr><td>NOTE</td><td>This is the first code sample in this chapter that involves modifying the auto-generated contents of the file <code>app.module.ts</code>.</td></tr>
</table>

Listing 2.8 shows the modified content of `app.module.ts`, which *must* import the class `ChildComponent` from `child.component.ts` and also specify the class `ChildComponent` in the `declarations` property. These additions to the default contents of `app.module.ts` are shown in bold in Listing 2.8.

*LISTING 2.8: app.module.ts*

```
import { NgModule }        from '@angular/core';
import { BrowserModule }   from '@angular/platform-browser';
import { AppComponent }    from './app.component';
import { ChildComponent } from './child.component';

@NgModule({
    imports:        [ BrowserModule ],
    declarations: [ AppComponent, ChildComponent ],
    bootstrap:      [ AppComponent ]
})
export class AppModule { }
```

Listing 2.8 contains a new `import` statement (shown in bold) that imports the `ChildComponent` component from the Typescript file `child.component.ts`. The second modification is the inclusion of `ChildComponent` (shown in bold) in the `declarations` array.

Listing 2.8 involves two very simple updates in order to include a child component in an Angular application. With practice, you will become familiar with the sequence of steps that are illustrated in this section.

## The Constructor and Storing State in Angular

This section contains a code sample that illustrates how to initialize a variable in a constructor and then reference the value of that variable via interpolation in the `template` property. Now copy the directory `StateComponent` from the companion files into a convenient location. Listing 2.9 shows the content of `app.component.ts`, which displays various attributes of an "employee."

### LISTING 2.9: app.component.ts

```
import {Component} from '@angular/core';

@Component({
  selector: 'app-root',
  template: '<h3>My name is {{emp.fname}} {{emp.lname}}</h3>'
})
export class AppComponent {
    public emp    = {fname:'John',lname:'Smith',city:'San Francisco'};
    public name = 'John Smith'

  constructor() {
    this.name = 'Jane Edwards'
    this.emp  = {fname:'Sarah',lname:'Smith',city:'San Francisco'};
  }
}
```

Listing 2.9 contains a `constructor()` method that initializes the variable name as well as the literal object emp. The emp variable is shown in bold in the template property and also in two other places inside the AppComponent class.

**Question:** Which name will be displayed when you launch the application?

**Answer:** The value that is assigned to the emp variable in the constructor. This behavior is the same as OO-oriented languages such as Java.

Launch this application to see the following output displayed in a Web browser:

## My name is Sarah Smith

Keen-eyed readers will notice how we "slipped in" the TypeScript keyword `public` in the declaration of the emp and name variables. Other possible keywords include `private` and `protected`; all three keywords have the same semantics that they have in Java. If you are unfamiliar with these keywords, you can find online TypeScript tutorials that explain their purpose. There is another handy TypeScript syntax for TypeScript variables that is discussed in the next section.

### Private Arguments in the Constructor: a Shortcut

TypeScript provides a short-hand notation for initializing private variables via a constructor. Consider the following TypeScript code block:

```
class MyStuff {
    private firstName: string;

    constructor(firstName: string) {
        this.firstName = firstName;
    }
}
```

A simpler and equivalent TypeScript code block is here:

```
class MyStuff {
    constructor(private firstName: string) {
    }
}
```

TypeScript support for the `private` keyword in a constructor is a convenient feature that reduces some boilerplate code and also eliminates a potential source of error (i.e., misspelled variable names).

As another example, the `constructor()` method in the following code snippet populates an employees object with data retrieved from an EmpService component (defined elsewhere and not important here):

```
constructor(private empService: EmpService) {
    this.employees = this.empService.getEmployees();
}
```

The next section shows you how to use the `*ngIf` directive for conditional logic in Angular applications.

## Conditional Logic in Angular

Although previous examples contain a `template` property with a single line of text, Angular enables you to specify multiple lines of text. If you place interpolated variables inside a pair of matching "back ticks," Angular will replace ("interpolate") the variables with their values.

Now copy the directory `IfLogic` from the companion files into a convenient location. Listing 2.10 shows the content of `app.component.ts`, which illustrates how to use the `*ngIf` directive.

*LISTING 2.10: app.component.ts*

```
import {Component} from '@angular/core';

@Component({
  selector: 'app-root',
  template: `
    <h3>Hello everyone!</h3>
    <h3>My name is {{emp.fname}} {{emp.lname}}</h3>
    <button (click)="moreInfo()">More Details</button>
    <div *ngIf="showMore === true">
      <h3>I live in {{emp.city}}</h3>
    </div>

    <div (click)="showDiv = !showDiv">Toggle Me</div>
    <div *ngIf="showDiv"
         style="color:white;background-color:blue;
width:25%">Content1</div>
    <div *ngIf="showDiv"
         style="background-color:red;
width:25%;">Content2</div>
    `
})
export class AppComponent {
  public emp = {fname:'John',lname:'Smith',city:'San
Francisco'};
  public showMore = false;
  public showDiv  = false;

  moreInfo() {
        this.showMore = true;
  }
}
```

Listing 2.10 contains some new code in the `template` property: a
`<button>` element that invokes the method `moreInfo()` whenever
users click on the button. After the click event, a `<div>` element with
city-related information inside an `<h3>` element is rendered. Notice that
this `<div>` element is only rendered when `showMore` is `true`, which is
controlled via the `ngIf` directive that checks for the value of `showMore`.
The initial value of `showMore` is `false`, and right after users click the
`<button>` element, its value is set to `true`, after which the `<div>` element is displayed.

The new code in `AppComponent` involves a Boolean variable `show-
More` (whose initial value is `false`) and the method `moreInfo()` that
initializes `showMore` to `true`.

The file `app.module.ts` contains auto-generated code that does not
require any modification, so we'll omit its contents in this section.

## Handling User Input

The code sample in this section shows you how to handle user input and
introduces the notion of a *service* in Angular. This code sample contains
custom code in the file `app.component.ts` and some updates to the
file `app.module.ts`, along with these three custom files (all of which
are discussed in this section):

- todoservice.ts
- todolist.ts
- todoinput.ts

The "source of truth" for a dynamically updated list of todo items is the
TypeScript `todos` array that is defined in `todoservice.ts`; this array
is accessed indirectly in the other two TypeScript classes. This coding
style conforms to object-oriented programming (OOP). If you are unfamiliar with OOP, it's worthwhile to learn this methodology and also highly
recommended for moderate and large Angular applications.

Before we look at the custom code, recall that Angular enables you to
create a reference to an HTML element, as shown here:

```
<input type="text" #user>
```

The `#user` syntax creates a reference to the `<input>` element that enables you to reference `{{user.value}}` to see its value or `{{user.`
`type}}` to see the type of the input. Moreover, you can use this reference in the following code block:

```
<p (click)="user.focus()">
  Get the input focus
</p>
<input type="text" #user (keyup)>
{{user.value}}
```

Whenever users click on the `<input>` element, the `focus()` method is invoked, and the `(keyup)` property updates the value in the input during the occurrence of a keyup event.

Now copy the directory `TodoInput` from the companion files into a convenient location. Listing 2.11 shows the content of `app.component.ts`, which illustrates how to reference a component that appends user input to an array in Angular.

### LISTING 2.11: app.component.ts

```
import {Component}   from '@angular/core';

@Component({
   selector: 'app-root',
   template: `<div>
                <todo-input></todo-input>
                <todo-list></todo-list>
              </div>`
})
export class AppComponent {}
```

Listing 2.11 contains a standard `import` statement. The `template` property specifies a `<div>` element that contains placeholders for the `TodoInput` and `TodoList` components.

Listing 2.12 shows the content of `todoinput.ts`, which illustrates how to display an `<input>` field and a `<button>` element to capture user input in Angular.

### LISTING 2.12: todoinput.ts

```
import {Component}    from '@angular/core';
import {TodoService } from './todoservice';

@Component({
  selector: 'todo-input',
  template: `
    <div>
```

```
    <input type="text" #myInput>
    <button (click)="mouseEvent(myInput.value)">Add Item</
button>
    </div>`
})
export class TodoInput{
    constructor(public todoService:TodoService) {}

    mouseEvent(value) {
        if((value != null) && (value.length > 0)) {
          this.todoService.todos.push(value);
          console.log("todos: "+this.todoService.todos);
        } else {
            console.log("value must be non-null");
        }
    }
}
```

Listing 2.12 contains a `template` property that consists of a `<div>` element that contains an `<input>` element for user input, followed by a `<button>` element for handling mouse click events.

The `TodoInput` class defines an empty constructor that also initializes an instance of the custom `TodoService` that is imported near the beginning of `todoinput.ts`. This instance contains an array `todos` that is updated with new to-do items whenever users click on the `<button>` element, provided that the new to-do item is not the empty string.

Now let's look at the custom files, starting with Listing 2.13, which displays the content of `todolist.ts` that keeps track of the items in a to-do list.

### LISTING 2.13: todolist.ts

```
import {Component}    from '@angular/core';
import {TodoService} from './todoservice';

@Component({
  selector: 'todo-list',
  template: `<div>
                <ul>
                    <li *ngFor="let todo of todoService.todos">
                      {{todo}}
                    </li>
                </ul>
```

```
        </div>`
})
export class TodoList {
   constructor(public todoService:TodoService) {}
}
```

Listing 2.13 contains a `template` property whose contents are a `<div>` element that contains an unordered list of items called `todos` (and defined in Listing 2.14), along with an empty constructor that initializes an instance of the `TodoService` custom component. This instance is used in the `template` property in order to iterate through the elements in the `todos` array.

Listing 2.14 shows the content of `todoservice.ts`, which keeps track of the current contents of a to-do list.

### LISTING 2.14: todoservice.ts

```
export class TodoService {
   todos = [];
}
```

Listing 2.14 contains a `todos` array that is updated with new to-do items when users click on the `<button>` element in the root component.

Finally, update the contents of `app.module.ts` to include the class shown in bold in Listing 2.15.

### Listing 2.15: app.module.ts

```
import { NgModule }        from '@angular/core';
import { BrowserModule }   from '@angular/platform-browser';
import { AppComponent }    from './app.component';
import { TodoInput }       from './todoinput';
import { TodoList }        from './todolist';
import { TodoService }     from './todoservice';

@NgModule({
   imports:       [ BrowserModule ],
   providers:     [ TodoService ],
   declarations:  [ AppComponent, TodoInput, TodoList ],
   bootstrap:     [ AppComponent ]
})
export class AppModule { }
```

As you probably expected, Listing 2.15 imports three `todo`-related classes and adds them to the `providers` property and the `declarations` property (shown in bold). Although the number of custom modifications to `app.module.ts` in this section is greater than in the Angular applications that you have seen earlier in this chapter, the updates make sense and are straightforward.

The output for this Angular application is similar to that shown in Figure 2.3, so it is not reproduced here. Keep in mind that although the output looks similar, the important point regarding the code sample in this section is its focus on Angular services and that it defines them following the methodology of object oriented programming.

## Click Events in Multiple Components

An Angular application can contain multiple components, each of which can declare event handlers with the same name. The Angular application in this section shows you how to add click events to different elements in an Angular application.

Copy the directory `ClickItems` from the companion files into a convenient location. Listing 2.16 shows the content of `app.component.ts`, which declares an `onClick()` event handler for each item in a list of items.

**LISTING 2.16: app.component.ts**

```
import {Component} from '@angular/core';
import {ClickItem} from './clickitem';


@Component({
    selector: 'app-root',
    styles:   [`li { display: inline; }`],
    template: `
    <div>
       <ul>
         <li><img (click)="onClick(100)"
                 width="100" height="100" src="src/sample1.
png"></li>
         <li><img (click)="onClick(200)"
                 width="100" height="100" src="src/sample2.
png"></li>
```

```
        <li><img (click)="onClick(300)"
                 width="100" height="100" src="src/sample3.
png"></li>
        </ul>
        </div>
    `
})
export class AppComponent {
    onClick(id) {
        console.log("you clicked me: "+id);
    }
}
```

The `template` property in Listing 2.16 displays an unordered list in which each item is a clickable PNG-based image. Whenever users click on one of the images, the `onClick()` method is invoked that simply displays a message via `console.log()`.

Listing 2.17 shows the content of `clickitem.ts`, which declares an `onClick()` event handler for each item in a list of items.

### LISTING 2.17: clickitem.ts

```
import {Component} from '@angular/core';

@Component({
    selector: 'cclick',
    styleUrl: [` li { inline: block } `],
    template: `
      <div>
       <ul>
        <li><img (click)="onClick(100)"
                 width="100" height="100" src="assets/sam-
ple1.png"></li>
        <li><img (click)="onClick(200)"
                 width="100" height="100" src="assets/sam-
ple2.png"></li>
        <li><img (click)="onClick(300)"
                 width="100" height="100" src="assets/sam-
ple3.png"></li>
        </ul>
        </div>
```

```
})
export class ClickItem {
  onClick(id) {
    console.log("app.component.ts: you clicked me: "+id);
  }
}
```

Listing 2.17 is very similar to Listing 2.16 in terms of functionality, so we won't repeat those details. In addition, the file `app.module.ts` contains the auto-generated code, along with two new code snippets. The first snippet is the following `import` statement that references the file `clickitem.ts`:

```
import { ClickItem }      from './clickitem';
```

The second code snippet specifies the preceding class in the providers element, as shown here:

```
providers: [ClickItem]
```

Now launch the application to see the three images that are displayed in Figure 2.4.

**FIGURE 2.4** Clicking on images in an Angular application

Click on the left-most image, then the middle image, and then the right-most image. Open the inspector for the current browser session, and you will see these messages:

```
you clicked me: 100
you clicked me: 200
you clicked me: 300
```

## Working with @Input, @Output, and EventEmitter

Angular supports the `@Input` and `@Output` annotations to pass values between components. The `@Input` annotation is for variables that receive values from a parent component, whereas the `@Output` annotation sends (or "emits") data from a component to its parent component whenever the value of the given variable is modified.

The output from this code sample is anti-climatic in the sense that there is a lot of code to produce the following output that is visible in the Inspector tab:

```
constructor parentValue = 77
```

However, the purpose of this code sample is to draw your attention to some of the non-intuitive code snippets (especially in `app.module.ts`). Moreover, this code sample works correctly for version 2.1.5 of the TypeScript compiler, but it's possible that future versions will require modifications to the code (so keep this detail in mind).

Copy the directory `ParentChildEmitters` from the companion files to a convenient location. Listing 2.18 shows the content of `app.component.ts`, which updates the value of a property of a child component from a parent component.

### LISTING 2.18: app.component.ts

```
import {Component}       from '@angular/core';
import {EventEmitter}    from '@angular/core';
import {ChildComponent} from './childcomponent';

@Component({
  selector: 'app-root',
  providers: [ChildComponent],
  template: `
    <div>
      <child-comp [childValue]="parentValue"
        (childValueChange)="reportValueChange($event)">
      </child-comp>
    </div>
  `
})
export class AppComponent {
  public parentValue:number = 77;

  constructor() {
        console.log("constructor  parentValue  =  "+this.
parentValue);
  }

  reportValueChange(event) {
    console.log(event);
  }
}
```

The `template` property in Listing 2.18 has a top-level `<div>` element that contains a `<child-comp>` element that has two attributes, as shown here:

```
<child-comp [childValue]="parentValue"
            (childValueChange)="reportValueChange($event)">
</child-comp>
```

The [childValue] attribute assigns the value of parentValue to the value of childValue. Notice that the variable parentValue is defined in AppComponent, whereas the variable childValue is defined in ChildComponent. This code shows how to pass a value from a parent component to a child component.

Next, the childValueChange attribute is assigned the value that is returned from ChildComponent to the current ("parent") component. The attribute childValueChange is updated only when the value of childValue (in the child component) is modified. This code shows how to pass a value from a child component to a parent component.

Keep in mind the following point: the child component *must* define a variable of type EventEmitter (such as childValueChange) in order to "emit" a modified value from the child component to the parent component.

The next portion of Listing 2.18 is a simple constructor, followed by the method reportValueChange that contains a console.log() statement.

Listing 2.19 displays the contents of childcomponent.ts that shows you how to update the value of a property of a child component from a parent component.

### LISTING 2.19: childcomponent.ts

```
import {Component}    from '@angular/core';
import {Input}        from '@angular/core';
import {Output}       from '@angular/core';
import {EventEmitter} from '@angular/core';

@Component({
   selector: 'child-comp',
   template: `
      <button (click)="decrement();">Subtract</button>
      <input type="text" [value]="childValue">
      <button (click)="increment();">Add</button>

})
```

```
export class ChildComponent {
  @Input() childValue:number = 3;
  @Output() childValueChange = new EventEmitter();

  constructor() {
    console.log("constructor childValue = "+this.
childValue);
  }
  increment() {
    this.childValue++;

    this.childValueChange.emit({
      value: this.childValue
    })
  }
  decrement() {
    this.childValue--;

    this.childValueChange.emit({
      value: this.childValue
    })
  }
}
```

Listing 2.19 contains a template property that specifies three elements: a "decrement" <button> element, an <input> field where users can enter a number, and an "increment" <button> element. The first <button> element increments the value <input> field whereas the second <button> element decrements the value.

The exported class ChildComponent class contains the numeric variable childValue that is decorated via @Input() and whose value is set by the parent.

As you can see, the methods increment() and decrement() increase and decrease the value of childValue, respectively. In both cases, the modified value of childValue is then "emitted" back to the parent with this code block:

```
this.childValueChange.emit({
    value: this.childValue
})
```

Update the content of app.module.ts as shown in Listing 2.20 (which is different from the content of this file in previous examples in this chapter).

### LISTING 2.20: app.module.ts

```
import { NgModule }           from '@angular/core';
import {CUSTOM_ELEMENTS_SCHEMA} from '@angular/core';
import { BrowserModule }  from '@angular/platform-browser';
import { AppComponent }    from './app.component';
import { ChildComponent } from './childcomponent';


@NgModule({
   imports:        [ BrowserModule ],
   providers:      [ ChildComponent ],
   declarations:   [ AppComponent ],
   bootstrap:      [ AppComponent ],
   schemas:        [CUSTOM_ELEMENTS_SCHEMA]
})
export class AppModule { }
```

When you launch the Angular application in this section, the value that is displayed in the <input> element is 77, which is the value in the parent component, and *not* the value that is assigned in the child component (which is 3). Open the inspector for the current browser session and you will see the following output:

```
constructor parentValue = 77
```

Keep in mind that if you specify ChildComponent in the declarations property instead of the providers property, you will probably see this error message:

```
"Can't bind to <child-comp> since it isn't a known
native property"
```

Listing 2.20 contains three code snippets shown in bold, all of which are required for this code sample. If you do not include them, you will see the following type of error message in the Inspector tab of your browser:

```
Error: Template parse errors:
Can't bind to 'childValue' since it isn't a known property
of 'child-comp'.
```

1) If `child-comp` is an Angular component and it has `childValue` input, then verify that it is part of this module.
2) If `child-comp` is a Web Component then add `CUSTOM_ELE-MENTS_SCHEMA` to the `@NgModule.schemas` of this component to suppress this message.
3) To allow any property add `NO_ERRORS_SCHEMA` to the `@NgModule.schemas` of this component. (`<div>` `<child-comp` [ERROR ->] [childValue]="parentValue" (childValueChange)="reportValueChange($event)"> </child-comp`): ng:///AppModule/AppComponent.html@2:18

## Presentational Components

Presentational components receive data as input and generate views as outputs (so they do not maintain the application state). Consider the following component:

```
@Component({
  selector: 'student-info',
  template: `<h2>{{studentDetails?.status}}</h2>
    <div class="container">
      <table class="table">
        <tbody>
        <tr *ngFor="let student of students">
            <td>{{student.fname}}</td>
            <td>{{student.lname}}</td>
        </tr>
        </tbody>
      </table>
</div>`
})
export class StudentDetailsComponent {
    @Input()
    studentDetails:StudentDetails;
}
```

The `StudentDetailsComponent` component has primarily presentational responsibilities: the component receives input data and displays that on the screen. As a result, this component is reusable.

By contrast, application-specific components (also called "smart" components) are tightly coupled to a specific Angular application. Thus, a smart component would have a presentation component (but not the converse).

Since data is passed to this component synchronously (not via an `Observable`), the data might not be present initially, which is the reason for including the so-called Elvis operator (i.e., the "?" in the template).

## Working with Pipes in Angular

Angular supports something called a `pipe` that is somewhat analogous to the Unix pipe "|" command. Angular pipes enable you to specify conditional logic that filters data, which is to say, you can display a subset of data items that is based on your conditional logic.

Angular supports built-in pipes, asynchronous pipes, and support for custom pipes. The next two sections show you some example of built-in pipes, followed by a description of asynchronous pipes. A separate section shows you how to define a custom Angular pipe.

### Working with Built-in Pipes

Angular supports various built-in pipes, such as `DatePipe`, `UpperCasePipe`, `LowerCasePipe`, `CurrencyPipe`, and `PercentPipe`. Each of these intuitively named pipes provides the functionality that you would expect: the `DatePipe` supports date values, the `UpperCasePipe` converts strings to uppercase, and so forth.

As a simple example, suppose that the variable food has the value `pizza`. Then the following code snippet displays the string `PIZZA`:

```
<p> I eat too much {{ food | UppercasePipe }} </p>
```

You can also parameterize some Angular pipes, an example of which is shown here:

```
</p> My brother's birthday is {{ birthday | date:"MM/dd/yy" }} </p>
```

In fact, you can even chain pipes, as shown here:

```
My brother's birthday is {{ birthday | date | uppercase}}
```

In the preceding code snippet, `birthday` is a custom pipe (written by you). As another example, suppose that an Angular application contains the variable `employees` array that contains JSON-based data. You can display the contents of the array with this code snippet:

```
<div>{{employees | json }}</div>
```

### The AsyncPipe

The Angular `AsyncPipe` accepts a `Promise` or `Observable` as input and subscribes to the input automatically, eventually returning the emitted values. Moreover, `AsyncPipe` is stateful: the pipe maintains a subscription to the input `Observable` and keeps delivering values from that `Observable` as they arrive.

The following code block gives you an idea of how to display stock quotes, where the variable `quotes$` is an `Observable`:

```
@Component({
    selector: 'stock-quotes',
    template: `
     <h2>Your Stock Quotes</h2>
     <p>Message: {{ quotes$ | async }}</p>
     `
})
```

Keep in mind that the `AsyncPipe` provides two advantages. First, `AsyncPipe` reduces boilerplate code. Second, there is no need to subscribe or to unsubscribe from an `Observable` (the latter feature can help avoid memory leaks).

Angular does not provide pipes for filtering or sorting lists (i.e., there is no `FilterPipe` or `OrderByPipe`) because both can be compute intensive, which would adversely affect the perceived performance of an application.

The code sample in the next section shows you how to create a custom pipe that displays a filtered list of users based on conditional logic that is defined in custom code.

## Creating a Custom Angular Pipe

Copy the directory `SimplePipe` from the companion files into a convenient location. Listing 2.21 shows the content of app.component. ts, which illustrates how to define and use a custom pipe in an Angular application that displays a subset of a hard-coded list of users.

*LISTING 2.21: app.component.ts*

```
import { Component } from '@angular/core';
import {User}        from './user.component';
```

```
import {MyPipe}        from './pipe.component';

@Component({
  selector: 'app-root',
  template: `
    <div>
      <h2>Complete List of Users:</h2>
      <ul>
       <li
       *ngFor="let user of userList"
         (mouseover)='mouseEvent(user)'
         [class.chosen]="isSelected(user)">
         {{user.fname}}-{{user.lname}}<br/>
       </li>
      </ul>

      <h2>Filtered List of Users:</h2>
      <ul>
       <li
       *ngFor="let user of userList|MyPipe"
         (mouseover)='mouseEvent(user)'
         [class.chosen]="isSelected(user)">
         {{user.fname}}-{{user.lname}}<br/>
       </li>
      </ul>
    </div>
  `
})
export class AppComponent {
  user:User;
  currentUser:User;
  userList:User[];

  mouseEvent(user:User) {
      console.log("current user: "+user.fname+" "+user.
lname);
      this.currentUser = user;
  }

  isSelected(user: User): boolean {
```

```
   if (!user || !this.currentUser) {
     return false;
   }

   return user.lname === this.currentUser.lname;
//return true;
   }

   constructor() {
     this.userList = [
                  new User('Jane','Smith'),
                  new User('John','Stone'),
                  new User('Dave','Jones'),
                  new User('Rick','Heard'),
                  ]
   }
}
```

Listing 2.21 imports the User custom class and the MyPipe custom class, where the latter is specified in the array of values for the pipes property.

Next, the template property displays two unordered lists of user names. The first list displayed the complete list, and whenever users hover (with their mouse) over a user in the first list, the current user is set equal to that user via the code in the mouseEvent() method (defined in the AppComponent class).

Note that the constructor in the AppComponent class (shown at the bottom of Listing 2.21) initializes the userList array with a set of users, each of which is an instance of the User custom component.

The second list displays a filtered list of users based on the conditional logic in the custom pipe called MyPipe. Listing 2.22 shows the content of pipe.component.ts, which defines the custom pipe MyPipe that is referenced in Listing 2.25.

### LISTING 2.22: pipe.component.ts

```
import {Component} from '@angular/core';
import {Pipe}      from '@angular/core';

@Pipe({
  name: "MyPipe"
})
```

```
export class MyPipe {
  transform(item) {
  return item.filter((item) => item.fname.startsWith("J"));
 //return item.filter((item) => item.lname.endsWith("th"));
 //return item.filter((item) => item.lname.contains("n"));
  }
}
```

Listing 2.22 contains the MyPipe class that contains the transform() method. There are three examples of how to define the behavior of the pipe, the first of which returns the users whose first name starts with an uppercase J (which is admittedly somewhat contrived, but nevertheless illustrative of pipe-related functionality).

Listing 2.23 shows the content of the custom component user.component.ts for creating User instances, which is also referenced via an import statement in app.component.ts.

### LISTING 2.23: user.component.ts

```
import {Component} from '@angular/core';
import { Inject } from '@angular/core';

@Component({
  selector: 'my-user',
  template: '<h1></h1>'
})
export class User {
  fname: string;
  lname: string;

  constructor(@Inject(String) fname: string,
              @Inject(String) lname: string) {
    this.fname = fname;
    this.lname = lname;
  }
}
```

The contents of Listing 2.23 are straightforward: there is a User class comprising the fields fname and lname for the first name and last name, respectively, for each new user, both of which are specified in the constructor whenever a new instance of the User class is created.

Finally, we need to update the contents of app.module.ts, as shown in Listing 2.24, where the modified contents are shown in bold.

### LISTING 2.24: app.module.ts

```
import { NgModule }        from '@angular/core';
import { BrowserModule }   from '@angular/platform-browser';
import { AppComponent }    from './app.component';
import { MyPipe }          from './pipe.component';
import { User }            from './user.component';

@NgModule({
  imports:       [ BrowserModule ],
  declarations:  [ AppComponent, MyPipe, User ],
  bootstrap:     [ AppComponent ]
})
export class AppModule { }
```

Listing 2.24 contains two new import statements so that the custom components MyPipe and User can be referenced in the declarations property. In addition, the declarations element includes MyPipe and User in its array of values.

Launch the application, navigate to localhost:4200 in a browser session, and after a few moments, you will see the following output:

Complete List of Users:

- Jane-Smith
- John-Stone
- Dave-Jones
- Rick-Heard

Filtered List of Users:

- Jane-Smith
- John-Stone

In the last portion of the preceding output, this Angular application performs a filtering operation that "filters out" the users whose first name does not start with the capital letter J.

Now that you understand how to define a basic Pipe in Angular, you can experiment with custom Pipes that receives data asynchronously. This type of functionality can be very useful when you need to display data (such as a list or a table) whenever it's updated without the need for "polling" the source of the data.

Additional information regarding Angular pipes is here:

*https://angular.io/docs/ts/latest/guide/pipes.html*

This concludes the portion of the chapter regarding Pipes in Angular. The next section discusses Services in Angular applications.

## Reading JSON Data via an Observable in Angular

This section shows you how to read data from a file that contains JSON-based data. Copy the directory ReadJSONFile from the companion files into a convenient location. Listing 2.25 shows the content of app.component.ts, which illustrates how to make an HTTP request (which returns an Observable) to read a JSON-based file with employee information.

### LISTING 2.25: app.component.ts

```
import { Component }   from '@angular/core';
import { Observable}   from 'rxjs';
import { Inject }      from '@angular/core';
import { HttpClient }  from '@angular/common/http';
import { HttpHeaders } from '@angular/common/http';
declare var $: any;

@Component({
  selector: 'app-root',
  template: `
    <button (click)="httpRequest()">Employee Info</button>
    <ul>
        <li *ngFor="let emp of employees">
           {{emp.fname}} {{emp.lname}} lives in {{emp.city}}
        </li>
    </ul>
`
})
export class AppComponent {
  employees : any;

//OLD STYLE: constructor(@Inject(Http) public http:Http)
{}
```

```
  constructor(@Inject(HttpClient) public http:HttpClient)
{}

  httpRequest() {
    this.http.get('assets/employees.json')
      .subscribe(
        // this function runs on success
        data => this.employees = data,
        // this function runs on error
        err => console.log('error reading data: '+err),
        // this function runs on completion
        () => this.userInfo()
      );
  }

  userInfo() {
  //console.log("employees = "+JSON.stringify(this.
employees));
  }
}
```

The template property in Listing 2.25 starts with a <button> element for making an HTTP GET request to retrieve information about employees from a JSON file. The template property also contains a <ul> element for displaying an unordered list of employee-based data.

The AppComponent class contains the variable employees, followed by a constructor that initializes the http variable that is an instance of the Http class. The httpRequest() method contains the code for making the HTTP GET request that returns an Observable. The subscribe() method contains the usual code, which in this case also initializes the employees array from the contents of the file employees.json in the subdirectory src/assets.

Listing 2.26 shows the content of employees.json, which contains employee-related information. This file is located in the src/assets subdirectory.

**LISTING 2.26: employees.json**

```
[
{"fname":"Jane","lname":"Jones","city":"San Francisco"},
{"fname":"John","lname":"Smith","city":"New York"},
```

```
{"fname":"Dave","lname":"Stone","city":"Seattle"},
{"fname":"Sara","lname":"Edson","city":"Chicago"}
]
```

Listing 2.27 shows the content of app.module.ts, which imports the Angular HttpModule.

### LISTING 2.27: *app.module.ts*

```
import { NgModule }          from '@angular/core';
import { BrowserModule }     from '@angular/platform-browser';
import { HttpClientModule } from '@angular/common/http';
import { AppComponent }      from './app.component';

@NgModule({
  imports:       [ BrowserModule, HttpClientModule ],
  declarations: [ AppComponent ],
  bootstrap:     [ AppComponent ]
})
export class AppModule { }
```

Listing 2.27 contains the familiar set of import statements, along with HttpClientModule that is listed in the array of elements in the imports property that is inside the @NgModule decorator.

Launch the Angular application and you will see a button element (not shown here) that you can click, after which you will see the following text:

- Jane Jones lives in San Francisco
- John Smith lives in New York
- Dave Stone lives in Seattle
- Sara Edson lives in Chicago

Angular applications prior to Angular 8 required two additional code snippets, the first of which is an import statement for the map() operator, as shown here:

```
import { map } from 'rxjs/operators';
```

The second code snippet involves an invocation of the map() operator immediately following the invocation of the get() method, as shown here:

```
this.http.get('assets/employees.json')
//.map(res => res.json()) redundant in Angular 8 and 9 and 10
```

However, the `map()` operator is automatically invoked for us, so it's no longer required; moreover, if you do include this code snippet, you see an error message.

## Upgrading Code from Earlier Angular Versions

Although Angular 10 is mostly backward compatible with earlier versions of Angular, sometimes code modifications are required, especially code that involves `HTTP` requests.

In particular, the previous section showed you that the invocation of the `map()` operator is no longer required in Angular 9 or in Angular 10. Another change pertains to a redundant `import` statement and a modification to another `import` statement.

Specifically, suppose that you see the following error messages when you compile an Angular application:

```
Error: Can't resolve 'rxjs/Rx'

Module not found Error: Can't resolve '@angular/http'
Error: Unexpected value 'HttpClient' imported by the module
'AppModule'. Please add a @NgModule annotation.
```

You need to update the code in `app.component.ts` as well as `app.module.ts` with the appropriate code for Angular 10, as shown here for `app.component.ts`:

```
// import { Observable }    from 'rxjs/Observable';    // old
import { Observable }    from 'rxjs';                  // new

// import { Http }            from '@angular/http';        // old
import { Http }            from '@angular/common/http'; // new

import { HttpClient }      from '@angular/common/http'; //
new

import { HttpHeaders }     from '@angular/common/http'; //
new

// import 'rxjs/Rx';                                       // old
```

Here are the changes to `app.module.ts`:

```
//import {HttpModule}      from '@angular/http';         // old
```

```
import {HttpClientModule} from '@angular/common/http'; //
new
imports: [
  BrowserModule,
  HttpClientModule,            // new
],
declarations: [
  AppComponent,
  HttpClientModule             // new
],
```

The preceding changes to app.component.ts and app.module. ts are precisely the changes that have been made to the Angular application ReadJSONFile (discussed in the previous section) to upgrade to an Angular 10 application. In the ideal scenario, these changes will work for your application as well, saving you some debugging effort. However, please keep in mind that you might need to make other modifications to the code in your Angular application.

## Reading Multiple Files with JSON Data in Angular

This section shows you how to read data from several files that contain JSON-based data. Copy the directory ReadMultipleJSONFiles from the companion files into a convenient location. Listing 2.28 shows the content of app.component.ts, which illustrates how to make multiple HTTP requests (which returns an Observable) to read a JSON-based files with customer information, employee information, and relative information.

**LISTING 2.28:** *app.component.ts*

```
import { Component }  from '@angular/core';
import { Observable } from 'rxjs';
import { HttpClient } from '@angular/common/http';

@Component({
  selector: 'app-root',
  styleUrls: ['./app.component.css'],
  template:`
    <h2>Angular HTTP and Observables</h2>
    <h3>Some of our Employees</h3>
```

```
    <ul>
      <li *ngFor="let emp of employees">
        {{emp.fname}} {{emp.lname}} lives in {{emp.city}}
      </li>
    </ul>
    <h3>Some of our Customers</h3>
    <ul>
      <li *ngFor="let cust of customers">
        {{cust.fname}} {{cust.lname}} lives in {{cust.city}}
      </li>
    </ul>
    <h3>Some of our Relatives</h3>
    <ul>
      <li *ngFor="let rel of relatives">
        {{rel.fname}} {{rel.lname}} lives in {{rel.city}}
      </li>
    </ul>
  `
})
export class AppComponent {
  public employees : any = [];
  public customers : any = [];
  public relatives : any = [];

  constructor(private http:HttpClient) {
   //this.getCustomers();
   //this.getEmployees();
   //this.getRelatives();
     this.getEveryone();
  }

  getCustomers() {
    this.http.get('assets/customers.json')
      .subscribe(
        // this function runs on success
        data => { this.customers = data },
        // this function runs on error
         err => console.log('error reading customer data:
'+err),
        // this function runs on completion
        () => console.log('Loading customers completed')
      );
  }
```

```
getEmployees() {
  this.http.get('assets/employees.json')
    .subscribe(
      // this function runs on success
      data => { this.employees = data },
      // this function runs on error
      err => console.log('error reading employee data:
'+err),
      // this function runs on completion
      () => console.log('Loading employees completed')
    );
}


getRelatives() {
  this.http.get('assets/relatives.json')
    .subscribe(
      // this function runs on success
      data => { this.relatives = data },
      // this function runs on error
      err => console.log('error reading relatives data:
'+err),
      // this function runs on completion
      () => console.log('Loading relatives completed')
    );
}


getEveryone() {
  this.getCustomers();
  this.getEmployees();
  this.getRelatives();
}


infoResults() {
  console.log('inside infoResults');
  console.log('this.customers:',this.customers);
  console.log('this.employees:',this.employees);
  console.log('this.relatives:',this.relatives);
}
}
```

The `template` property in Listing 2.28 contains three very similar blocks of code that all use `ngFor` to display information about customers, employees, and relatives. Since each code block resembles the code with `ngFor` in Listing 2.25, read the associated description for the details about their contents.

The `AppComponent` class contains the array-based variables `customers`, `employees`, and `relatives`. Next, a constructor initializes the `http` variable that is an instance of the `HttpClient` class, as shown here:

```
constructor(private http:HttpClient) {
  //this.getCustomers();
  //this.getEmployees();
  //this.getRelatives();
    this.getEveryone();
}
```

The constructor contains three commented-out methods, and these three methods retrieve data from the JSON-based files `customers.json`, `employees.json`, and `relatives.json`. In addition, the `getEveryone()` method is a convenience method that invokes the other three methods to retrieve all three types of data.

Although these three methods are similar to the code in Listing 2.25, let's take a look at the contents of the `getCustomers()` method:

```
getCustomers() {
    this.http.get('assets/customers.json')
      .subscribe(
        // this function runs on success
        data => { this.customers = data },
        // this function runs on error
        err => console.log('error reading customer
data:'+err),
        // this function runs on completion
        () => console.log('Loading customers completed')
      );
}
```

The preceding code makes an HTTP GET request when the `subscribe()` method is invoked, and if it's successful, the variable `customers` is populated with the contents of the file `customers.json`. In fact, these are the only two lines that you need to modify in the `getEmployees()` method (which involves the `employees.json` file) and the `getRelatives()` method (which involves the `relatives.json` file).

The `httpRequest()` method contains the code for making the HTTP GET request that returns an `Observable`. The `subscribe()` method contains the usual code, which in this case also initializes the `employees` array from the contents of the file `employees.json` in the subdirectory `src/assets`.

Listing 2.29, Listing 2.30, and Listing 2.31 show the contents of the JSON-based files `customers.json`, `employees.json`, and `relatives.json`, respectively.

### LISTING 2.29: *customers.json*

```
[
{"fname":"Paolo","lname":"Friulano","city":"Maniago"},
{"fname":"Luigi","lname":"Napoli","city":"Vicenza"},
{"fname":"Miko","lname":"Tanaka","city":"Yokohama"},
{"fname":"Yumi","lname":"Fujimoto","city":"Tokyo"}
]
```

### LISTING 2.30: *employees.json*

```
[
{"fname":"Jane","lname":"Jones","city":"San Francisco"},
{"fname":"John","lname":"Smith","city":"New York"},
{"fname":"Dave","lname":"Stone","city":"Seattle"},
{"fname":"Sara","lname":"Edson","city":"Chicago"}
]
```

### LISTING 2.31: *relatives.json*

```
[
{"fname":"Beppi","lname":"Guarda","city":"Vicenza"},
{"fname":"Paolo","lname":"Fermi","city":"Padova"},
{"fname":"Antonio","lname":"Gatto","city":"Brescia"},
{"fname":"Pasquale","lname":"Fritto","city":"Verona"}
]
```

Listing 2.32 shows the content of `app.module.ts`, which imports the Angular `HttpModule`.

### LISTING 2.32: *app.module.ts*

```
import { BrowserModule }    from '@angular/
platform-browser';
import { NgModule }         from '@angular/core';
```

```
import { AppComponent }      from './app.component';
import { HttpClientModule } from '@angular/common/http';

@NgModule({
  declarations: [
    AppComponent
  ],
  imports: [
    BrowserModule,
    HttpClientModule,
  ],
  providers: [ ],
  bootstrap: [AppComponent]
})
export class AppModule { }
```

Listing 2.32 contains the standard set of import statements, along with HttpClientModule that is listed in the array of imports in the @ NgModule decorator.

Launch this Angular application to see the following output displayed in a browser session:

## Angular HTTP and Observables

### Some of our Employees

■ Jane Jones lives in San Diego
■ John Smith lives in New York
■ Dave Stone lives in Seattle
■ Sara Edson lives in Chicago

### Some of our Customers

■ Paolo Friulano lives in Maniago
■ Luigi Napoli lives in Vicenza
■ Miko Tanaka lives in Yokohama
■ Yumi Fujimoto lives in Tokyo

### Some of our Relatives

■ Beppi Guarda lives in Vicenza
■ Paolo Fermi lives in Padova

- Antonio Gatto lives in Brescia
- Pasquale Fritto lives in Verona

The JSON files in Angular applications are located in the `src/assets` subdirectory, and in this example, there are three JSON files. These files are referenced in each of the three methods `getCustomers()`, `getEmployees()`, and `getRelatives()`, with the following code snippets:

```
this.http.get('assets/customers.json')
this.http.get('assets/employees.json')
this.http.get('assets/relatives.json')
```

As you can probably infer, the prefix `assets` in the preceding code snippet refers to the subdirectory `src/assets` in an Angular application. If you see a blank screen when you launch an Angular application, you most likely did not place your JSON files in the correct subdirectory.

## Reading CSV Files in Angular

The code sample in this section shows you how to read the contents of a CSV file and display the contents of that file. This Angular application is very useful in Chapter 6 for a machine learning task that involves reading the contents of a dataset from a CSV file.

Copy the directory `ReadWineCSV` from the companion files into a convenient location. Listing 2.33 shows the content of `app.component.ts`, which illustrates how to read the contents of `assets/wine.csv` and then display the data in tabular form.

**LISTING 2.33: app.component.ts**

```
import { Component }    from '@angular/core';
import { Inject }       from '@angular/core';
import { HttpClient }   from '@angular/common/http';
import { Observable }   from 'rxjs';


@Component({
  selector: 'app-root',
  styleUrls: ['./app.component.css'],
  template: `
    <table>
      <thead>
        <tr>
```

```
          <th>{{headers[0]}}</th>
          <th>{{headers[1]}}</th>
          <th>{{headers[2]}}</th>
        </tr>
      </thead>
      <tbody>
        <tr *ngFor="let record of records;let i = index;">
          <td> <span>{{record[0]}}</span> </td>
          <td> <span>{{record[1]}}</span> </td>
          <td> <span>{{record[2]}}</span> </td>
        </tr>
      </tbody>
    </table>
    `,
})
export class AppComponent {
  public headers: any = [];
  public records: any = [];
  public csvUrl = 'assets/wine.csv';

  constructor(@Inject(HttpClient) public http:HttpClient)
{
    this.readCsvData ();
  }

  readCsvData () {
    this.http.get(this.csvUrl, {responseType: 'text'})
      .subscribe(
        data => { this.extractData(data) },
        err => { console.log(err) }
      );
  }

  private extractData(res: any) {
    let csvData = res || '';
    let allTextLines = csvData.split(/\r\n|\n/);

    // headers: Alcohol, Malic acid, class
    this.headers = allTextLines[0].split(',');
    // console.log("headers: "+this.headers)

    let lines = [];

    // skip the header row: start from index 1
```

```
for (let i=1; i < allTextLines.length; i++) {
    // split content based on comma
    let data = allTextLines[i].split(',');

    if (data.length == headers.length) {
        let tarr = [];
        for ( let j = 0; j < headers.length; j++) {
            tarr.push(data[j]);
        }
        lines.push(tarr);
    }
}
// console.log("lines: "+lines)
this.records = lines;
    }
}
```

Listing 2.33 contains an assortment of `import` statements, some standard properties, and a `template` property that consists of two parts. The first part displays header-related information, and the second part contains a loop that iterates through the data that was retrieved from the CSV file `wine.csv`.

The next portion of Listing 2.33 defines a constructor that invokes the `readCsvData()` method, which in turn makes an `HTTP GET` request in order to read the contents of the CSV file `wine.csv` in the `src/assets` subdirectory.

After the `HTTP GET` request has completed, the code invokes the `extractData()` method that contains a loop that creates a one-dimensional array for each row of data in the CSV file `wine.csv`. Each array is appended to the `lines` array, and when the loop has completed, the `records` array is initialized with the contents of the `lines` array.

Take a look at the `template` property in Listing 2.33 to see a loop in the `<tbody>` element that creates and displays a `<tr>` element for each row in the `records` array.

Listing 2.34 shows the updated content of `app.module.ts`, which contains the usual code that you have seen in previous code samples.

### LISTING 2.34: app.module.ts

```
import { BrowserModule }    from '@angular/
platform-browser';
```

```
import { NgModule }          from '@angular/core';
import { AppComponent }      from './app.component';
import { HttpClientModule } from '@angular/common/http';

@NgModule({
  declarations: [
    AppComponent
  ],
  imports: [
    BrowserModule,
    HttpClientModule
  ],
  providers: [],
  bootstrap: [AppComponent]
})
export class AppModule { }
```

There are two additions to the auto-generated file app.module.ts that are shown in Listing 2.34: the first snippet is an import statement and the second snippet references HttpClientModule in the imports element.

Launch this Angular application. In the browser session, you will see the following output:

```
Alcohol Malic acid class
14.23   1.71    1
13.2    1.78    1
13.16   2.36    1
14.37   1.95    1
13.24   2.59    1
// detailed omitted for brevity
13.71   5.65    3
13.4    3.91    3
13.27   4.28    3
13.17   2.59    3
14.13   4.1     3
```

The output above is a "bare bones" display consisting of three columns of numeric data. Feel free to define CSS-related code for better styling of the output.

## Summary

This chapter showed you how to use UI Controls in Angular applications. You saw how to render buttons, how to render lists of names, and also how to add and delete names from those lists. You also learned about conditional logic and how to create child components.

Then you learned about communicating between parent and child components, followed by a discussion of presentational components. In addition, you were briefly introduced to Angular `Pipes` and code samples that illustrate how to use them in Angular applications. Finally, you learned how to make `HTTP GET` requests from an Angular application to retrieve the contents of a JSON file as well as the contents of a CSV file that are in the `src/assets` subdirectory.

# CHAPTER 3

# FORMS AND SERVICES

This chapter shows you how to create Angular applications that use Angular Forms and Services. The code samples rely on an understanding of functionality that is discussed in the previous chapter, such as how to make HTTP requests in Angular.

The first section in this chapter contains Angular applications that use Angular Controls and Control Groups. This section also provides an example of an Angular application that contains a form that makes HTTP GET requests.

The second part of this chapter contains code samples that retrieve data from an external endpoint. Specifically, this section shows you how to retrieve GitHub details for a hard-coded user, and also how to provide a GitHub user name in a text field and then search GitHub for additional details regarding that user.

The focus of the code samples in this book is on Angular-specific features, which means that there is a "no frills" approach to the UI portion of the applications. Hence, the UI portion is minimalistic, but you can enhance the UI by providing your own custom code.

## Overview of Angular Forms

An Angular FormControl represents a single input field, a FormGroup consists of multiple logically related fields, and an NgForm component represents a <form> element in an HTML Web page. The ngSubmit action for submitting a form has this syntax:

```
(ngSubmit)="onSubmit(myForm.value)".
```

Note that NgForm provides the ngSubmit event, whereas you must define the onSubmit() method in the component class. The expression myForm. value consists of the key/value pairs in the form. Later in the chapter, you will see examples involving these controls, as well as FormBuilder that supports additional useful functionality.

Angular also supports template-driven forms (with a FormsModule) and reactive forms (with a ReactiveFormsModule), both of which belong to @angular/forms. However, reactive forms are synchronous whereas template-driven forms are asynchronous.

## Reactive forms

Reactive forms involve the explicit management of the data flowing between a non-UI data model and a UI-oriented form model that retains the states and values of the HTML controls on screen. Reactive forms offer the ease of using reactive patterns, testing, and validation.

Reactive Forms involve the creation of a tree of Angular form control objects in the component class app.component.ts, which are also bound them to native form control elements in the component template app.component.html.

The component class has access to the data model and the form control structure, which enables you to propagate data model values into the form controls and also retrieve user-supplied values in the HTML controls. The component can observe changes in the form control state and react to those changes.

One advantage of working with form control objects directly is that value and validity updates are always synchronous and under your control. You won't encounter the timing issues that sometimes plague a template-driven form and reactive forms are easier to unit test. Since reactive forms are created directly via code, they are always available, which enables you to immediately update values and "drill down" to descendant elements.

## Template-driven forms

Template-driven forms involve placing HTML form controls (such as <input>, <select>, and so forth) in the component template. In addition, the form controls are bound to the data model properties in the component via directives such as ngModel. Note that Angular directives create Angular form objects based on the information in the provided data bindings. Angular uses `ngModel` to handle the transfer of data values, and also updates the mutable data model with user changes as they happen. Consequently, the `ngModel` directive does not belong to the `ReactiveFormsModule`.

Before delving into the material in this section, you should access the Angular application `MasterForm` that has the form-related code on the companion files. Although this code sample does not use an `FormGroup`, you might find some useful features in the code.

The next section shows you how to use the Angular `ngForm` component to create a form "the Angular way." Then you will see an example that shows you how to use an Angular `FormGroup` in an Angular Application.

## An Angular Form Example

This section contains a simple example of creating a form in an Angular application. Copy the directory `NGForm` from the companion files into a convenient location. Listing 3.1 shows the content of `app.component.ts`, which illustrates how to use `<input>` elements with an `ngModel` attribute in an Angular application.

*LISTING 3.1: app.component.ts*

```
import { Component } from '@angular/core';

@Component({
  selector: 'app-root',
  template: `
    <div>
      <h2>A Sample Form</h2>
      <form #f="ngForm"
            (ngSubmit)="onSubmit(f.value)"
            class="ui form">
        <div class="field">
          <label for="fname">fname</label>
          <input type="text"
                 id="fname"
                 placeholder="fname"
                 name="fname" ngModel>

          <label for="lname">lname</label>
```

```
            <input type="text"
                   id="lname"
                   placeholder="lname"
                   name="lname" ngModel>
        </div>

        <button type="submit">Submit</button>
      </form>
    </div>

})
export class AppComponent {
  myForm: any;

  onSubmit(form: any): void {
    console.log('you submitted value:', form);
  }
}
```

Listing 3.1 defines a template property that contains a <form> element that contains two <div> elements, each of which contains an <input> element. The first <input> element is for the first name and the second <input> element is for the last name of a new user.

Angular provides the NgModel directive that enables you to use the instance variable myForm in an Angular form. For example, the following code snippet specifies myForm as the control group for the given form:

```
<form [ngModel]="myForm"
    (ngSubmit)="onSubmit(myForm.value)"
```

Notice that onSubmit specifies myForm and that a Control is bound to the input element.

*Add the attribute novalidate to the <form> element to disable the browser validation.*

Listing 3.2 shows the content of app.module.ts, which imports a FormsModule and includes it in the imports property.

**LISTING 3.2: app.module.ts**

```
import { NgModule }       from '@angular/core';
import { FormsModule }    from '@angular/forms';
import { BrowserModule }  from '@angular/platform-browser';
import { AppComponent }   from './app.component';
```

```
@NgModule({
  imports:      [ BrowserModule, FormsModule ],
  declarations: [ AppComponent ],
  bootstrap:    [ AppComponent ]
})
export class AppModule { }
```

Listing 3.2 is straightforward: it contains two lines (shown in bold) involving the FormsModule that is required for this code sample.

Launch this application and navigate to localhost:4200 in a browser session, where you will see a simple form with two input fields labeled fname and lname. Enter a pair of values – let's say tom and jones – for these two fields. Open the inspector for this browser session to see the following information displayed:

```
you submitted value: Object { fname: "tom", lname:
"jones" }
you submitted value: Object { fname: "tom", lname:
"jones" }
```

## Data Binding and ngModel

Angular supports three types of binding in a form: no binding, one-way binding, and two-way binding. Here are some examples:

```
<!-- no binding -->
<input name="fname" ngModel>

<!-- one-way binding -->
<input name="fname" [ngModel]="fname">

<!-- two-way binding -->
<input name="fname" [ngModel]="fname"
       (ngModelChange)="fname=$event">

<!-- two-way binding -->
<input name="fname" [(ngModel)]="fname">
```

The *one-way binding* example looks for the fname property in the associated component and initializes the <input> field with the value of the fname property.

The *two-way binding* example fires the ngModelChange event when users alter the value of the <input> field, which causes an update to the fname property in the component, thereby ensuring that the input value and its associated component value are the same. You can also replace the value of ngModelChange with the output of a function (e.g., capitalizing the text string that users enter in the input field).

The second example of two-way data binding uses the "banana in a box" syntax, which is a shorthand way of achieving the same result as the first two-way data binding example. However, this syntax does not support the use of a function that is possible with the longer syntax for two-way data binding.

The next section in this chapter shows you how to work with forms in the "Angular way."

## Angular Forms with FormBuilder

The FormBuilder class and the FormGroup class are built-in Angular classes for creating forms. FormBuilder supports the control() function for creating a FormControl and the group() function for creating a FormGroup.

Copy the directory FormBuilder from the companion files to a convenient location. Listing 3.3 shows the content of app.component.ts, which illustrates how to use an Angular form in an Angular application.

*LISTING 3.3: app.component.ts*

```
import { Component }   from '@angular/core';
import { FormBuilder } from '@angular/forms';
import { FormGroup }   from '@angular/forms';

@Component({
  selector: 'app-root',
  template: `
    <div>
      <h2>A FormBuilder Form</h2>

      <form [formGroup]="myForm"
            (ngSubmit)="onSubmit(myForm.value)"
            class="ui form">

        <div class="field">
          <label for="fname">fname</label>
          <input type="text"
                 id="fname"
```

```
          placeholder="fname"
          [formControl]="myForm.controls['fname']">
    </div>

    <div class="field">
      <label for="lname">lname</label>
      <input type="text"
             id="lname"
             placeholder="lname"
         [formControl]="myForm.controls['lname']">
    </div>

    <button type="submit">Submit</button>
  </form>
</div>
`
})
export class AppComponent {
  myForm: FormGroup;

  constructor(fb: FormBuilder) {
    this.myForm = fb.group({
      'fname': ['John'],
      'lname': ['Smith']
    });
  }

  onSubmit(value: string): void {
    console.log('you submitted value:', value);
  }
}
```

Listing 3.3 contains a <form> element with two <div> elements, each of which contains an <input> element. The first <input> element is for the first name and the second <input> element is for the last name of a new user.

In Listing 3.3, FormBuilder is injected into the constructor, which creates an instance of FormBuilder that is assigned to the fb variable in the constructor. Next, myForm is initialized by invoking the group() method that takes an object of the key/value pairs. In this case, fname and lname are keys, and both of them appear as <input> elements in the template property. The values of these keys are optional initial values.

Launch this application and navigate to `localhost:4200` in a browser session, where you will see a simple form with two input fields labeled `fname` and `lname` that are pre-populated with the values `John` and `Smith`, respectively. Open the inspector for this browser session to see the following information displayed:

```
you submitted value: Object { fname: "John", lname:
"Smith" }
```

Obviously, you can add many other properties inside the `group()` method (such as address-related fields). Moreover, you can add a different form for each new entity. For example, you could create separate forms for a `Customer`, `PurchaseOrder`, and `LineItems`.

## Angular Reactive Forms

This section contains a code sample for creating a reactive Angular form, whose purpose will become clear after you see the `Form`-related code in Listing 3.6.

Copy the directory `ReactiveForm` from the companion files to a convenient location. Listing 3.4 shows the content of `app.component.ts`, which illustrates how to define a reactive Angular form in an Angular application.

**LISTING 3.4:** *app.component.ts*

```
import { Component }   from '@angular/core';
import { FormBuilder } from '@angular/forms';
import { FormGroup }   from '@angular/forms';
import { FormControl } from '@angular/forms';

@Component({
  selector:     'app-root',
  templateUrl: './app.component.html',
  styleUrls:    ['./app.component.css']
})
export class AppComponent {
    userForm: FormGroup;
    disabled:boolean;

    constructor(fb: FormBuilder) {
      this.userForm = fb.group({
        name:     'Jane',
```

```
      email:    'jsmith@yahoo.com',
      address: fb.group({
        city:   'San Francisco',
        state: 'California'
      })
   });
}

onFormSubmitted(theForm : FormGroup) {
    console.log("name    = "+theForm.controls['name'].
value);
    console.log("email = "+theForm.controls['email'].
value);
    console.log("city   = "+theForm.get('address.city').
value);
    console.log("city   = "+theForm.get('address.state').
value);
  }
}
```

Listing 3.4 contains the usual import statements, and notice how the variable userForm, which has type FormBuilder, is initialized in the constructor. In addition to two text fields, userForm contains the address element, which also has type FormBuilder.

Listing 3.5 shows the contents of app.module.html with an Angular form that contains <input> elements that correspond to the fields in the userForm variable.

### LISTING 3.5: *app.component.html*

```
<form    [formGroup]="userForm"    (ngSubmit)="onFormSubmit-
ted(userForm)">
  <label>
    <span>Name</span>
    <input type="text" formControlName="name" placehold-
er="Name" required>
  </label>

  <div>
    <label>
      <span>Email</span>
        <input type="email" formControlName="email" place-
holder="Email" required>
```

```
        </label>
      </div>

      <div formGroupName="address">
        <div>
          <label>
            <span>City</span>
              <input type="text" formControlName="city" place-
holder="City" required>
          </label>
        </div>
        <label>
          <span>Country</span>
            <input type="text" formControlName="state" placehold-
er="State" required>
        </label>
      </div>
        <br />
      <input type="submit" [disabled]="userForm.invalid">
    </form>
```

Listing 3.5 contains very simple HTML markup that enables users to change the default values for each of the input fields.

Listing 3.6 shows the updated content (shown in bold) of app.module. ts, which involves just two code snippets.

### LISTING 3.6: app.module.ts

```
import { BrowserModule } from '@angular/platform-browser';
import { NgModule }            from '@angular/core';
import { FormsModule }         from '@angular/forms';
import { ReactiveFormsModule } from '@angular/forms';
import { AppComponent }        from './app.component';

@NgModule({
  declarations: [
    AppComponent
  ],
  imports: [
    BrowserModule,
    FormsModule,
    ReactiveFormsModule
  ],
```

```
  providers: [],
  bootstrap: [AppComponent]
})
export class AppModule { }
```

Listing 3.6 contains one new import statement for ReactiveFormsModule (which can be combined with the import statement for FormsModule) that is also referenced in the imports property.

Launch this application and navigate to localhost:4200 in a browser session, where you will see a simple form with several pre-populated input fields. Click the submit button. When you open the inspector for this browser session, you will see the following information displayed:

```
name  = Jane
email = jsmith@yahoo.com
city  = San Francisco
state = California
```

### FormGroup versus FormArray

A FormGroup aggregates the values of FormControl elements into one object, where the control name is the key. Angular also supports FormArray (a "variation" of FormGroup) that aggregates the values of FormControl elements into an array.

FormGroup data is serialized as an array, whereas FormArray data is serialized as an object). If you do not know how many controls are in a given group, consider using a FormArray (otherwise use a FormGroup). The following link contains an example of using a FormArray:

*https://alligator.io/angular/reactive-forms-formarray-dynamic-fields/*

## Other Form Features in Angular

The preceding section gave you a glimpse into the modularized style of Angular forms, and this brief section highlights some additional form-related features in Angular, such as the following:

- Form validation
- Custom validators
- Nested forms
- Dynamic forms
- Template-driven forms

Validators enable you to perform validation on form fields, such specifying mandatory fields the minimum and maximum lengths of fields. You can also specify a regular expression that a field must match, which is very useful for zip codes, email addresses, and so forth. Alternatively, you can also specify validators programmatically.

Angular forms provide event listeners that detect various events pertaining to the state of a form, as shown in the following code snippets:

```
{{myform.form.touched}}
{{myform.form.untouched}}
{{myform.form.pristine}}
{{myform.form.dirty}}
{{myform.form.valid}}
{{myform.form.invalid}}
```

For example, the following <span> element is displayed if one or more form fields is invalid:

```
<span *ngIf="!myform.form.valid">The Form is Invalid</span>
```

You can also display error messages using the *ngIf directive to display the status of a specific field, as shown here:

```
<label>
  <span>First Name</span>
    <input type="text" formControlName="fname" placehold-
er="First Name">
    <p *ngIf="userForm.controls.fname.errors">
      This value is invalid
    </p>
</label>
```

An example of a dynamic Angular form is here:

*https://angular.io/docs/ts/latest/cookbook/dynamic-form.html*

Instead of using plain CSS for styling effects for field-related error messages, consider using something like Bootstrap.

## What are Angular Services?

This section contains a brief description of Angular Services, along with a list of some built-in services, followed by an example of defining a custom service in Angular in a subsequent section.

Sometimes the front-end of Web applications contains a combination of presentation logic and some business logic. Angular components comprise the presentation tier and services belong to the business-logic tier. Define your Angular services in such a way that they are decoupled from the presentation tier.

Angular services are classes that implement some business logic and are designed so that they can be used by components, models, and other services. In other words, services can be providers for other parts of an application.

Because of the "dependency injection" mechanism in Angular, services can be invoked in other sections of an Angular application. Moreover, Angular ensures that services are singletons, which means that each service consumer accesses the same instance of the service class.

A sample Angular custom service is shown here:

```
@Injectable()
export class UpperCaseService {
  public upper(message: string): string {
    return message.toUpperCase();
  }
}
```

The preceding class `UpperCaseService` is a service with one method that takes a string as an argument and returns the uppercase version of that string. The `@Injectable()` decorator is required so that this class can be injected as a dependency. Although this decorator is not mandatory in all cases, it's a good idea to mark your services in this manner. Use the `@Injectable` decorator only when a service (or class) receives an injection.

`app.component.ts`, which invokes the method in the preceding service, is here:

```
import {UpperCaseService} from "./path/to/service/
UpperCaseService";

@Component({
  selector: "convert",
  template: "<button (click)='greet()'>Greet</button>";
})
export class UpperComponent {
  // inject the custom service in the constructor
  constructor(private upperCaseService: UpperCaseService {
```

```
    }

    // invoke the method in the uppercaseService class
    public greet(): void {
      alert(this.upperCaseService.upper("Hello world"));
    }
}
```

The preceding code block imports the UpperCaseService class (shown in bold) via an import statement and then injects an instance of this class into the constructor of the UpperComponent class. Next, the template property contains a <button> element with a click handler that invokes the greet() method defined in the preceding code block. The greet() method displays an alert whose contents are the result of invoking the upper() method in the custom UpperCaseService class.

## Built-in Angular services

Angular supports various built-in services that are organized in different modules. For example, the http module (in @angular/common/http) contains support for HTTP requests that involve typical verbs, such as GET, POST, PUT, and DELETE. In fact, you saw examples of HTTP-based requests in Chapter 2. In addition, the routing module (in @angular/router) provides routing support, which includes HTML5 and hash routing. The form module (in @angular/forms) provides form-related services. Check the Angular documentation for a complete list of built-in services.

## An Angular Service Example

Copy the directory ServiceExample from the companion files into a convenient location. Listing 3.7 shows the content of app.component.ts, which contains an example of defining a basic custom service in Angular.

### LISTING 3.7: app.component.ts

```
import {Component}  from '@angular/core';
import {Injectable} from '@angular/core';

@Injectable()
class Service {
  somedata = ["one", "two", "three"];
  constructor() { }

  getData()  { return this.somedata; }
```

```
    toString() { return "From toString"; }
}

@Component({
  selector: 'app-root',
  providers: [ Service ],
  template: `Here is the data: {{ service.getData() }}`
})
export class AppComponent {
  constructor(public service: Service) { }
}
```

Listing 3.7 contains a `Service` class that is preceded by the `@Injectable` decorator, which enables us to inject an instance of the `Service` class in the constructor of the `AppComponent` class in Listing 3.7.

Launch this application and navigate to `localhost:4200` in a browser session, where you will see the following information displayed:

```
Data from the service: one,two,three
```

## A Service with an EventEmitter

This section contains a code sample that uses `EventEmitters` for communicating between a component and its child component. Now copy the directory `UserServiceEmitter` from the companion files to a convenient location. Listing 3.8 shows the content of `user.component.ts`, which defines a custom component for an individual user.

**LISTING 3.8: user.component.ts**

```
import {Component} from '@angular/core';
import { Inject } from '@angular/core';

@Component({
  selector: 'user',
  template: '<h2></h2>'
})
export class User {
  fname: string;
  lname: string;
  imageUrl: string;

    constructor(@Inject(String) fname: string,
                @Inject(String) lname: string,
```

```
            @Inject(String) imageUrl: string) {
    this.fname = fname;
    this.lname = lname;
    this.imageUrl = imageUrl;
  }
}
```

Listing 3.8 is straightforward: the custom User class has a constructor with three arguments that represent the first name, last name, and image url for a single user.

Listing 3.9 shows the content of user.service.ts, which creates a list of users, where each user has a first name, last name, and an associated PNG file.

### LISTING 3.9: user.service.ts

```
import {Component} from '@angular/core';
import {User}      from './user.component';

@Component({
  selector: 'user-comp',
  template: '<h2></h2>'
})
export class UserService {
  userList:User[];

  constructor() {
    this.userList = [
              new User('Jane','Smith','assets/sample1.
png'),
              new User('John','Stone','assets/sample2.
png'),
              new User('Dave','Jones','assets/sample3.
png'),
                    ]
  }

  getUserList() {
    return this.userList;
  }
}
```

Listing 3.9 imports the User custom component (shown in Listing 3.11) and then defines the UserService custom component that uses the userList array of User elements to keep track of users. This array is initialized in the constructor, and it contains three new `User` instances that are created and populated with data. The `getUserList()` method performs the "service" that returns the `userList` array.

Listing 3.10 shows the content of `app.component.ts`, which references the two preceding custom components and renders user-related information in an unordered list.

*LISTING 3.10: app.component.ts*

```
import {Component}     from '@angular/core';
import {EventEmitter}  from '@angular/core';
import {UserService}   from './user.service';
import {User}          from './user.component';

@Component({
  selector: 'app-root',
  providers: [User, UserService],
  template: `
    <div class="ui items">
      <user-comp
        *ngFor="let user of userList; let i=index"
        [user]="user"
        (mouseover)='mouseEvent(user)'
        [class.chosen]="isSelected(user)">
        USER {{i+1}}: {{user.fname}}-{{user.lname}}
        <img class="user-image" [src]="user.imageUrl"
             (mouseenter)="mouseEnter(user)"
             width="50" height="50">
      </user-comp>
    </div>
  `
})
export class AppComponent {
  user:User;
  currentUser:User;
  userList:User[];
  onUserSelected: EventEmitter<User>;

  mouseEvent(user:User) {
      console.log("current user: "+user.fname+" "+user.
lname);
    this.currentUser = user;
```

```
    this.onUserSelected.emit(user);
  }

mouseEnter(user:User) {
    console.log("image name: "+user.imageUrl);
    alert("Image name: "+user.imageUrl);
  }

isSelected(user: User): boolean {
  if (!user || !this.currentUser) {
    return false;
  }

  return user.lname === this.currentUser.lname;
//return true;
  }

constructor(userService:UserService) {
    this.onUserSelected = new EventEmitter();
    this.userList = userService.getUserList();
  }
}
```

Listing 3.10 contains a `template` property that displays the current list of users (i.e., the three users that are initialized by executing the code in the constructor in Listing 3.10). Notice the syntax to display information about each user in the list of users:

```
USER {{i+1}}: {{user.fname}}-{{user.lname}}
<img class="user-image" [src]="user.imageUrl"
    (mouseenter)="mouseEnter(user)"
    width="50" height="50">
```

Whenever users move their mouse over the displayed list, the `mouseEvent()` method is invoked to set `currentUser` to refer to the current user. In addition, when users move their mouse over one of the images, the `mouseEnter()` method is invoked, which displays a message via `console.log()` and also displays an alert.

Listing 3.11 shows the content of `app.module.ts`, which references the custom component and custom service.

### LISTING 3.11: app.module.ts

```
import { NgModule }      from '@angular/core';
import {CUSTOM_ELEMENTS_SCHEMA} from '@angular/core';
```

```
import { BrowserModule } from '@angular/platform-browser';
import { AppComponent }  from './app.component';
import { UserService }   from './user.service';

@NgModule({
   imports:       [ BrowserModule ],
   providers:     [ UserService ],
   declarations: [ AppComponent ],
   bootstrap:     [ AppComponent ],
   schemas:       [CUSTOM_ELEMENTS_SCHEMA]
})
export class AppModule { }
```

Listing 3.11 has essentially the same contents as the example in Chapter 2 that contains the schemas property. The lines shown in bold are the modifications that are required for the code sample in this section. You can refresh your memory by reading the comments that follow Listing 2.20 in Chapter 2 that pertain to the code snippets that are shown in bold in Listing 3.11.

## Searching for a GitHub User

This section shows you how to read a GitHub user name from an input field, perform a GitHub search for that user, and then append a subset of the details pertaining to that user in a list.

Copy the directory SearchGithubUsers from the companion files into a convenient location. Listing 3.12 shows the content of app.component. ts, which illustrates how to make an HTTP GET request to retrieve information about GitHub users.

**LISTING 3.12: app.component.ts**

```
import { Component }       from '@angular/core';
import { Inject }          from '@angular/core';
import { HttpClient }      from '@angular/common/http';
import { UserComponent } from './user.component';
import { Observable }      from 'rxjs';

@Component({
   selector: 'app-root',
   template: `
     <div>
```

```
<form>
  <h3>Search GitHub For User:</h3>
  <div class="field">
    <label for="guser">GitHub Id</label>
    <input type="text" #guser>
  </div>

  <button (click)="findGitHubUser(guser)">
    >>> Find User <<<
  </button>
</form>

<div id="container">
 <div class="onerow">
  <h3>List of Users:</h3>
  <ul>
   <li *ngFor="let user of users"
       (mouseover)="currUser(user)">
     {{user.field1}} {{user.field2}}</li>
  </ul>
 </div>
 </div>
</div>
})
export class AppComponent {
   currentUser:UserComponent = new UserComponent('ABC',
'DEF', '');
  users: UserComponent[];
  GitHubUserInfo : any;
  GitHubUserJSON:JSON;
  user:UserComponent;
  userStr:string = "";
  guserStr:string = "";

  constructor(@Inject(HttpClient) public http:HttpClient)
{
    this.users = [
      new UserComponent('Jane', 'jsmith', ''),
      new UserComponent('John', 'jstone', ''),
    ];
  }

  currUser(user) {
```

```
        console.log("fname: "+user.field1+" lname: "+user.
field2);
    this.currentUser = new UserComponent(user.field1,
                                         user.field2,
                                         user.field3);

  }

  findGitHubUser(guser: HTMLInputElement): boolean {
    if((guser.value == undefined) || (guser.value == "")) {
      alert("Please enter a user name");
      return;
    }

    // guser.value is not available in the 'subscribe'
method
    this.guserStr = guser.value;

    this.http.get('https://api.GitHub.com/users/'+guser.
value)
      .subscribe(data => {
        this.GitHubUserInfo = data;
    //console.log("GitHub info = "+JSON.stringify(data));

        // create a new User instance:
        this.user = new UserComponent(this.GitHubUserInfo.
name,
                                     this.guserStr,
                                     this.GitHubUserInfo.
created_at);

          // append new User instance to list of users:
          this.users.push(this.user); },
        err => {
          console.log("Lookup error: "+err);
          alert("Lookup error: "+err);
        }
      );

    // reset the input field to an empty string
    guser.value = "";

    // prevent a page reload:
    return false;
  }
}
```

Listing 3.12 contains the usual `import` statements, followed by an `@ Component` decorator that contains the usual `selector` property and an extensive code block for the `template` property.

The `template` property consists of a top-level `<div>` element that contains a `<form>` element and another `<div>` element. The `<form>` element contains an `<input>` element where users can enter a `GitHub` username, whereas the `<div>` element contains a `<ul>` element that in turn renders the list of current users. Notice that each `<li>` element in the `<ul>` element handles a `mouseover` event by setting the current user to the element that users have highlighted with their mouse.

The next portion of Listing 3.12 defines the exported class `AppComponent` that initializes some instance variables, followed by a constructor that initializes the `users` array with two hard-coded users. Next, the `currUser()` method "points" to the user that users have highlighted with their mouse. This functionality is not essential, but it's available in case you need to keep track of the user that is currently highlighted.

The `findGitHubUser()` method displays an alert if there the `<input>` element is empty (which prevents a redundant invocation of the `http()` method). If a user is specified in the `<input>` element, the code invokes an `HTTP GET` request from the `GitHub` website and appends the new user (as an instance of the `UserComponent` class) to the `users` array. In addition, an alert is displayed if there is no `GitHub` that matches the input string.

Another small but important detail is the following code snippet that keeps track of the user-specified input string:

```
this.guserStr = guser.value;
```

The preceding snippet is required because of the context change that occurs inside the invocation of the `get()` method, which loses the reference to the `guser` argument.

Listing 3.13 shows the content of `user.component.ts`, which contains three strings for keeping track of three user-related fields.

### LISTING 3.13: user.component.ts

```
import {Component} from '@angular/core';
import { Inject } from '@angular/core';

@Component({
  selector: 'current-user',
```

```
   template: '<h1></h1>'
})
export class UserComponent {
  constructor(@Inject(String) private field1: string,
              @Inject(String) private field2: string,
              @Inject(String) private field3: string) {
    this.field1 = field1;
    this.field2 = field2;
    this.field3 = field3;
  }

}
```

Listing 3.13 contains the string properties field1, field2, and field3 for keeping track of three attributes from the JSON-based string of information for a GitHub user. The property names in the UserComponent class are generic so that you can store different properties from the JSON string, such as followers, following, and created_at.

You now have a starting point for displaying additional details regarding a user, and you can improve the styling of the output by using Bootstrap or some other toolkit for UI-related layouts.

### Search Github For User:

Github Id ocampesato

>>> Find User <<<

### List of Users:

- Jane jsmith
- John jstone

**FIGURE 3.1** Search and display GitHub users in a list

Figure 3.1 shows the output from launching this Angular application and adding information about GitHub users. One thing to notice is that duplicates are allowed in the current sample (the code for preventing duplicates is an exercise for you).

## Other Service-related Use Cases

As you saw in the previous section, services are useful for retrieving external data. In addition, there are other situations that involve sharing data and services in an Angular application. In particular, one Angular application might need multiple instances of a service class, whereas another Angular application might need to enforce a single instance of a service class. Yet another situation involves sharing data between components in an Angular application.

These three scenarios are discussed briefly in the following subsections, and they are based on a very simple `UserService` class that is defined as follows:

```
export class UserService {
    private users: string[];

    adduser(user: string) {
        this.users.push(user);
    }

    getUsers() {
        return this.users;
    }
}
```

## Multiple Service Instances

Suppose that `UserService`, `MyComponent1`, and `MyComponent2` are defined in the TypeScript files `user.service.ts`, `component1.ts`, and `component2.ts`, respectively. If you need a different instance of the `UserService` class in each component, inject this class in their constructors, as shown here:

```
// component1.ts
export class MyComponent1 {
  constructor(private userService: UserService) {
  }
}

// component2.ts
export class MyComponent2 {
  constructor(private userService: UserService) {
  }
}
```

In the preceding code block, the instance of the `UserService` class in `MyComponent1` is different from the instance of the `UserService` class in `MyComponent2`.

## Single Service Instance

Consider the situation in which two Angular components must share the same instance of the `UserService` class. For simplicity, let's assume that the two components are children of the root component. In this scenario, perform the following sequence of steps:

1) Create a new service component (ng g s service).
2) Include UserService in the providers array in app.module.ts.
3) Import MyComponent1 and MyComponent2 in service.component. ts.
4) Remove the UserService class from the providers array in MyComponent1.
5) Remove the UserService class from the providers array in MyComponent2.

Step #2 ensures that the UserService class is available to all components in this Angular application, and there is only one instance of the UserService class throughout the application.

### Services and Inter-Component Communication

There are three steps required to send a new user from MyComponent1 to MyComponent2.

Step #1: Define a variable sendUser that is an instance of EventEmitter and a sendNewUser() method in UserService:

```
export class UserService {
    sendUser = new EventEmitter<string>();
    ...
    sendNewUser(user:string) {
        this.sendUser.emit(user);
    }
}
```

Step #2: Define an onSend() method in MyComponent1 to send a new user to MyComponent2:

```
onSend(user:string) {
    this.userService.sendNewUser(user);
}
```

Step #3: Define an Observable in MyComponent2 to "listen" for data that is emitted from MyComponent1:

```
ngOnInit() {
  this.userService.subscribe(...);
}
```

Another way to summarize the logical flow in the preceding code blocks is shown here:

- Users click a button to add a new user.
- The `UserService` instance sends the data to `Component1`.
- The `Component1` instance "emits" the new user.
- The `Component2` instance "listens" for the new user via an `Observable`.

## Injecting Services into Services

You have seen how to use DI to inject a service into a component via its constructor. In addition, you can inject services into other services. In order to do so, use the `@Injectable` decorator in the "injected service":

```
@Injectable
@Component({
})
export MyService(...)
```

> **NOTE**  *DI in Angular only works in classes that have a suitable decorator as part of the class definition.*

# Flickr Image Search Using jQuery and Angular

The code sample in this section shows you how to use jQuery in an Angular application, which is relevant for existing HTML Web pages that perform HTTP GET requests via jQuery.

Copy the directory `SearchFlickr` from the companion files into a convenient location. Now "cd" inside this application and install jQuery as shown here:

```
npm install jquery --save
```

Listing 3.14 shows the content of `app.component.ts`, which illustrates how to make an HTTP GET request to retrieve images from `Flickr` that are based on text string that users enter in a search box.

**LISTING 3.14:** *app.component.ts*

```
import {Component} from '@angular/core';

// remember: npm install jquery --save
import * as $ from "jquery";

@Component({
```

```
    selector: 'app-root',
    template: `
        Enter a word and search for related images:
        <br />
        <input id="searchterm" />
        <button (click)="httpRequest()">Search</button>
        <div id="images"></div>
})
export class AppComponent {
  imageCount = 4;
  url = "http://api.flickr.com/services/feeds/photos_pub-
lic.gne?jsoncallback=?";

  constructor() {}

  httpRequest() {
    $.getJSON(this.url,
    {
      tags: $("#searchterm").val(),
      tagmode: "any",
      format: "json"
    },
    function(data) {
      $.each(data.items, function(i,item){
                    $("<img/>").attr("src",   item.media.m).
prependTo("#images");
      //if ( i == this.imageCount ) return false;
      });
    });
  }
}
```

Listing 3.14 contains a standard import statement, followed by this code snippet:

```
import * as $ from "jquery";
```

The preceding snippet is necessary for TypeScript to "find" jQuery, which is possible after you have installed via the npm command. However, keep in mind that if you remove the preceding code snippet, you will see the following error (or something similar):

```
ERROR ReferenceError: "$ is not defined"
```

NOTE *The code in this section works for Angular 6 onward, whereas the code for Angular 4 requires a different syntax.*

The next portion of Listing 3.14 is the `@Component` decorator, whose `template` property contains `<input>`, `<button>`, and `<div>` elements to a capture user's search string, perform a search with that string, and display the results of the search, respectively.

The next portion of Listing 3.14 is the exported class `@AppComponent` that defines the `url` variable that is initialized with a hard-coded string value that "points" to the Flickr website.

Next, an empty constructor is defined, followed by the `httpRequest()` method that is invoked when users click on the `<button>` element. This method invokes the jQuery `getJSON()` method that performs a Flickr image search based on the text string entered in the `<input>` element because of this code snippet:

```
tags: $("#searchterm").val()
```

When the matching images are retrieved, they are available via `data.items`, and the jQuery `each()` method iterates through the list of images. Each image is dynamically inserted in the `<images>` element via this snippet:

```
$("<img/>").attr("src" item.media.m).prependTo("#images");
```

Take a minute to absorb the compact manner in which jQuery achieves the desired result.

Figure 3.2 shows the output from launching this Angular application and searching Flickr with the keyword `pasta`.

**FIGURE 3.2** A partial list of figures with pasta

# HTTP GET Requests with a Simple Server

This section shows you how to work with the command line utility json-server that can serve JSON-based data. This program performs the function of a very simple server: clients can make GET requests to retrieve JSON data from a server. Moreover, a simple command in the console where json-server was launched enables you to save the in-memory data to a file.

Although json-server does not perform the functions of a Node-based application that contains Express and MongoDB, json-server is a convenient program that helps you learn how an Angular application can interact with a file server.

You need to perform the following steps before you launch the Angular application in this section:

- Step 1: Install json-server.
- Step 2: Launch json-server.
- Step 3: Launch the Angular application.

Install json-server via the following command:

```
[sudo] npm install -g json-server
```

Navigate to the src/assets directory that contains the JSON file posts. json and invoke this command:

```
json-server posts.json
```

The preceding command launches a file server at port 3000 and reads the contents of posts.json into memory, making that data available to HTTP GET requests.

Now copy the directory JSONServerGET from the companion files into a convenient location. Listing 3.15 shows the content of app.component. ts, which illustrates how to make an HTTP GET request to retrieve data from a file server.

*LISTING 3.15: app.component.ts*

```
import {Component}      from '@angular/core';
import {Inject}         from '@angular/core';
import {HttpClient}     from '@angular/common/http';
import {HTTP_BINDINGS}  from '@angular/common/http';

@Component({
    selector: 'app-root',
```

```
      template: `
          <button (click)="httpRequest()">Get Information</
button>
        <div>
          <li *ngFor="let post of postData">
            {{post.author}}
            {{post.title}}
          </li>
        </div>
      `
})
export class AppComponent {
  postData = "";

    constructor(@Inject(HttpClient) public http:HttpClient)
  {
  }

  httpRequest() {
    this.http.get('http://localhost:3000/posts')
      .subscribe(
        data => this.postData = JSON.stringify(data),
        err => console.log('error'),
        () => this.postInfo()
      );
  }

  postInfo() {
      //-----------------------------------------------
      // the 'eval' statement is required to
      // convert the data retrieved from json-server
      // to an array of JSON objects (else an error)
      //-----------------------------------------------
      var myObject = eval('(' + this.postData + ')');
      console.log("myObject = "+JSON.stringify(myObject));
      this.postData = myObject;
  }
}
```

Listing 3.15 contains code that is similar to earlier code samples. The first difference involves the details of the unordered list that is displayed in the template property.

The second difference is the endpoint `http://localhost:3000/posts` in the `HTTP GET` request. This endpoint provides `JSON` data via the `json-server` that is listening on port 3000.

Listing 3.16 shows the content of `posts.json`, which is retrieved during the `HTTP GET` request in Listing 3.15.

**LISTING 3.16: posts.json**

```
{
  "posts": [
  {"id": 100,"title": "json-server","author": "smartguy"},
  {"id": 200,"title": "pizza-maker","author": "chicago"},
  {"id": 300,"title": "good-beer",  "author": "escondido"}
  ]
}
```

The next section shows you how to make an `HTTP POST` request to a local file server in an Angular application.

## HTTP POST Requests with a Simple Server

The Angular application in this section makes an `HTTP POST` request with the utility `json-server` that can serve `JSON`-based data. Keep in mind that the server in this code sample only handles basic data requests: "universal" JavaScript (sometimes also called "isomorphic" JavaScript) is not covered in this chapter.

Please note that this application is not production-ready code, partly because the ID value is based on a randomly generated integer.

Copy the directory `JSONServerPOST` from the companion files into a convenient location. Navigate to the `src/assets` subdirectory, which contains the `JSON` file `authors.json`, and launch this command:

```
json-server authors.json
```

The preceding command launches a file server at port 3000 and reads the contents of `authors.json` into memory, making that data available to `HTTP GET` requests.

**NOTE**    *You must launch json-server before you launch the Angular application in this section.*

Listing 3.17 shows the content of app.component.ts, which illustrates how to make an HTTP POST request to a local file server.

**LISTING 3.17: app.component.ts**

```
import { Component } from '@angular/core';
import {Inject}      from '@angular/core';
import {HttpClient}  from '@angular/common/http';

// remember: npm install jquery --save
import * as $ from "jquery";

@Component({
   selector: 'app-root',
   template: `
    <button (click)="getEmpData()">Click to Display Author
Info</button>
      <div>
        <table>
          <thead *ngIf="foundData">
            <th>AUTHORID</th>
            <th>Title</th>
            <th>Author</th>
          </thead>
          <tbody>
            <tr *ngFor="let author of authorData">
              <td>{{author.id}}</td>
              <td>{{author.title}}</td>
              <td>{{author.author}}</td>
            </tr>
          </tbody>
        </table>
        <button (click)="postAuthorData()">Click to Add New
Author Info</button>
      </div>
      `
})
export class AppComponent {
   foundData   = false;
   authorData  : any;
   currData    = {};
   idIncr      = 100;
   newAuthorId = 0;
```

```
  newTitle    = "";
  newAuthor   = "";
  largestId   = 0;

  constructor(@Inject(HttpClient) public http:HttpClient)
{}

  postAuthorData() {
    this.newAuthorId = 0+this.largestId+this.idIncr;
    this.newTitle   = "The Book of "+this.newAuthorId;
    this.newAuthor  = "My New Title"+this.newAuthorId;

    var postNewAuthor = {id:this.newAuthorId,
                         title:this.newTitle,
                         author:this.newAuthor};
//console.log("postNewAuthor: "+JSON.
stringify(postNewAuthor));
    $.post("http://localhost:3000/authors",
        postNewAuthor,
        function(result, textStatus, jqXHR) {
//console.log("2returned result: "+JSON.stringify(result));
            this.authorData.push(postNewAuthor);
        }.bind(this),"json")
          .fail(function(jqXHR, textStatus, errorThrown) {
        console.log("error:   "+errorThrown+"   textStatus:
"+textStatus);
          });
  }

  getAuthorData() {
    this.http.get('http://localhost:3000/authors')
      .subscribe(
        data => this.authorData = data,
        err => console.log('error'),
        () => this.authorInfo()
      );
  }

  authorInfo() {
    this.largestId =
      parseInt(this.authorData[this.authorData.length-1].
id,10);
```

```
      //console.log("largestId    = "+ this.largestId);
      //console.log("authorData1  =  "+  JSON.stringify(this.
authorData));
         this.foundData = true;
     }
  }
```

Listing 3.17 contains the usual import statements, followed by a template property that displays a table of author-based data. When users click on the <button> element, the postAuthorData() adds a hard-coded new author to the list of authors. This method performs a standard jQuery POST request instead of using an Observable. Note that this method increments the value of the id property of each author so that they are treated as distinct authors (even though the names of the new users are almost the same).

On the other hand, the getAuthorData() method does involve an Observable for retrieving author-related data (shown in Listing 3.18) from the file server that is running on port 3000.

The browser is reloaded after each invocation of the postAuthorData() method, so you need to click the "Author Info" button to see the newly-added author. However, you can prevent a page reload by issuing either of the following commands from the command line:

```
ng serve --live-reload false OR
ng serve --no-live-reload
```

Listing 3.18 shows a portion of the contents of authors.json, whose contents are given in this Angular application.

### LISTING 3.18: authors.json

```
{
  "authors": [
    {
      "id": 100,
      "title": "json-server",
      "author": "typicode"
    },
    {
      "id": 200,
      "title": "pizza-maker",
      "author": "chicago"
```

```
    },
// sections omitted for brevity
    {
        "id": "900",
        "title": "The Book of 900",
        "author": "My New Title900"
    }
  ]
}
```

Listing 3.18 is a very simple collection of JSON-based data items, where each item contains the elements id, title, and author.

## An SVG Line Plot from Simulated Data in Angular (optional)

The Angular application in this section reads the contents of a CSV file (located in the src/assets subdirectory) and then uses that data to display an SVG-based line graph. However, if you are not interested in generating SVG-based line graphs, then you can skip this section with no loss of continuity.

Copy the directory ReadDataCSVLRPlot from the companion files into a convenient location. Listing 3.19 shows the content of app.component. ts, which illustrates how to read the contents of assets/wine.csv and then display the data in tabular form.

*LISTING 3.19: app.component.ts*

```
import { Component }  from '@angular/core';
import { Inject }     from '@angular/core';
import { Observable } from 'rxjs';
import { HttpClient } from '@angular/common/http';

@Component({
  selector: 'app-root',
  styleUrls: ['./app.component.css'],
  template: `
    <svg width="600" height="200">
      <rect x="0" y="0" width="600" height="200"
            stroke="black" stroke-width="4" fill="white" />
      <polyline [attr.points]="polyPts"
```

```
                    style="fill:none;stroke:red;stroke-width:4"
    />
      </svg>
      <table>
        <tbody>
          <p>Data points for this line graph:</p>
          <tr *ngFor="let record of records;let i = index;">
            <td> <span>{{record[0]}}</span> </td>
            <td> <span>{{record[1]}}</span> </td>
          </tr>
        </tbody>
      </table>
      `,
})
export class AppComponent {
  public xValue:number    = 0;
  public yValue:number    = 0;

  // points for an SVG polyline
  public polyPts : any = "";

  // populate an array with CSV data
  public records : any = [];
  public csvUrl  = 'assets/rand20.csv';
  public allTextLines:any = "";

  constructor(@Inject(HttpClient) public http:HttpClient)
{
      this.readCsvData ();
  }

  readCsvData () {
    this.http.get(this.csvUrl, {responseType: 'text'})
      .subscribe(
          data => { this.extractData(data) },
          err => { console.log(err) }
        );
  }

  //---------------------------------------------------
  // After the readCsvData reads the CSV file in the
  // assets directory, the extractData method is invoked
  // to populate an array with that CSV data.
```

```
// This method also invokes constructLineGraph, which
// constructs a line graph of the set of datapoints
//----------------------------------------------------
private extractData(res: any) {
  let csvData = res || '';
  this.allTextLines = csvData.split(/\r\n|\n/);

  let lines = [];
  let onerow = this.allTextLines[0].split(',');
  let columnCount = onerow.length;

  for ( let i = 0; i < this.allTextLines.length-1; i++) {
    // split content based on comma
    let data = this.allTextLines[i].split(',');

    let tarr = [];
    for ( let j = 0; j < columnCount; j++) {
      tarr.push(data[j]);
    }
    lines.push(tarr);
  }
  this.records = lines;

  this.constructLineGraph();
}

private constructLineGraph() {
  // construct a line graph
  for ( let i = 0; i < this.records.length; i++) {
  //console.log("this.xValue:",  this.records[i][0]);
  //console.log("this.yValue:",  this.records[i][1]);

    // append current point to the SVG polyline:
    this.polyPts += this.xValue.toString() + "," +
                    this.yValue.toString() + " ";

    this.xValue += +this.records[i][0];
    this.yValue = +this.records[i][1];
  }
}
}
```

Listing 3.19 starts with the usual import statements, followed by the template property that contains two main parts. The first part consists of an SVG <svg> element, as shown here:

```
<svg width="600" height="200">
    <rect x="0" y="0" width="600" height="200"
          stroke="black" stroke-width="4" fill="white" />
    <polyline [attr.points]="polyPts"
              style="fill:none;stroke:red;stroke-width:4" />
</svg>
```

The SVG <svg> element in the preceding code block has a width of 600 pixels and a height of 200 pixels, both of which you can adjust if you need to do so. In addition, the SVG <svg> element contains an SVG <rect> element that is essentially just an outer border, followed by an SVG <polyline> element that represents a line graph.

The second portion of the <template> property displays header information about the data in the CSV file, followed by an ngFor code block that displays the contents of the CSV file.

Next, the constructor invokes the readCsvData() method, which in turn involves an Observable that reads the content of the CSV file rand20.csv, which is in the src/assets subdirectory.

After the data is successfully read from the CSV file, the extractData() method is invoked to populate the records variable with an array of values from the retrieved data. This step is necessary because the data that is retrieved in the readCsvData() is simply a collection of strings, each of which contains comma-separated values. Keep in mind that each row in the records array consists of a pair of numbers that is treated as an (x,y) point in the plane.

The final code snippet in the readCsvData() method invokes the method constructLineGraph() that appends each row in the records array to the variable polyPts, which constructs a contiguous set of line segments that is rendered as a line graph. This technique works because the values in rand20.csv are sorted in increasing order, based on the values in the first column.

Listing 3.20 shows a portion of the contents of rand20.csv, which is located in the src/assets subdirectory.

**LISTING 3.20: rand20.csv**

```
46,8
46,13
70,40
92,55
```

```
174,74
// details omitted for brevity
536,204
543,208
553,220
572,246
596,247
```

Figure 3.3 shows the output from launching the Angular application in this section.

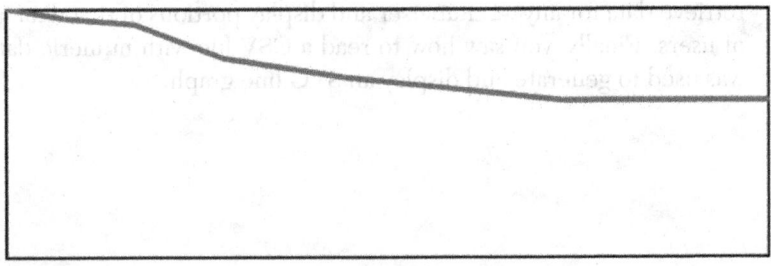

Data points for this line graph:

| | |
|-----|-----|
| 46 | 8 |
| 56 | 13 |
| 70 | 40 |
| 92 | 55 |
| 174 | 74 |
| 179 | 74 |
| 193 | 115 |
| 198 | 127 |
| 283 | 154 |
| 340 | 159 |
| 405 | 160 |
| 414 | 164 |
| 418 | 169 |
| 432 | 183 |
| 506 | 197 |
| 536 | 204 |
| 543 | 208 |
| 553 | 220 |
| 572 | 246 |
| 596 | 247 |

**FIGURE 3.3** A line graph from a list of numbers

## Summary

This chapter showed you how to create Angular applications with HTML5 Forms, as well as Forms that contain Angular Controls and FormGroups. You also saw how to save form-based data in local storage. Next you learned about Angular Pipes, along with an example that showed you how to implement this functionality.

You also learned about Angular Services and worked through an example that illustrated how to use Services. Next, you saw an example of the http() method (which returns an Observable) of the Http class to retrieve data for any GitHub user and display portions of that data in a list of users. Finally, you saw how to read a CSV file with numeric data that was used to generate and display an SVG line graph.

# CHAPTER 4

# DEEP LEARNING INTRODUCTION

This chapter introduces you to deep learning, which includes MLPs (MultiLayer Perceptrons) and CNNs (Convolutional Neural Networks). Chapter 5 contains information about more complex deep learning architectures, such as RNNs (Recurrent Neural Networks) and LSTMs (Long Short Term Memory). Most of this chapter contains descriptive content, along with some Keras-based code samples that assume you have read the Keras material in the previous chapters. This chapter is meant to be a cursory introduction to a diverse set of topics, along with suitable links to additional information.

If you are new to deep learning, many topics in this chapter will probably require additional study for you to become comfortable with them: think of this chapter as a modest step of toward your mastery of deep learning.

The first portion of this chapter briefly discusses deep learning, the problems it can solve, and the challenges for the future. The second part of this chapter briefly introduces perceptrons, which are essentially the core building blocks for neural networks. ANNs, MLPs, RNNs, LSTMs, and VAEs are all based on multiple layers that contain multiple perceptrons.

The third part of this chapter provides an introduction to CNNs, followed by an example of training a Keras-based CNN with the MNIST dataset: this code sample will make more sense if you have read the section pertaining to activation functions in Chapter 5.

## Keras and the XOR Function

The XOR function is a well-known function that is not linearly separable in the plane. The truth table for the XOR ("exclusive OR") function is straightforward: given two binary inputs, the output is 1 if at most one input is a 1; otherwise, the output is 0. If we treat XOR as the name of a function with two binary inputs, here are the outputs:

```
XOR(0,0) = 0
XOR(1,0) = 1
XOR(0,1) = 1
XOR(1,1) = 0
```

We can treat the output values as labels that are associated with the input values. Specifically, the points (0,0) and (1,1) are in class 0 and the points (1,0) and (0,1) are in class 1. Draw these points in the plane, and you have the four vertices of a unit square whose lower-left vertex is the origin. Moreover, each pair of diagonal elements belongs to the same class, which makes the XOR function non-linear separable in the plane. If you're skeptical, try to find a linear separator for the XOR function in the Euclidean plane.

Listing 4.1 shows the content of tf2_keras_xor.py, which illustrates how to create a Keras-based NN to train the XOR function.

### LISTING 4.1: tf2_keras_xor.py

```
import tensorflow as tf
import numpy as np

# Logical XOR operator and "truth" values:
x = np.array([[0., 0.],[0., 1.],[1., 0.],[1., 1.]])
y = np.array([[0.], [1.], [1.], [0.]])

model = tf.keras.models.Sequential()
model.add(tf.keras.layers.Dense(2, input_dim=2,
activation='relu'))
model.add(tf.keras.layers.Dense(1))

print("compiling model...")
model.compile(loss='mean_squared_error', optimizer='adam')
print("fitting model...")
model.fit(x,y,verbose=0,epochs=1000)
pred = model.predict(x)

# Test final prediction
print("Testing XOR operator")
p1 = np.array([[0., 0.]])
p2 = np.array([[0., 1.]])
```

```
p3 = np.array([[1., 0.]])
p4 = np.array([[1., 1.]])

print(p1,":", model.predict(p1))
print(p2,":", model.predict(p2))
print(p3,":", model.predict(p3))
print(p4,":", model.predict(p4))
```

Listing 4.1 initializes the NumPy array x with four pairs of numbers that are the four combinations of 0 and 1, followed by the NumPy array y that contains the logical OR of each pair of numbers in x.

The next portion of Listing 4.1 defines a Keras-based model with two Dense layers. Next, the model is compiled, trained, and then the variable pred is populated with a set of predictions based on the trained model.

The next code block initializes the points p1, p2, p3, and p4 and then displays the values that are predicted for those points. The output from launching the code in Listing 4.1 is here:

```
compiling model...
fitting model...
Testing XOR operator
[[0. 0.]] : [[0.36438465]]
[[0. 1.]] : [[1.0067574]]
[[1. 0.]] : [[0.36437267]]
[[1. 1.]] : [[0.15084022]]
```

Experiment with different values for epochs and see how they affect the predictions. Use the code in Listing 4.1 as a template for other logical functions. The only modification to Listing 4.1 that is required is the replacement of the variable y in Listing 4.1 with the variable y that is specified as the labels for several other logic gates that are listed below.

The labels for the NOR function:
```
y = np.array([[1.], [0.], [0.], [1.]])
```
The labels for the OR function:
```
y = np.array([[0.], [1.], [1.], [1.]])
```
The labels for the XOR function:
```
y = np.array([[0.], [1.], [1.], [0.]])
```
The labels for the ANDR function:
```
y = np.array([[0.], [0.], [0.], [1.]])
mnist = tf.keras.datasets.mnist
```

The preceding code snippets are the only required code changes to Listing 4.1 needed to train a model for a different logical function. If you are familiar with the NOR, OR, and AND functions, you can easily modify the values in the y vector in Listing 4.1 to create the corresponding Python code samples.

Now that you have seen an example of the limitations of a neural network with a single hidden layer, the usefulness of architectures with multiple hidden layers makes more sense.

# What is Deep Learning?

Deep learning is a subset of machine learning that focuses on neural networks and algorithms for training neural networks. Deep learning comprises many types of neural networks, such as CNNs, RNNs, LSTMs, GRUs, Variational Autoencoders (VAEs), and GANs. A deep learning model requires at least two hidden layers in a neural network ("very deep learning" involves neural networks with at least 10 hidden layers).

From a high-level perspective, deep learning with supervised learning involves defining a model (aka neural network) as well as

- making an estimate for a datapoint
- calculating the loss or error of each estimate
- reducing the error via gradient descent

We also need to initialize variables for the training data (often named x_train and y_train) and the test-related data (often named x_test and x_test), which is typically an 80/20 or 75/25 split between the training data and test data.

## What are Hyperparameters?

Deep learning involves *hyperparameters*, which are sort of like knobs and dials whose values are initialized by you prior to the actual training process. For instance, the number of hidden layers and the number of neurons in hidden layers are examples of hyperparameters. You will encounter many hyperparameters in deep learning models, some of which are listed here:

- Number of hidden layers
- Number of neurons in hidden layers
- Weight initialization
- An activation function
- A loss function

- An optimizer
- A learning rate
- A dropout rate

The first three hyperparameters in the preceding list are required for the initial set-up of a neural network. The fourth hyperparameter is required for forward propagation. The next three hyperparameters (i.e., the loss function, optimizer, and learning rate) are required to perform backward error propagation (aka backprop) during supervised learning tasks. This step calculates a set of numbers that are used to update the values of the weights in the neural network to improve the accuracy of the neural network. The final hyperparameter is useful if you need to reduce overfitting in your model. In general, the loss function is the most complex of all these hyperparameters.

During back propagation, *the vanishing gradient problem* can occur, after which some weights are no longer updated, in which case the neural network is essentially inert (and debugging this problem is generally non-trivial). Another consideration involves deciding whether a local minima is good enough and preferable to expending the additional time and effort that is required to find an absolute minima.

## Deep Learning Architectures

As discussed previously, deep learning supports various architectures, including MLPs, CNNs, RNNs, and LSTMs. Although there is overlap in terms of the types of tasks that these architectures can solve, each one has a specific reason for its creation. As you progress from MLPs to LSTMs, the architectures become more complex. Sometimes combinations of these architectures are well-suited for solving tasks. For example, capturing video and making predictions typically involves a CNN (for processing each input image in a video sequence) and an LSTM to make predictions of the position of objects that are in the video stream.

In addition, neural networks for NLP (natural language processing) can contain one or more CNNs, RNNs, LSTMs, and biLSTMs (bidirectional LSTMs). The combination of reinforcement learning with these architectures is called *deep reinforcement learning*. Note that the Transformer architecture and the Reformer architecture (both created by Google) are two more recent architectures for NLP whose performance results are state of the art.

Although MLPs have been popular for a long time, they suffer from two disadvantages: they are not scalable for computer vision tasks, and they are somewhat difficult to train. However, CNNs do not require adjacent layers to be fully connected. Another advantage of CNNs is called the *translation invariance*, which means that an image (such as a digit, cat, dog, and so forth) is recognized as such, regardless of where it appears in a bitmap.

## Problems that Deep Learning Can Solve

Back propagation involves updating the weights of the edges between consecutive layers, which is performed in a right-to-left fashion (i.e., from the output layer toward the input layer). The updates involve the chain rule (a rule for computing derivatives) and an arithmetic product of parameters and gradient values. There are two anomalous results that can occur: the product of terms approaches zero (which is called the vanishing gradient problem) or the product of terms becomes arbitrarily large (which is called the *exploding gradient problem*). The former problem can arise with the sigmoid activation function.

Deep learning can mitigate both of these problems via LSTMs. Deep learning models usually replace the sigmoid activation function with the ReLU activation function. ReLU is a very simple continuous function that is differentiable (with a value of 1 to the right of the y-axis and a value of -1 to the left of the y-axis) everywhere except the origin. Hence, it's necessary to perform some tweaking to make things work nicely at the origin (such as ELU instead of ReLU).

## Challenges in Deep Learning

Although deep learning is powerful and has produced impressive results in many fields, there are some important on-going challenges that are being explored, including:

- Bias in algorithms
- Susceptibility to adversarial attacks
- Limited ability to generalize
- Lack of explainability
- Correlation but not causality

Algorithms can contain unintentional bias, and even if the bias is removed from an algorithm, there can be unintentional bias in the data. For example, one neural network was trained on a dataset containing pictures of Caucasian males and females. The outcome of the training process determined that males were physicians and that females were housewives and did so with a high probability. The reason was simple: the dataset depicted males and females almost exclusively in those two roles. The following article contains more information regarding bias in algorithms:

*https://www.technologyreview.com/s/612876/this-is-how-ai-bias-really-happensand-why-its-so-hard-to-fix*

Deep learning focuses on finding patterns in datasets, but generalizing those results is a difficult task. There are some initiatives that attempt to provide explainability for the outcomes of neural networks, but such work is still in its infancy. Deep learning finds patterns and can determine correlation, but it's incapable of determining causality.

Now that you have a bird's eye view of deep learning, let's rewind and discuss an important cornerstone of machine learning called the perceptron, which is the topic of the next section.

## What are Perceptrons?

DNNs (deep neural networks) contain at least two hidden layers, and they can solve logistic regression problems as well as classification problems. In fact, the output layer of a model for classification problems actually consists of a set of probabilities (one for each class in the dataset) whose sum equals 1.

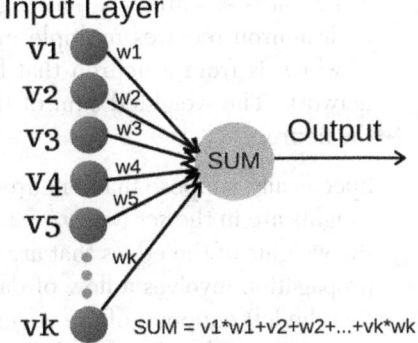

**FIGURE 4.1** An example of a perceptron

Figure 4.1 shows a perceptron with incoming edges that have numeric weights.

The next section delves into the details of perceptrons, and how they form the backbone of MLPs.

### Definition of the Perceptron Function

A perceptron involves a function f(x) where the following holds:

f(x) = 1 if w*x + b > 0 (otherwise f(x) = 0)

In the previous expression, w is a vector of weights, x is an input vector, b is a vector of biases. The product w*x is the inner product of the vectors w and x, and activating a perceptron is an all-or-nothing decision (e.g., a light bulb is either on or off, with no intermediate states).

Notice that the function f(x) checks the value of the linear term w*x+b, which is also specified in the sigmoid function for logistic regression. The same term appears as part of the calculation of the sigmoid value, as shown here:

```
1/[1 + e^(w*x+b)]
```

Given a value for w*x+b, the preceding expression generates a numeric value. However, in the general case, w is a weight matrix, and x and b are vectors.

The next section digresses slightly in order to describe artificial neural networks, after which we'll discuss MLPs.

## A Detailed View of a Perceptron

A *neuron* is essentially a building block for neural networks. In general, each neuron receives multiple inputs (which are numeric values), each of which is from a neuron that belongs to a previous layer in a neural network. The weighted sum of the inputs is calculated and assigned to the neuron.

Specifically, suppose that a neuron N' (N "prime") receives inputs whose weights are in the set {w1, w2, w3, . . . , wn}, where these numbers specify the weights of the edges that are connected to neuron N'. Since forward propagation involves a flow of data in a left-to-right fashion, this means that the left endpoint of the edges are connected to neurons {N1, N2, . . ., Nk} in a preceding layer, and the right endpoint of these edges is N'. The weighted sum is calculated as follows:

```
x1*w1 + x2*w2 + . . . + xn*wn
```

After the weighted sum is calculated, it's "passed" to an activation function that calculates a second value. This step is required for artificial neural networks, and it's explained later in the chapter. This process of calculating a weighted sum is repeated for every neuron in a given layer, and then the same process is repeated on the neurons in the next layer of a neural network.

The entire process is called *forward propagation* (also called *forward prop*), which is complemented by the *backward error propagation* step (also called *backward prop*). During the backward error propagation step, new weight values are calculated for the entire neural network. The combination of forward prop and backward prop is repeated for each data point (e.g., each row of data in a CSV file). The goal is to finish this training process so that the finalized neural network (also called a *model*) accurately represents the data in a dataset and can also accurately predict values for the test data. Of course, the accuracy of a neural network depends on the dataset in question, and the accuracy can be higher than 99%.

## The Anatomy of an Artificial Neural Network (ANN)

An ANN consists of an input layer, an output layer, and one or more hidden layers. For each pair of adjacent layers in an ANN, neurons in the left layer are connected with neurons in the right layer via an edge that has a numeric weight. If all neurons in the left layer are connected to all neurons in the right layer, it's called an MLP (discussed later).

Keep in mind that the perceptrons in an ANN are stateless: they do *not* retain any information about previously processed data. Furthermore, an ANN does not contain cycles (hence ANNs are acyclic). By contrast, RNNs and LSTMs *do* retain state and they do have cycle-like behavior, as you will see later in this chapter.

Incidentally, if you have a mathematics background, you might be tempted to think of an ANN as a set of contiguous bipartite graphs in which data flows from the input layer (think "multiple sources") toward the output layer ("the sink"). Unfortunately, this viewpoint doesn't prove useful for understanding ANNs. A better way to understand ANNs is to think of their structure as a combination of the hyperparameters in the following list:

1) the number of hidden layers
2) the number of neurons in each hidden layer
3) the initial weights of edges connecting pairs of neurons
4) the activation function
5) a loss function
6) an optimizer (used with the loss function)
7) the learning rate (a small number)
8) dropout rate (optional)

Figure 4.2 shows the contents of an ANN (there are many variations: this is simply one example).

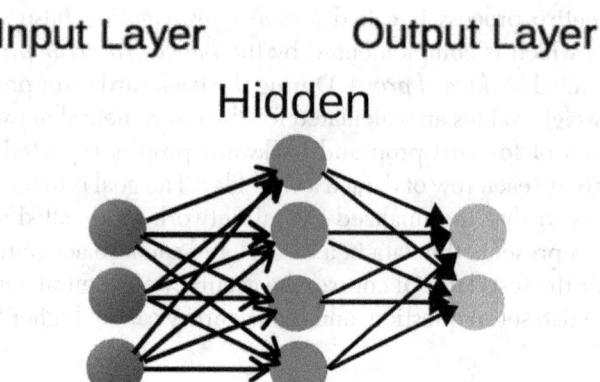

**FIGURE 4.2** An example of an ANN

Since the output layer of the ANN in Figure 4.2 contains more than one neuron, we know that it's a model for a classification task.

## The Model Initialization Hyperparameters

The first three parameters in the list of bullet items in the previous section are required for initializing the neural network. The hidden layers are intermediate computational layers, each of which is composed of neurons. The number of edges between each pair of adjacent layers is flexible and determined by you. More information about network initialization is here:

*http://www.deeplearning.ai/ai-notes/initialization/*

The edges that connect neurons in each pair of adjacent layers (including the input layer and the output layer) have numeric weights. The initial values of these weights are often small random numbers between 0 and 1. Keep in mind that the connections between adjacent layers can affect the complexity of a model. The purpose of the training process is to fine-tune edge weights to produce an accurate model.

An ANN is not necessarily fully connected, which is to say that some edges between pairs of neurons in adjacent layers might be missing. By contrast, neural networks such as CNNs share edges (and their weights), which can make them more computationally feasible (but even CNNs can require significant training time). Note that the Keras `tf.keras.layers.Dense()` class handles the task of fully connecting two adjacent layers. As discussed later, MLPs are fully connected, which can greatly increase the training time for such a neural network.

## The Activation Hyperparameter

The fourth parameter is the activation function that is applied to weights between each pair of consecutive layers. Neural networks with many layers typically involve different activation functions. For instance, CNNs use the ReLU activation function on feature maps (created by applying filters to an image), whereas the penultimate layer is connected to the output layer via the softmax function (which is a generalization of the sigmoid function).

## The Loss Function Hyperparameter

The fifth, sixth, and seventh hyperparameters are required for the backward error propagation that starts from the output layer and moves in a right-to-left toward the input layer. These hyperparameters perform the heavy lifting of machine learning frameworks: they compute the updates to the weights of the edges in neural networks.

The *loss function* is a function in multi-dimensional Euclidean space. For example, the MSE loss function is a bowl-shaped loss function that has a global minimum. In general, the goal is to minimize the MSE function in order to minimize the loss, which in turn helps us maximize the accuracy of a model (but this is not guaranteed for other loss functions). However, sometimes a local minimum might be considered good enough instead of finding a global minimum: you must make this decision (i.e., it's not a purely programmatic decision).

Alas, loss functions for larger datasets tend to be very complex, which is necessary in order to detect potential patterns in datasets. Another loss function is the cross-entropy function, which involves maximizing the likelihood function (contrast this with MSE). Search for online articles for more details about loss functions.

## The Optimizer Hyperparameter

An *optimizer* is an algorithm that is chosen in conjunction with a loss function, and its purpose is to converge to the minimum value of the loss function during the training phase (see the comment in the previous section regarding a local minimum). Different optimizers make different assumptions regarding the manner in which new approximations are calculated during the training process. Some optimizers involve only the most recent approximation, whereas other optimizers use a rolling average that takes into account several previous approximations.

There are several well-known optimizers, including SGD, RMSprop, Adagrad, Adadelta, and Adam. Check online for details regarding the advantages and trade-offs of these optimizers.

## The Learning Rate Hyperparameter

The *learning rate* is a small number, usually between 0.001 and 0.05, which affects the magnitude of a number that is added to the current weight of an edge in order to train the model with these updated weights. The learning rate has a sort of throttling effect. If the value is too large, the new approximation might overshoot the optimal point; if it's too small, the training time can increase significantly. By analogy, imagine you are in a passenger jet and you're 100 miles away from an airport. The speed of the airplane decreases as you approach the airport, which corresponds to decreasing the learning rate in a neural network.

## The Dropout Rate Hyperparameter

The *dropout rate* is the eighth hyperparameter, which is a decimal value between 0 and 1, typically between 0.2 and 0.5. Multiply this decimal value with 100 to determine the percentage of randomly selected neurons to ignore during each forward pass in the training process. For example, if the dropout rate is 0.2, then 20% of the neurons are selected randomly and ignored during each step of the forward propagation. A different set of neurons is randomly selected whenever a new datapoint is processed in the neural network. Note that the neurons are not removed from the neural network: they still exist, and ignoring them during forward propagation has the effect of thinning the neural network. In TF 2, the Keras tf.keras. layers.Dropout class performs the task of thinning a neural network.

There are additional hyper parameters that you can specify, but they are optional and not required in order to understand ANNs.

## What is Backward Error Propagation?

An ANN is typically drawn in a *left-to-right* fashion, where the left-most layer is the input layer. The output from each layer becomes the input for the next layer. The term forward propagation refers to supplying values to the input layer and the progress through the hidden layers toward the output layer. The output layer contains the results (which are estimated numeric values) of the forward pass through the model.

Here is a key point: backward error propagation involves the calculation of numbers that are used to update the weights of the edges in the neural network. The update process is performed by means of a loss function (and an optimizer and a learning rate), starting from the output layer (the right-most layer) and then moving in a right-to-left fashion to update the weights of the edges between consecutive layers. This procedure trains the neural network, which involves reducing the error between the estimated values at the output layer and the true values (in the case of supervised learning). This procedure is repeated for each data point in the training portion of the dataset. Processing the dataset is called an *epoch*, and many times a neural network is trained via multiple epochs.

The previous paragraph did not explain what the loss function is or how it is chosen: that's because the loss function and the optimizer and the learning rate are hyperparameters that are discussed in previous sections. However, two commonly used loss functions are MSE and cross entropy; a commonly used optimizer is the Adam optimizer (and SGD and RMSprop and others); and a common value for the learning rate is 0.01.

## What is a Multilayer Perceptron (MLP)?

A multilayer perceptron (MLP) is a feed forward artificial neural network that consists of at least three layers of nodes: an input layer, a hidden layer, and an output layer. An MLP is fully connected: given a pair of adjacent layers, every node in the left layer is connected to every node in the right layer. Apart from the nodes in the input layer, each node is a neuron and each layer of neurons involves a nonlinear activation function. In addition, MLPs use backward error propagation for training, which is also true for CNNs (Convolutional Neural Networks).

Figure 4.3 shows the contents of an MLP with two hidden layers.

One point to keep in mind: the non-linear activation function of an MLP differentiates an MLP from a linear perceptron. In fact, an MLP can handle data that is not linearly separable. For instance, the OR function and the AND function involve linearly separable data, so they can be represented via a linear perceptron. However, the XOR function involves data that is not linearly separable, and therefore requires a neural network such as an MLP.

# MLP (Two Hidden Layers)

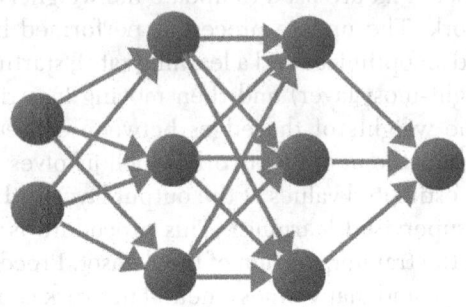

**FIGURE 4.3** An example of an MLP

## Activation Functions

An MLP without an activation function between any adjacent pair of layers is a linear system: at each layer, simply multiply the vector from the previous layer with the current matrix (which connects the current layer to the next layer) to produce another vector.

It's straightforward to multiply a set of matrices to produce a *single* matrix. Since a neural network without activation functions is a linear system, we can multiply those matrices (one matrix for each pair of adjacent layers) together to produce a single matrix: the original neural network is thereby reduced to a two-layer neural network consisting of an input layer and an output layer, which defeats the purpose of having a multi-layered neural network.

In order to prevent such a reduction of the layers of a neural network, an MLP must include a nonlinear activation function between adjacent layers (this is also true of any other deep neural network). The choice of the non-linear activation function is typically sigmoid, tanh (which is a hyperbolic tangent function), or ReLU (Rectified Linear Unit).

The output of the sigmoid function ranges from 0 to 1, which has the effect of squashing the data values. Similarly, the output of the tanh function ranges from -1 to 1. However, the ReLU activation function (or one of its variants) is preferred for ANNs and CNNs, whereas sigmoid and tanh are used in LSTMs.

Several upcoming sections contain the details of constructing an MLP, such as how to initialize the weights of an MLP, storing weights and biases, and how to train a neural network via backward error propagation.

## How are Datapoints Correctly Classified?

A *datapoint* refers to a row of data in a dataset, which can be a dataset for real estate, a dataset of thumbnail images, or some other type of dataset. Suppose that we want to train an MLP for a dataset that contains four classes (aka labels). In this scenario, the output layer must also contain four neurons, where the neurons have index values 0, 1, 2, and 3 (a ten-neuron output layer has index values from 0 to 9, inclusive). The sum of the probabilities in the output layer always equals 1 because of the softmax activation function that is used when transitioning from the penultimate layer to the output layer.

Find the index of the largest probability and the index of the "1" in the one-hot encoding of the label (of the current datapoint) and compare them. If the index values are equal, then the NN has correctly classified the current datapoint (otherwise, it's a mismatch).

For example, the MNIST dataset contains images of hand-drawn digits from 0 through 9, inclusive, which means that a NN for the MNIST dataset has ten outputs in the final layer, one for each digit. Suppose that an image containing the digit 3 is currently being passed through the NN. The one-hot encoding for 3 is [0,0,0,1,0,0,0,0,0,0], and the index value with the largest value in the one-hot encoding is also 3. Now suppose that output layer of the NN is [0.05,0.05,0.2,0.6,0.2,0.2,0.1,0.1,0.238] after processing the digit 3. As you can see, the index value with the maximum value (which is 0.6) is also 3. In this scenario, the NN has correctly identified the input image. One other point: the TF API tf.argmax() is used to calculate the total number of images that have been correctly labeled by a NN.

A *binary classifier* involves two outcomes for handling tasks, such as determining spam/not-spam, fraud/not-fraud, or stock increase/decrease (or temperature, or barometric pressure). Predicting the future value of a stock price is a regression task, whereas predicting whether the price will increase or decrease is a classification task.

In machine learning, the multi-layer perceptron is a NN for supervised learning of binary classifiers (and it's a type of linear classifier). However, single layer perceptrons are only capable of learning linearly separable patterns. In fact, a famous book entitled *Perceptrons* by Marvin Minsky and Seymour Papert (written in 1969) showed that it was impossible for these classes of network to learn an XOR function. However, an XOR function can be learned by a two-layer perceptron.

## A High-Level View of CNNs

CNNs are deep NNs (with one or more convolutional layers) that are well-suited for image classification, along with other use cases, such as audio and NLP.

Although MLPs were successfully used for image recognition, they do not scale well because every pair of adjacent layers is fully connected, which in turn can result in massive neural networks. For large images (or other large inputs) the complexity becomes significant and adversely affects performance.

Figure 4.4 displays the contents of a CNN (there are many variations: this is simply one example).

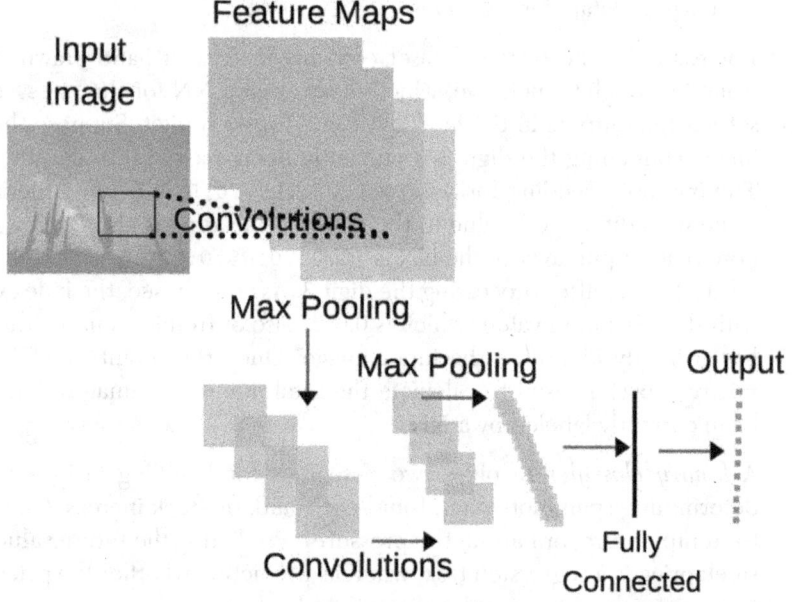

**FIGURE 4.4** An example of a CNN

## A Minimalistic CNN

A production quality CNN can be very complex, comprising many hidden layers. However, in this section, we're going to look at a minimalistic

CNN (essentially a "toy" neural network), which consists of the following layers:

- Conv2D (a convolutional layer)
- ReLU (activation function)
- Max Pooling (reduction technique)
- Fully Connected (FC) Layer
- Softmax activation function

The next subsections briefly explain the purpose of each bullet point in the preceding list of items.

### The Convolutional Layer (Conv2D)

The convolutional layer is typically labeled as Conv2D in Python and TF code. The Conv2D layer involves a set of filters, which are small square matrices whose dimensions are often 3x3 but can also be 5x5, 7x7, or even 1x1. Each filter is scanned across an image (think of tricorders in *Star Trek* movies), and at each step, an inner product is calculated with the filter and the portion of the image that is currently underneath the filter. The result of this scanning process is called a *feature map* that contains real numbers.

Figure 4.5 shows a 6x6 grid of numbers and the inner product of a 2x2 filter with a 2x2 subregion that results in the number -4 that appears in the feature map.

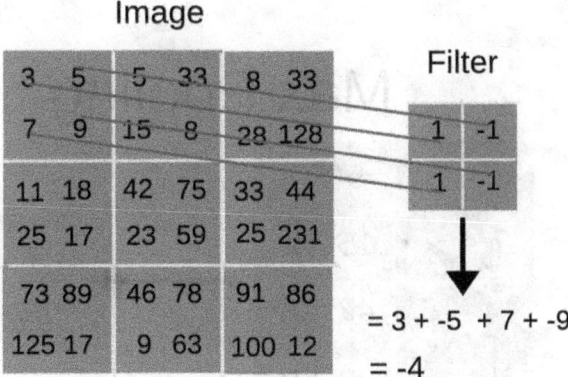

**FIGURE 4.5** Performing a convolution

### The ReLU Activation Function

After each feature map is created, it's possible that some of the values in the feature map are negative. The purpose of the ReLU activation function is to replace negative values (if any) with zero. Recall the definition of the ReLU function:

```
ReLU(x) = x if x >=0 and ReLU(x) = 0 if x < 0
```

If you draw a 2D graph of ReLU, it consists of two parts: the horizontal axis for x less than zero and the identity function (which is a line) in the first quadrant for x greater than or equal to 0.

### The Max Pooling Layer

The third step involves max pooling, which is simple to perform: after processing the feature map with the ReLU activation function in the previous step, partition the updated feature map into 2x2 rectangles, and select the largest value from each of those rectangles. The result is a smaller array that contains 25% of the feature map (i.e., 75% of the numbers are discarded). There are several algorithms that you can use to perform this extraction: the average of the numbers in each square; the square root of the sum of the squares of the numbers in each square; or the maximum number in each square.

In the case of CNNs, the algorithm for max pooling selects the maximum number from each 2x2 rectangle. Figure 4.6 shows the result of max pooling in a CNN.

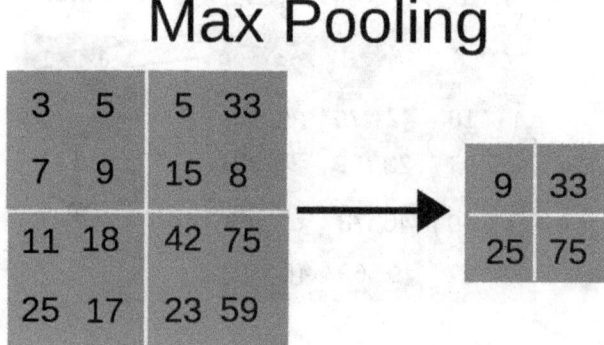

*FIGURE 4.6* An example of max pooling in a CNN

The result is a small square array whose size is only 25% of the previous feature map. This sequence is performed for each filter in the set of filters that were chosen in the Conv2D layer. This set can have 8, 16, 32, or more filters (usually a power of 2).

If you feel puzzled or skeptical about this technique, consider the analogy involving compression algorithms, which can be divided into two types: lossy and lossless. In case you didn't already know, JPEG is a lossy algorithm (i.e., data is lost during the compression process), and yet it works just fine for compressing images. Think of max pooling as the counterpart to lossy compression algorithms, and perhaps that will persuade you of the efficacy of this algorithm.

However, your skepticism is valid. In fact, Geoffrey Hinton (often called the "godfather" of deep learning) proposed a replacement for max pooling called *capsule networks*. This architecture is more complex and more difficult to train, and also beyond the scope of this book (you can find online tutorials that discuss capsule networks in detail). However, capsule networks tend to be more resistant to GANs (Generative Adversarial Networks).

Repeat the previous sequence of steps (as in LeNet), and then perform a rather non-intuitive action: flatten all these small arrays so that they are one-dimensional vectors, and concatenate these vectors into one (very long) vector. The resulting vector is then fully connected with the output layer, where the latter consists of 10 buckets. In the case of MNIST, these placeholders are for the digits from 0 to 9, inclusive. Note that the Keras tf.keras.layers.Flatten class performs this flattening process.

The softmax activation function is applied to the long vector of numbers to populate the 10 buckets of the output layer. The result is that the 10 buckets are populated with a set of non-zero (and non-negative) numbers whose sum equals one. Find the index of the bucket containing the largest number, and compare this number with the index of the one-hot encoded label associated with the image that was just processed. If the index values are equal, then the image was successfully identified.

More complex CNNs involve multiple Conv2D layers, multiple FC (fully connected) layers, different filter sizes, and techniques for combining previous layers (such as ResNet) to boost the data values' current layer. Additional information about CNNs is here: *https://en.wikipedia.org/wiki/ Convolutional_neural_network*

Now that you have a high-level understanding of CNNs, let's look at a code sample that illustrates an image in the MNIST dataset (and the pixel values of that image), followed by two code samples that use Keras to train a model on the MNIST dataset.

## Displaying an Image in the MNIST Dataset

Listing 4.2 shows the content of tf2_keras-mnist_digit.py, which illustrates how to create a neural network in TensorFlow that processes the MNIST dataset.

*LISTING 4.2: tf2_keras-mnist_digit.py*

```
import tensorflow as tf

mnist = tf.keras.datasets.mnist

(X_train, y_train), (X_test, y_test) = mnist.load_data()

print("X_train.shape:",X_train.shape)
print("X_test.shape: ",X_test.shape)

first_img = X_train[0]

# uncomment this line to see the pixel values
#print(first_img)

import matplotlib.pyplot as plt
plt.imshow(first_img, cmap='gray')
plt.show()
```

Listing 4.2 starts with some import statements and then populates the training data and test data from the MNIST dataset. The variable first_img is initialized as the first entry in the X_train array, which is the first image in the training dataset. The final block of code in Listing 4.2 displays the pixel values for the first image. The output from Listing 4.2 is here:

```
X_train.shape: (60000, 28, 28)
X_test.shape:  (10000, 28, 28)
```

Figure 4.7 shows the contents of the first image in the MNIST dataset.

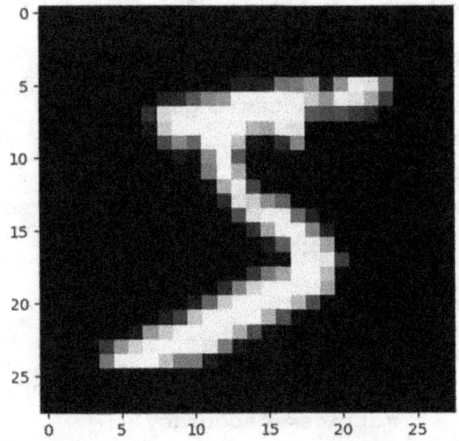

*FIGURE 4.7* The first image in the MNIST dataset

## Keras and the MNIST Dataset

When you read code samples that contain Keras-based models that use the MNIST dataset, the models use a different API in the input layer.

Specifically, a model that is not a CNN flattens the input images into a one-dimensional vector via the tf.keras.layers.Flatten() API, an example of which is here (see Listing 4.3 for details):

```
tf.keras.layers.Flatten(input_shape=(28,28))
```

A CNN uses the tf.keras.layers.Conv2D() API, an example of which is here (see Listing 4.4 for details):

```
tf.keras.layers.Conv2D(32,(3,3),activation='relu',input_
shape=(28,28,1))
```

Listing 4.3 shows the content of keras_mnist.py, which illustrates how to create a Keras-based neural network in TensorFlow that processes the MNIST dataset.

### *LISTING 4.3: keras_mnist.py*

```
import tensorflow as tf

mnist = tf.keras.datasets.mnist
(x_train, y_train),(x_test, y_test) = mnist.load_data()
```

```
x_train, x_test = x_train / 255.0, x_test / 255.0

model = tf.keras.models.Sequential([
  tf.keras.layers.Flatten(input_shape=(28, 28)),
  tf.keras.layers.Dense(512, activation='relu'),
  tf.keras.layers.Dropout(0.2),
  tf.keras.layers.Dense(10, activation='softmax')
])

model.summary()

model.compile(optimizer='adam',
              loss='sparse_categorical_crossentropy',
              metrics=['accuracy'])

model.fit(x_train, y_train, epochs=5)
model.evaluate(x_test, y_test)
```

Listing 4.3 starts with some import statements and then initializes the variable mnist as a reference to the built-in MNIST dataset. Next, the training-related and test-related variables are initialized with their respective portions of the MNIST dataset, followed by a scaling transformation for x_train and x_test.

The next portion of Listing 4.3 defines a very simple Keras-based model with four layers that are created from classes in the tf.keras.layers package. The next code snippet displays a summary of the model definition, as shown here:

```
Model: "sequential"
```

| Layer (type) | Output Shape | Param # |
|---|---|---|
| flatten (Flatten) | None, 784) | 0 |
| dense (Dense) | (None, 512) | 401920 |
| dropout (Dropout) | None, 512) | 0 |
| dense_1 (Dense) | (None, 10) | 5130 |

```
Total params: 407,050
Trainable params: 407,050
Non-trainable params: 0
```

The remaining portion of Listing 4.3 compiles, fits, and evaluates the model, which produces the following output:

```
Epoch 1/5
60000/60000 [====================] - 14s 225us/step - loss:
0.2186 - acc: 0.9360
Epoch 2/5
60000/60000 [====================] - 14s 225us/step - loss:
0.0958 - acc: 0.9704
Epoch 3/5
60000/60000 [====================] - 14s 232us/step - loss:
0.0685 - acc: 0.9783
Epoch 4/5
60000/60000 [====================] - 14s 227us/step - loss:
0.0527 - acc: 0.9832
Epoch 5/5
60000/60000 [====================] - 14s 225us/step - loss:
0.0426 - acc: 0.9861
10000/10000 [====================] - 1s 59us/step
```

The final accuracy for this model is 98.6%, which is a respectable value.

## Keras, CNNs, and the Mnist Dataset

Listing 4.4 shows the content of keras_cnn_mnist.py, which illustrates how to create a Keras-based neural network in TensorFlow that processes the MNIST dataset.

### LISTING 4.4: keras_cnn_mnist.py

```python
import tensorflow as tf
import numpy as np
import matplotlib.pyplot as plt

(train_images, train_labels), (test_images, test_labels) =
tf.keras.datasets.mnist.load_data()

train_images = train_images.reshape((60000, 28, 28, 1))
test_images = test_images.reshape((10000, 28, 28, 1))

# Normalize pixel values: from the range 0-255 to the range 0-1
train_images,    test_images    =    train_images/255.0,
test_images/255.0
```

```
model = tf.keras.models.Sequential()
model.add(tf.keras.layers.Conv2D(32,    (3,   3),   activa-
tion='relu', input_shape=(28, 28, 1)))
model.add(tf.keras.layers.MaxPooling2D((2, 2)))
model.add(tf.keras.layers.Conv2D(64,         (3,        3),
activation='relu'))
model.add(tf.keras.layers.MaxPooling2D((2, 2)))
model.add(tf.keras.layers.Conv2D(64,        (3,       3),
activation='relu'))
model.add(tf.keras.layers.Flatten())
model.add(tf.keras.layers.Dense(64, activation='relu'))
model.add(tf.keras.layers.Dense(10, activation='softmax'))

model.summary()

model.compile(optimizer='adam',
              loss='sparse_categorical_crossentropy',
              metrics=['accuracy'])

model.fit(train_images, train_labels, epochs=1)
test_loss, test_acc = model.evaluate(test_images,
test_labels)
print(test_acc)

# predict the label of one image
test_image = np.expand_dims(test_images[300],axis = 0)
plt.imshow(test_image.reshape(28,28))
plt.show()

result = model.predict(test_image)
print("result:", result)
print("result.argmax():", result.argmax())
```

Listing 4.4 initializes the training data and labels, as well as the test data and labels, via the load_data() function. Next, the images are reshaped so that they are 28x28 images, and then the pixel values are rescaled from the range 0-255 (all integers) to the range 0-1 (decimal values).

The next portion of Listing 4.4 uses the Keras Sequential() API to define a Keras-based model called model, which contains two pairs of Conv2D and MaxPooling2D layers, followed by the Flatten layer, and then two consecutive Dense layers.

Next, the model is compiled, trained, and evaluated via the compile(), fit(), and evaluate() methods, respectively. The final portion of

Listing 4.4 successfully predicts the image whose label is 4, which is then displayed via `Matplotlib`. Launch the code in Listing 4.4 to see the following output on the command line:

```
Model: "sequential"
```

| Layer (type) | Output Shape | Param # |
| --- | --- | --- |
| conv2d (Conv2D) | (None, 26, 26, 32) | 320 |
| max_pooling2d (MaxPooling2D) | (None, 13, 13, 32) | 0 |
| conv2d_1 (Conv2D) | (None, 11, 11, 64) | 18496 |
| max_pooling2d_1 (MaxPooling2 | (None, 5, 5, 64) | 0 |
| conv2d_2 (Conv2D) | (None, 3, 3, 64) | 36928 |
| flatten (Flatten) | (None, 576) | 0 |
| dense (Dense) | (None, 64) | 36928 |
| dense_1 (Dense) | (None, 10) | 650 |

```
Total params: 93,322
Trainable params: 93,322
Non-trainable params: 0
```

```
60000/60000 [==========================] - 54s 907us/sample
- loss: 0.1452 - accuracy: 0.9563
10000/10000 [=========================] - 3s 297us/sample -
loss: 0.0408 - accuracy: 0.9868
0.9868
Using TensorFlow backend.
result:    [[6.2746993e-05    1.7837329e-03    3.8957372e-04
4.6143982e-06 9.9723744e-01
   1.5522403e-06 1.9182076e-04 3.0044283e-04 2.2602901e-05
5.3929521e-06]]
result.argmax(): 4
```

Figure 4.8 shows the image that is displayed when you launch the code in Listing 4.4.

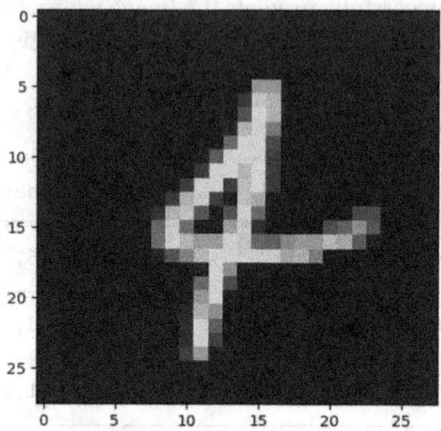

***FIGURE 4.8*** An image in the MNIST dataset

You might be asking yourself how the model in Listing 4.4 can achieve such a high accuracy when every input image is flattened into a one-dimensional vector, which loses the adjacency information that is available in a two-dimensional image. Before CNNs became popular, one technique involved using MLPs and another technique involved SVMs as models for images. In fact, if you don't have enough images to train a model, you can still use an SVM. Another option is to generate synthetic data using a GAN (which was its original purpose).

## CNNS with Audio Signals

In addition to image classification, you can train CNNs with audio signals, which can be converted from analog to digital. Audio signals have various numeric parameters (such as decibel level and voltage level) that are described here:

*https://en.wikipedia.org/wiki/Audio_signal*

If you have a set of audio signals, the numeric values of their associated parameters become the dataset for a CNN. Remember that CNNs have no "understanding" of the numeric input values: the numeric values are processed in the same fashion, regardless of the source of the numeric values.

One use case involves a microphone outside of a building detects and identifies various sounds. Obviously, it's important to identify the sound of a backfire from a vehicle versus the sound of a gunshot. In the latter case, the police should be notified about a potential crime. There are companies that use CNNs to identify different types of sounds; other companies are exploring the use of RNNs and LSTMs instead of CNNs.

## Summary

In this chapter, you got a brief introduction to deep learning, how it differs from machine learning, and some of the problems it can solve. You learned about the challenges that exist in deep learning, which includes bias in algorithms, susceptibility to adversarial attacks, limited ability to generalize, lack of explainability in neural networks, and the lack of causality.

Next you learned about the XOR function, which is an example of a non-linearly separable set of four points in the plane. Despite its simplicity in the 2D case, the XOR function cannot be solved with a single layer shallow network: instead, two hidden layers are required. Next you learned about perceptrons, which are essentially the core building blocks of neural networks.

You also saw a Keras-based code sample for training a neural network on the MNIST dataset. In addition, you learned how CNNs are constructed, along with a Keras-based code sample for training a CNN with the MNIST dataset: this code sample will make more sense after you have read the section pertaining to activation functions in Chapter 5.

# DEEP LEARNING: RNNs AND LSTMs

This chapter extends the introduction from Chapter 4 by discussing RNNs (Recurrent Neural Networks) and LSTMs (Long Short Term Memory). Although most of this chapter contains descriptive content regarding these architectures, there are Keras-based code samples. Hence, this would be a good point to read the Keras material in the associated appendix in case you haven't already done so.

The first part of this chapter introduces you to the architecture of RNNs, BPTT (back propagation through time), and a short Keras-based code sample. As you will see, RNNs can keep track of information from earlier time periods, which makes them useful for a variety of tasks, including NLP tasks.

The second part of this chapter introduces you to the architecture of LSTMs, which is more complex than RNNs. Specifically, LSTMs includes a forget gate, an input gate, and an output gate, as well as a long-term memory cell. We also discuss the advantages of LSTMs over RNNs. In addition, we cover bi-directional LSTMs that are used in some well-known NLP-related models (see Chapter 6).

The third part of this chapter introduces you to the architecture of auto-encoders and the rationale for using them, as well as an introduction to variational autoencoders.

Please keep in mind that the code samples in this chapter assume that you have some familiarity with Keras (discussed in one of the appendices).

## What is an RNN?

An RNN is a Recurrent Neural Network, which is a type of architecture that was developed during the 1980s. RNNs are suitable for datasets that contain sequential data and also for NLP tasks, such as language modeling, text generation, or auto-completion of sentences. In fact, you might be surprised to learn that you can even perform image classification (such as MNIST) via an RNN. Figure 5.1 shows the contents of a simple RNN.

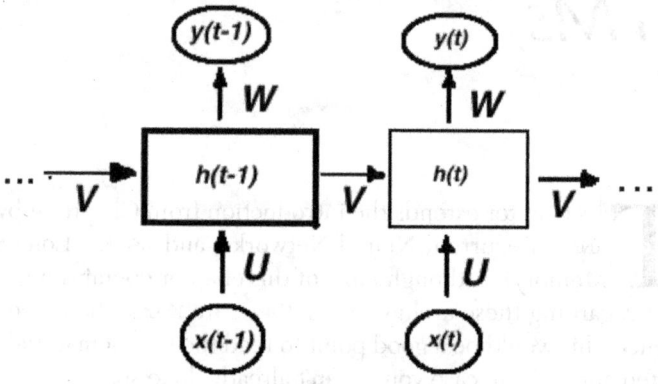

**FIGURE 5.1** An example of an RNN

In addition to simple RNNs, there are more powerful constructs, such as LSTMs and GRUs. A basic RNN has the simplest type of feedback mechanism (described later), and involves a sigmoid activation function.

RNNs (which includes LSTMs and GRUs) differ from ANNs in several important ways, as listed here:

- Statefulness (all RNNs)
- Feedback mechanism (all RNNs)
- A sigmoid or tanh activation function
- Multiple gates (LSTMs and GRUs)
- BPTT (Back Propagation Through Time)
- Truncated BPTT (simple RNNs)

First, ANNs and CNNs are essentially "stateless," whereas RNNs are "stateful" because they have an internal state. Hence, RNNs can process more complex sequences of inputs, which makes them suitable for tasks such as handwriting recognition and or speech recognition.

## Anatomy of an RNN

Consider the RNN in Figure 5.1. Suppose that the sequence of inputs is labeled x1, x2, x3, ... , x(t), .... and also that the sequence of "hidden states" is labeled h1, h2, h3, ..., h(t). Note that each input sequence and hidden state is a 1xn vector, where n is the number of features.

At time period t, the input is based on a combination of h(t-1) and x(t), after which an activation function is applied to this combination (which can also involve adding a bias vector).

Another difference is the feedback mechanism for RNNs that occurs between consecutive time periods. Specifically, the output at a *previous* time period is combined with the new input of the *current* time period in order to calculate the new internal state. Let's use the sequence {h(0), h(1), h(2), . . . h(t-1), h(t)} to represent the set of internal states of an RNN during time periods {0, 1, 2, ... , t-1, t}, and let's also suppose that the sequence {x(0), x(1), x(2), ... , x(t-1), x(t)} is the input during the same time periods.

The fundamental relationship for an RNN at time period t is here:

h(t) = f(W*x(t) + U*h(t-1))

In the preceding formula, W and U are weight matrices and f is typically the tanh activation function.

Here is a code snippet of a TF 2 Keras-based model that is based on the tf.keras.layers.SimpleRNN class:

```
import tensorflow as tf

...

model = tf.keras.models.Sequential()
model.add(tf.keras.layers.SimpleRNN(5, input_shape=(1,2),
batch_input_shape=[1,1,2], stateful=True))

...
```

Perform an online search for more information and code samples involving Keras and RNNs.

## What is BPTT?

BPTT (back propagation through time) in RNNs is the counterpart to backprop for CNNs. The weight matrices of RNNs are updated during to train the neural network.

However, there is a problem called the exploding gradient that can occur in RNNs, which is to say that the gradient becomes arbitrarily large (versus the gradient becoming arbitrarily small in the vanishing gradient scenario). One way to deal with the exploding gradient problem is to use a *truncated BPTT*, which means that BPTT is computed for a small number of steps instead of all time steps. Another technique is to specify a maximum value for the gradient, which involves simple conditional logic.

The good news is that there is another way to overcome both the exploding gradient and vanishing gradient problem, which involves LSTMs that are discussed later in this chapter.

## Working with RNNs and Keras

Listing 5.1 shows the contents of `keras_rnn_model.py`, which illustrates how to create a simple Keras-based RNN model.

*LISTING 5.1: keras_rnn_model.py*

```
import tensorflow as tf

timesteps = 30
input_dim = 12

# number of units in RNN cell
units = 512

# number of classes to be identified
n_classes = 5

# Keras Sequential model with RNN and Dense layer
model = tf.keras.models.Sequential()
model.add(tf.keras.layers.SimpleRNN(units=units,
                      dropout=0.2,
                      input_shape=(timesteps, input_dim)))
model.add(tf.keras.layers.Dense(n_classes,
activation='softmax'))

# model loss function and optimizer
model.compile(loss='categorical_crossentropy',
              optimizer=tf.keras.optimizers.Adam(),
              metrics=['accuracy'])

model.summary()
```

Listing 5.1 first initializes the variables timesteps (the number of time steps), input_dim (the number of elements in each input vector of numbers), units (the number of hidden units in the RNN neuron), and n_classes (the number of classes in the dataset).

The next portion of Listing 5.1 creates a Keras-based model that looks similar to earlier Keras-based models, with the exception of the code snippet for the RNN layer, as shown here:

```
model.add(tf.keras.layers.SimpleRNN(units=units,
          dropout=0.2,
          input_shape=(timesteps, input_dim)))
```

The preceding code snippet adds an instance of the SimpleRNN class as well as the variables that are defined in the preceding code block.

The final portion of code invokes the compile() method, followed by the summary() method to display the structure of the model.

Launch the code in Listing 5.1 to see the following output:

```
Model: "sequential"
```

| Layer (type) | Output Shape | Param # |
|---|---|---|
| simple_rnn (SimpleRNN) | (None, 512) | 268800 |
| dense (Dense) | (None, 5) | 2565 |

```
Total params: 271,365
Trainable params: 271,365
Non-trainable params: 0
```

Now that you see how easy it is to create an RNN-based model in Keras, let's look at an example of an RNN-based model in Keras that will be trained on the MNIST dataset, which is the topic of the next section.

## Working with **Keras**, RNNs, and MNIST

Listing 5.2 displays the contents of keras_rnn_mnist.py that illustrates how to create a simple Keras-based RNN model that is trained on the MNIST dataset.

*LISTING 5.2: keras_rnn_mnist.py*

```python
# this code works with TensorFlow 2.1 and Python 3.6
import tensorflow as tf
import numpy as np

# get an instance of the TF 2 built-in mnist dataset:
mnist = tf.keras.datasets.mnist

# load the mnist dataset and split into training and test:
(x_train, y_train), (x_test, y_test) = mnist.load_data()

# compute the number of training labels:
num_labels = len(np.unique(y_train))

# make sure that all labels are one-hot encoded:
y_train = tf.keras.utils.to_categorical(y_train)
y_test  = tf.keras.utils.to_categorical(y_test)

# resize the training and test data x_train and x-test
# and then divide pixel values by 255 (normalization)
image_size = x_train.shape[1]
x_train = np.reshape(x_train,[-1, image_size, image_size])
x_test = np.reshape(x_test,[-1, image_size, image_size])
x_train = x_train.astype('float32') / 255
x_test = x_test.astype('float32') / 255

# initialize some standard parameters:
input_shape = (image_size, image_size)
batch_size = 128
units = 256
dropout = 0.2

# create a Keras RNN model with:
# 256 units
# input is 28-dimensional vector
# having 28 timesteps
# with a few simple layers

model = tf.keras.models.Sequential()
model.add(tf.keras.layers.SimpleRNN(units=units,
                    dropout=dropout,
                    input_shape=input_shape))
model.add(tf.keras.layers.Dense(num_labels))
model.add(tf.keras.layers.Activation('softmax'))
model.summary()
```

```
tf.keras.utils.plot_model(model,      to_file='my-rnn-mnist.
png', show_shapes=True)

# loss function for one-hot vector: sgd optimizer
# accuracy is good metric for classification tasks
model.compile(loss='categorical_crossentropy',
              optimizer='sgd',
              metrics=['accuracy'])

# train the network: increase epochs for better results
model.fit(x_train, y_train, epochs=5, batch_size=batch_size)

loss, acc = model.evaluate(x_test, y_test,
batch_size=batch_size)
print("\nTest accuracy: %.1f%%" % (100.0 * acc))
```

Listing 5.2 contains the usual import statements, followed by the initialization of the mnist variable as a reference to the MNIST dataset, after which the four variables for the training data and the test data are initialized.

The next portion of Listing 5.2 ensures that the training images and test images are resized as 28x28 images, after which the pixel values (which are in the range of 0 to 255) in these images are scaled down so that they are in the range of 0 to 1. The next portion of Listing 5.2 is very similar to Listing 5.1: some hyperparameters are initialized and then an RNN-based model in Keras is created.

At this point we have new code, starting with the code snippet that saves the model structure in the rnn-mnist.png file. A second new code block invokes the compile() method to sync up the model with the training data, followed by the fit() method that trains the model.

The final portion of Listing 5.2 evaluates the trained model on the test data and displays the values of loss and acc that correspond to the loss and the accuracy, respectively, of the model on the test data. Launch the code in Listing 5.2 to see the following output:

```
Model: "sequential"
```

| Layer (type) | Output Shape | Param # |
| --- | --- | --- |
| simple_rnn (SimpleRNN) | (None, 256) | 72960 |
| dense (Dense) | (None, 10) | 2570 |
| activation (Activation) | (None, 10) | 0 |

```
Total params: 75,530
Trainable params: 75,530
Non-trainable params: 0
Epoch 1/5
60000/60000 [==============================] - 33s 542us/
sample - loss: 0.8198 - accuracy: 0.7605
Epoch 2/5
6528/60000 [==>...........................] - ETA: 27s -
loss: 0.4661 - accuracy: 0.8627
60000/60000 [==============================] - 34s 559us/
sample - loss: 0.3724 - accuracy: 0.8917
Epoch 3/5
60000/60000 [==============================] - 33s 545us/
sample - loss: 0.2764 - accuracy: 0.9183
Epoch 4/5
60000/60000 [==============================] - 33s 545us/
sample - loss: 0.2269 - accuracy: 0.9327
Epoch 5/5
60000/60000 [==============================] - 34s 561us/
sample - loss: 0.1983 - accuracy: 0.9407
10000/10000 [==============================] - 2s 237us/
sample - loss: 0.1396 - accuracy: 0.9577
Test accuracy: 95.8%
```

## Working with TensorFlow and RNNs (Optional)

The code sample in this section is optional because it's based on TensorFlow 1.x. Currently TensorFlow 2.3 is available, and TensorFlow 1.x is considered legacy code (starting from late 2019 for a period of one additional year). Keep this in mind when you encounter any other code samples in this book that involve TensorFlow 1.x.

However, this code sample does provide some low-level details regarding the output and the state for each hidden layer in an RNN neuron, which can give you some insight into how the calculations are performed and the values that are generated. Keep in mind that the data for the two time steps is simulated, which is to say that the data does not reflect any meaningful use case. The purpose of the simplified data is to help you focus on the way in which calculations are performed.

Listing 5.3 shows the content of dynamic_rnn_2TP.py, which illustrates how to create a simple TensorFlow-based RNN model.

*LISTING 5.3: dynamic_rnn_2TP.py*

```python
import tensorflow as tf
import numpy as np

n_steps = 2     # number of time steps
n_inputs = 3    # number of inputs per time unit
n_neurons = 5   # number of hidden units
X_batch = np.array([
  # t = 0        t = 1
  [[0, 1, 2], [9, 8, 7]], # instance 0
  [[3, 4, 5], [0, 0, 0]], # instance 1
  [[6, 7, 8], [6, 5, 4]], # instance 2
  [[9, 0, 1], [3, 2, 1]], # instance 3
])

#sequence_length <= # of elements in each batch
seq_length_batch = np.array([2, 1, 2, 2])
X = tf.placeholder(dtype=tf.float32, shape=[None, n_steps,
n_inputs])
seq_length = tf.placeholder(tf.int32, [None])

basic_cell=tf.nn.rnn_cell.BasicRNNCell(num_units=n_neurons)
outputs, states = tf.nn.dynamic_rnn(basic_cell, X,
sequence_length=seq_length, dtype=tf.float32)

with tf.Session() as sess:
  sess.run(tf.global_variables_initializer())
  outputs_val, states_val = sess.run([outputs, states],
        feed_dict={X:X_batch, seq_length:seq_length_batch})

  print("X_batch     shape:", X_batch.shape)     # (4,2,3)
  print("outputs_val shape:", outputs_val.shape) # (4,2,5)
  print("states_val  shape:", states_val.shape)    # (4,5)

  print("outputs_val:",outputs_val)
  print("--------------------------\n")
  print("states_val: ",states_val)

############################################################
# outputs => output of ALL RNN states
# states  => output of LAST ACTUAL RNN state (ignores zero
vector)
# state = output[1] for full sequences
# state = output[0] for short sequences
############################################################
```

Listing 5.3 starts by initializing n_steps (the number of time steps), n_inputs (the number of inputs), and n_neurons (the number of neurons) to 2, 3, and 5, respectively.

Next the NumPy array X_batch is a 4x2x3 array that is initialized with integers. As you can see from the comment line, the first column of values is for time step 0, and the second column of values is for time step 1. You can also think of each row of data in X_batch as an instance of data for both time steps.

Next, the variable seq_length_batch is a one-dimensional vector of integers, each of which specifies that number of time steps that appear to the left of a vector consisting of purely zero values. As you can see, this vector contains the value 2 for instances number 0, 2, and 3, and the value 0 for instance number 1.

The next portion of Listing 5.3 defines the placeholder X that can hold an arbitrary number of arrays whose shape is [n_steps, n_inputs]. Now we're ready to define an RNN cell and specify its outputs and states, as shown here:

```
basic_cell = tf.nn.rnn_cell.BasicRNNCell(num_units=n_neu-
rons)
outputs, states = tf.nn.dynamic_rnn(basic_cell, X,
sequence_length=seq_length, dtype=tf.float32)
```

The key point to remember is that the final output value from the rightmost hidden unit is the value that is passed to the next neuron.

Launch the code in Listing 5.3 to see the following output, where the value of the interest is shown in bold:

```
#-----------------------------
#outputs_val:
#[[[-0.09700205    0.7671716     0.6775758     0.01522888
0.5460828 ]
#   [ 0.92776424   -0.5916748    0.67824966    0.99423325
0.9999991 ]]
#
# [[ 0.24040672   0.81568515    0.8890421     0.780813
0.99762475]
#   [ 0.           0.            0.            0.         0.
]]
#
# [[ 0.5282535    0.8549201     0.9647311     0.9692446
0.99999046]
```

```
#   [ 0.9725177    -0.7165484     0.46688017     0.9411293
0.9999323 ]]
#
# [[ 0.81080747   -0.9926888     0.56612366     0.9561879
0.9997731 ]
#   [ 0.48786768   -0.7099759    -0.7283263      0.76442945
0.9971904 ]]]
#--------------------------
#states_val:
#[[ 0.92776424   -0.5916748     0.67824966     0.99423325
0.9999991 ]
# [ 0.24040672    0.81568515     0.8890421      0.780813
0.99762475]
# [ 0.9725177    -0.7165484      0.46688017     0.9411293
0.9999323 ]
# [ 0.48786768   -0.7099759     -0.7283263      0.76442945
0.9971904 ]]
#--------------------------
```

In the preceding output, notice that the row count of the rows shown in bold is 2, 1, 2, and 2, which includes exactly the same values as in `seq_length_batch`. As you can see, these highlighted rows appear (also in bold) in the array labeled `states_val`.

Listing 5.3 is a very small and artificial example of an RNN, and hopefully this example gives you a better understanding of the inner workings of an RNN. There are many variants of RNNs, and you can read about some of them here:

*https://en.wikipedia.org/wiki/Recurrent_neural_network*

## What is an LSTM?

LSTMs are a special type of RNN, and they are well-suited for many use cases, including NLP, speech recognition, and handwriting recognition. LSTMs are well-suited for handling the *long term dependency*, which refers to the distance gap between the relevant information and the location where that information is required. This situation arises when information in one section of a document needs to be "linked" to information that is in a more distant location of the document.

LSTMs were developed in 1997 and went on to exceed the accuracy performance of state-of-the-art algorithms. LSTMs also began revolutionizing speech recognition (circa 2007). Then, in 2009, an LSTM won pattern recognition contests, and in 2014, Baidu used RNNs to exceed speech recognition records. The following site has an example of an LSTM: *https://commons.wikimedia.org/w/index.php?curid=60149410*

## Anatomy of an LSTM

LSTMs are "stateful" and they contain three gates (forget gate, input gate, and an output gate) that involve a sigmoid function, and also a cell state that involves the tanh activation function. At time period t, the input to an LSTM is based on a combination of the two vectors h(t-1) and x(t). This pair of inputs is combined, after which a sigmoid activation function is applied to this combination (which can also include a bias vector) in the case of the forget gate, input gate, and the output gate.

The processing that occurs at time step t is the "short term" memory of an LSTM. The internal cell state of LSTMs maintains "long term" memory. Updating the internal cell state involves the tanh activation function, whereas the other gates use the sigmoid activation function, as mentioned in the previous paragraph. Here is a TF 2 code block that defines Keras-based model for an LSTM (with the LSTM shown in bold):

```
import tensorflow as tf
. . .
model = tf.keras.models.Sequential()
model.add(tf.keras.layers.LSTMCell(6,batch_input_
shape=(1,1,1),kernel_initializer='ones',stateful=True))
model.add(tf.keras.layers.Dense(1))
. . .
```

You can learn about the difference between an LSTM and an LSTMCell here:

*https://stackoverflow.com/questions/48187283/whats-the-difference-between-lstm-and-lstmcell*

Additional information about LSTMs and how to define a custom LSTM cell can be found at the following sites:

- *https://en.wikipedia.org/wiki/Recurrent_neural_network*
- *https://stackoverflow.com/questions/54231440/define-custom-lstm-cell-in-keras*

## BiDirectional LSTMs

In addition to one-directional LSTMs, you can also define a "bi-directional" LSTM that consists of two "regular" LSTMs: one LSTM for the forward direction and one LSTM in the backward or opposite direction. You might be surprised to discover that bi-directional LSTMs are well-suited for solving NLP tasks.

For instance, ELMO is a deep word representation for NLP tasks that uses bi-directional LSTMs. An even newer architecture in the NLP world is called a *transformer*, and bidirectional transformers are used in BERT, which is a very well-known system (released by Google in 2018) that can solve complex NLP problems.

The following TF 2 code block contains a Keras-based model that involves bidirectional LSTMs:

```
import tensorflow as tf
. . .
model = tf.keras.models.Sequential()
model.add(tf.keras.layers.Bidirectional(LSTM(10,
return_sequences=True), input_shape=(5,10)))
model.add(tf.keras.layers.Bidirectional(LSTM(10)))
model.add(tf.keras.layers.Dense(5))
model.add(tf.keras.layers.Activation('softmax'))
model.compile(loss='categorical_crossentropy',
optimizer='rmsprop')
. . .
```

The previous code block contains two bidirectional LSTM cells, both of which are shown in bold.

## LSTM Formulas

The formulas for LSTMs are more complex than the update formula for a simple RNN, but there are some patterns that can help you understand those formulas.

Visit the following site to see the formulas for an LSTM:

*https://en.wikipedia.org/wiki/Long_short-term_memory#cite_note-lstm1997-1*

The formulas show you how the new weights are calculated for the forget gate f, the input gate i, and the output gate i during time step t. In addition, the preceding link shows you how the new internal state and the hidden state (both at time step t) are calculated.

Notice the pattern for gates f, i, and o: all of them calculate the sum of two terms, each of which is a product involving $x(t)$ and $h(t)$, after which the sigmoid function is applied to that sum. Specifically, here's the formula for the forget gate at time t:

```
f(t) = sigma(W(f)*x(t) + U(f)*h(t) + b(f))
```

In the preceding formula, W(f), U(f), and b(f) are the weight matrices associated with x(t), the weight matrix associated with h(t), and the bias vector for the forget gate f, respectively.

Notice that the calculations for i(t) and o(t) have the same pattern as the calculation for f(t). The difference is that i(t) has the matrices W(i) and U(i), whereas o(t) has the matrices W(o) and U(o). Thus, f(t), i(t), and o(t) have a parallel construction.

The calculations for c(t), i(t), and h(t) are based on the values for f(t), i(t), and o(t), as shown here:

```
c(t)  = f(t) * c(t-1) + i(t) * tanh(c'(t))
c'(t) = sigma(W(c) * x(t) + U(c) * h(t-1))
h(t)  = o(t) * tanh(c(t))
```

The final state of an LSTM is a one-dimensional vector that contains the output from all the other layers in the LSTM. If you have a model that contains multiple LSTMs, the final state vector for a given LSTM becomes the input for the next LSTM in that model.

## LSTM Hyperparameter Tuning

LSTMs are also prone to overfitting, and here is a list of considerations if you are manually optimizing hyperparameters for LSTMs:

- overfitting (use regularization, such as L1 or L2)
- larger networks are more prone to overfitting
- more data tends to reduce overfitting
- train the networks over multiple epochs
- the learning rate is vitally important
- stacking layers can be helpful
- use softsign instead of softmax for LSTMs
- RMSprop, AdaGrad, or momentum are good choices
- Xavier weight initialization

Perform an online search to obtain more information about the optimizers in the preceding list.

## Working with TensorFlow and LSTMs (Optional)

Listing 5.4 shows the content of dynamic_lstm_2TP.py, which illustrates how to create a simple LSTM model with TensorFlow 1.x code.

### *LISTING 5.4: dynamic_lstm_2TP.py*

```
import tensorflow as tf
import numpy as np

n_steps = 2    # number of time steps
n_inputs = 3   # number of inputs per time unit
n_neurons = 5  # number of hidden units

X_batch = np.array([
  # t = 0        t = 1
  [[0, 1, 2], [9, 8, 7]], # instance 0
  [[3, 4, 5], [0, 0, 0]], # instance 1
  [[6, 7, 8], [6, 5, 4]], # instance 2
  [[9, 0, 1], [3, 2, 1]], # instance 3
])

seq_length_batch = np.array([2, 1, 2, 2])

X = tf.placeholder(dtype=tf.float32,shape=[None,n_steps,
n_inputs])
seq_length = tf.placeholder(tf.int32, [None])

basic_cell = tf.nn.rnn_cell.
BasicLSTMCell(num_units=n_neurons)

outputs, states = tf.nn.dynamic_rnn(basic_cell, X,
sequence_length=seq_length, dtype=tf.float32)

with tf.Session() as sess:
  sess.run(tf.global_variables_initializer())
  outputs_val, states_val = sess.run([outputs, states],
      feed_dict={X:X_batch, seq_length:seq_length_batch})

  print("X_batch      shape:", X_batch.shape)      # (4,2,3)
  print("outputs_val shape:", outputs_val.shape)  # (4,2,5)
  print("states:            ", states_val)            #
LSTMStateTuple(...)
```

```
print("outputs_val:",outputs_val)
print("--------------------------\n")
print("states_val: ",states_val)
```

The first half of Listing 5.4 is identical to the first half of Listing 5.3, and the first line of code that is different involves defining basic_cell as an LSTM (shown in bold), which is reproduced here:

```
basic_cell = tf.nn.rnn_cell.BasicLSTMCell(num_units=
n_neurons)
outputs, states = tf.nn.dynamic_rnn(basic_cell, X,
sequence_length=seq_length, dtype=tf.float32)
```

Notice that outputs and states in Listing 5.4 are initialized in exactly the same fashion as shown in Listing 5.3. The next portion of code is a tf. Session() code block that is the training loop.

Another difference to notice in Listing 5.4 is that during each computation in the training loop, states_val is actually an instance of LSTMStatesTuple, whereas states_val in Listing 5.3 is a 4x5 tensor. Launch the code in Listing 5.4 to see the following output:

```
('X_batch     shape:', (4, 2, 3))
('outputs_val shape:', (4, 2, 5))

('states:              ', LSTMStateTuple(c=array(
   [[-1.0492262 , -0.1059267 , -0.27163735, -0.64399946,
0.06018598],
    [-0.7445494 ,  0.00723887, -0.11805946, -0.26550752,
0.21816696],
    [-1.4126835 ,  0.05187892, -0.07408151, -0.66379607,
0.1348486 ],
    [-0.5987958 ,  0.24536057, -0.16916996, -0.8177415 ,
0.39747238]],

       dtype=float32), h=array(
   [[-7.33636796e-01, -6.07701950e-02, -1.40444040e-01,
      -2.65002381e-02, 5.37334010e-04],
     [-4.83454257e-01, 3.39480606e-03, -3.36034223e-02,
      -2.59866733e-02, 4.49425131e-02],
     [-7.36429453e-01, 2.63450593e-02, -4.42487188e-02,
      -1.05846934e-01, 5.22684120e-03],
     [-3.73311013e-01, 1.35892674e-01, -9.72046256e-02,
     -2.79455721e-01, 5.36275432e-02]], dtype=float32)))
```

```
('outputs_val:', array([
    [[-1.39581457e-01, -8.17378387e-02, -8.70967656e-02,
      -3.05497926e-02,  1.16406225e-01],
     [-7.33636796e-01, -6.07701950e-02, -1.40444040e-01,
      -2.65002381e-02,  5.37334010e-04]],

    [[-4.83454257e-01,  3.39480606e-03, -3.36034223e-02,
      -2.59866733e-02,  4.49425131e-02],
     [ 0.00000000e+00,  0.00000000e+00,  0.00000000e+00,
       0.00000000e+00,  0.00000000e+00]],

    [[-6.21303201e-01,  4.13885061e-03, -6.17417134e-03,
      -8.89408588e-03,  4.83810157e-03],
     [-7.36429453e-01,  2.63450593e-02, -4.42487188e-02,
      -1.05846934e-01,  5.22684120e-03]],

    [[-1.01410240e-01,  4.99857590e-02, -9.47358180e-03,
      -3.74739647e-01,  9.64458846e-03],
     [-3.73311013e-01,  1.35892674e-01, -9.72046256e-02,
      -2.79455721e-01,  5.36275432e-02]]], dtype=float32))

-----------------------------

('states_val: ', LSTMStateTuple(c=array(
    [[-1.0492262 , -0.1059267 , -0.27163735, -0.64399946,
0.06018598],
     [-0.7445494 ,  0.00723887, -0.11805946, -0.26550752,
0.21816696],
     [-1.4126835 ,  0.05187892, -0.07408151, -0.66379607,
0.1348486 ],
     [-0.5987958 ,  0.24536057, -0.16916996, -0.8177415 ,
0.39747238]],
    dtype=float32), h=array(
    [[-7.33636796e-01, -6.07701950e-02, -1.40444040e-01,
      -2.65002381e-02,  5.37334010e-04],
     [-4.83454257e-01,  3.39480606e-03, -3.36034223e-02,
      -2.59866733e-02,  4.49425131e-02],
     [-7.36429453e-01,  2.63450593e-02, -4.42487188e-02,
      -1.05846934e-01,  5.22684120e-03],
     [-3.73311013e-01,  1.35892674e-01, -9.72046256e-02,
      -2.79455721e-01,  5.36275432e-02]], dtype=float32)))
```

There are two things in particular to notice about the output. First, examine the middle portion displayed in bold in the preceding output, and notice that these are the same values that are displayed in the final output block in the output section labeled `states_val`.

Next, the second code block that is displayed in bold contains two vectors: a non-zero vector followed by a zero vector, which corresponds to the data labeled `instance 1` in Listing 5.4.

## What are GRUs?

A GRU (Gated Recurrent Unit) is an RNN that is a simplified type of LSTM. The key difference between a GRU and an LSTM is that a GRU has two gates (reset and update gates) whereas an LSTM has three gates (reset, output, and forget gates). The reset gate in a GRU performs the functionality of the input gate and the forget gate of an LSTM.

Keep in mind that GRUs and LSTMs both have the goal of tracking long-term dependencies effectively, and they both address the problem of vanishing gradients and exploding gradients. Visit the following site to see an example of a GRU:

*https://commons.wikimedia.org/wiki/File:Gated_Recurrent_Unit,_base_type.svg*

Visit the following site to see the formulas for a GRU (which are similar to the formulas for an LSTM):

*https://en.wikipedia.org/wiki/Gated_recurrent_unit*

## What are Autoencoders?

An *autoencoder* (AE) is a neural network that is similar to an MLP, where the output layer is the same as the input layer. The simplest type of AE contains a single hidden layer that has fewer neurons than either the input layer or the output layer. However, there are many different types of AEs in which there are multiple hidden layers, sometimes containing more neurons than the input layer (and sometimes containing fewer neurons).

An AE uses unsupervised learning and back propagation to learn efficient data encoding. Their purpose is dimensionality reduction: AEs set the input values equal to the inputs and then try to find the identity function. Figure 5.2 shows a simple AE that involves a single hidden layer.

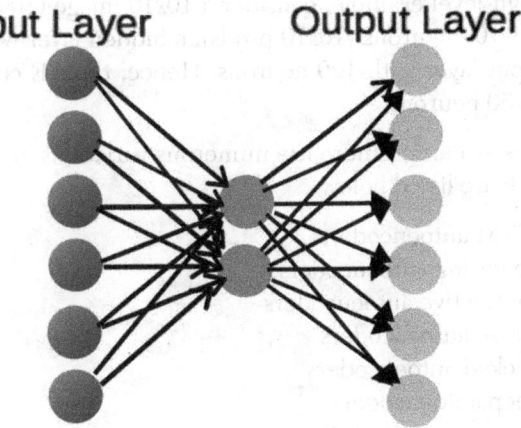

*FIGURE 5.2* A basic autoencoder

In essence, a basic AE compresses the input to an intermediate vector with fewer dimensions than the input data, and then transforms that vector into a tensor with the same shape as the input. Several use cases for AEs are listed below:

- document retrieval
- classification
- anomaly detection
- adversarial autoencoders
- image denoising (generating clear images)

An example of using TensorFlow and Keras with an autoencoder to perform fraud detection is here:

*https://www.datascience.com/blog/fraud-detection-with-tensorflow*

AEs can also be used for feature extraction because they can yield better results than PCA. Keep in mind that AEs are data-specific, which means that they only work with similar data. However, they differ from image compression (and are mediocre for data compression). For example, an autoencoder trained on faces would work poorly on pictures of trees. In summary, an AE involves the following:

- "squeezing" the input to a smaller layer
- learning a representation for a set of data
- is typically used for dimensionality reduction (PCA)
- keeps only the middle compressed layer

As a high-level example, consider a 10x10 image (100 pixels), and an AE that has 100 neurons (10x10 pixels), a hidden layer with 50 neurons, and an output layer with 100 neurons. Hence, the AE compresses 100 neurons to 50 neurons.

As you saw earlier, there are numerous variations of the basic AE, some of which are listed below:

- LSTM autoencoders
- Denoising autoencoders
- Contractive autoencoders
- Sparse autoencoders
- Stacked autoencoders
- Deep autoencoders
- Linear autoencoders

The following site contains a wide assortment of autoencoders, including those that are mentioned in this section:

*https://www.google.com/search?sa=X&q=Autoencoder&tbm=isch&source=univ&ved=2ahUKEwjo-8zRrIniAhUGup4KHVgvC10QiR-56BAgMEBY&biw=967&bih=672*

Perform an online search for code samples and more details regarding AEs and their associated use cases.

## Autoencoders and PCA

The optimal solution to an autoencoder is strongly related to principal component analysis (PCA) if the autoencoder involves linear activations or only a single sigmoid hidden layer.

The weights of an autoencoder with a single hidden layer of size p (where p is less than the size of the input) span the same vector subspace as the one spanned by the first p principal components.

The output of the autoencoder is an orthogonal projection onto this subspace. The autoencoder weights are not equal to the principal components, and are generally not orthogonal, yet the principal components may be recovered from them using the singular value decomposition.

## What are Variational Autoencoders?

In very brief terms, a *variational autoencoder* is sort of an enhanced "regular" autoencoder in which the "left side" acts as an encoder, and the "right side" acts as a decoder. Both sides have a probability distribution associated with the encoding and decoding process.

In addition, both the encoder and the decoder are actually neural networks. The input for the encoder is a vector x of numeric values, and its output is a hidden representation z that has weights and biases. The decoder has input a (i.e., the output of the encoder), and its output is the parameters of a probability distribution of the data, which also has weights and biases. Note that the probability distributions for the encoder and the decoder are different.

Figure 5.3 shows a high-level and simplified VAE that involves a single hidden layer.

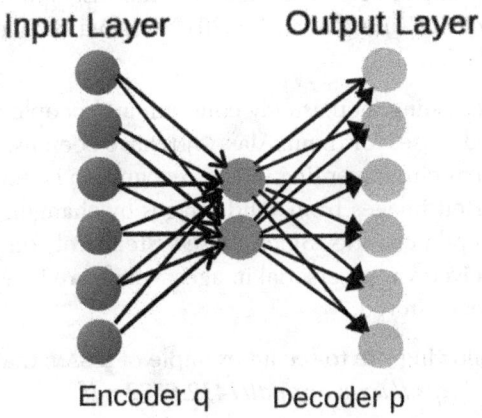

**FIGURE 5.3**  A variational autoencoder

Another interesting model architecture is a combination of a CNN and a VAE, which you can read about here:

*https://towardsdatascience.com/gans-vs-autoencoders-comparison-of-deep-generative-models-985cf15936ea*

In the next section, you will learn about GANs, and also how to combine a VAE with a GAN.

## What are GANs?

A GAN is an acronym for Generative Adversarial Network whose original purpose was to generate synthetic data, typically for augmenting small datasets or unbalanced datasets. One use case pertains to missing persons:

supply the available images of those persons to a GAN in order to generate an image of how those people might look today. There are many other use cases for GANs, some of which are listed here:

- Generating art
- Creating fashion styles
- Improving images of low quality
- Creating artificial faces
- Reconstructing incomplete/damaged images

Ian Goodfellow (who has a PhD in machine learning from the University of Montreal) created GANs in 2014. Yann LeCun (the AI research director at Facebook) called adversarial training "the most interesting idea in the last 10 years in ML." (Incidentally, Yann LeCun was one of the three recipients of the Turing Award in 2019: Yoshua Bengio, Geoffrey Hinton, and Yann LeCun.)

GANs are becoming increasingly common and people are finding creative (unexpected?) uses for them. Alas, GANs have been used for nefarious purposes, such as circumventing image-recognition systems. GANs can generate counterfeit images from valid images by changing the pixel values to deceive neural networks. Since those systems rely on pixel patterns, they can be deceived via adversarial images, which are images whose pixel values have been altered.

Visit the following site to see an example of a GAN that distorts the image of a Panda: *https://arxiv.org/pdf/1412.6572.pdf*

An article that delves into details of adversarial examples (including the misclassified Panda) is here:

*https://openai.com/blog/adversarial-example-research/*

According to an MIT paper, the modified values that trigger misclassifications exploit precise patterns that the image system associates with specific objects. The researchers noticed that data sets contain two types of correlations: patterns that are correlated with the dataset data and non-generalizable patterns in the dataset data. GANs successfully exploit the latter correlations to deceive image-recognition systems. Details of the MIT paper are here: *https://gandissect.csail.mit.edu*

## Can Adversarial Attacks be Stopped?

Unfortunately, there are no long-term solutions to adversarial attacks, and given their nature, it might never be possible to completely defend against them. Although various techniques are being developed to thwart adversarial attacks, their effectiveness tends to be short-lived: new GANs are created that can outwit those techniques. The following article contains more information about adversarial attacks:

*https://www.technologyreview.com/s/613170/emtech-digital-dawn-song-adversarial-machine-learning*

Interestingly, GANs can have problems in terms of convergence, just like other neural networks. One technique for addressing this problem is called *minibatch discrimination*, the details of which are here:

*https://www.inference.vc/understanding-minibatch-discrimination-in-gans/*

Please note that the preceding link involves Kullback-Leibler divergence and JS divergence, which are more advanced topics (for more information, visit *https://gist.github.com/fhuszar/a91c7d0672036335c1783d02c3a3dfe5*).

If you're interested in working with GANs, GitHub contains Python and TensorFlow code samples for constructing attacks and defenses:

*https://github.com/tensorflow/cleverhans*

## Creating a GAN

A GAN has two main parts: a *generator* and a *discriminator*. The generator can have a CNN-like architecture for the purpose of generating images, whereas the discriminator can have a CNN-like architecture to detect whether an image (provided by the generator) is real or fake. By way of analogy, a generator is analogous to a person who makes counterfeit money, and a discriminator is analogous to a law enforcement officer who tries to distinguish between valid currency and counterfeit currency.

The generator (which has previously been initialized) sends fake images to the discriminator (already trained but no longer updateable) for analysis. If the discriminator is highly accurate in terms of detecting real and fake images, then the generator needs to be modified to improve the quality of fake images that are produced. The modification to the generator is performed by backward error propagation. If the discriminator performs poorly, then the generator is generating high quality fake images, and therefore the generator does not require significant modification.

Listing 5.5 shows the content of keras_create_gan.py, which defines a Python function for creating a GAN.

### LISTING 5.4: *keras_create_gan.py*

```python
import tensorflow as tf
def build_generator(img_shape, z_dim):
  model = tf.keras.models.Sequential()
  # Fully connected layer
  model.add(tf.keras.layers.Dense(128, input_dim=z_dim))
  # Leaky ReLU activation
  model.add(tf.keras.layers.LeakyReLU(alpha=0.01))
  # Output layer with tanh activation
   model.add(tf.keras.layers.Dense(28    *    28    *    1,
activation='tanh'))
   # Reshape the Generator output to image dimensions
   model.add(tf.keras.layers.Reshape(img_shape))
   return model

def build_discriminator(img_shape):
  model = tf.keras.models.Sequential()
  # Flatten the input image
  model.add(tf.keras.layers.Flatten(input_shape=img_shape))
  # Fully connected layer
  model.add(tf.keras.layers.Dense(128))
  # Leaky ReLU activation
  model.add(tf.keras.layers.LeakyReLU(alpha=0.01))
  # Output layer with sigmoid activation
  model.add(tf.keras.layers.Dense(1, activation='sigmoid'))
  return model

def build_gan(generator, discriminator):
  # ensure that the discriminator is not trainable
  discriminator.trainable = False

  # the GAN connects the generator and descriminator
  gan = tf.keras.models.Sequential()

  # start with the generator:
  gan.add(generator)

  # then add the discriminator:
  gan.add(discriminator)

  # compile gan
  opt = tf.keras.optimizers.Adam(lr=0.0002, beta_1=0.5)
  gan.compile(loss='binary_crossentropy', optimizer=opt)
  return gan
```

```
gen = build_generator(...)
dis = build_discriminator(...)
gan = build_gan(gen, dis)
```

The Python function in Listing 5.5 contains three Python methods for `build_generator()`, `build_discriminator()`, and `build_gan()` for creating a generator, a discriminator, and a GAN, respectively.

The GAN is initialized with a generator and then a discriminator, both of which are parameters for this function. Notice that the discriminator in the `build_gan()` method is not trainable, which is ensured with this code snippet:

```
discriminator.trainable = False
```

Another point to notice is that the preceding Python functions do not create CNN-like architectures. A different way to create a discriminator is shown in the following code block (details are omitted):

```
dis = build_discriminator(...)
gen_model = tf.keras.models.Sequential()
gen_model.add(tf.keras.layers.Dense(...)
gen_model.add(tf.keras.layers.LeakyReLU(alpha=0.2))
gen_model.add(tf.keras.layers.Reshape(...)

# code for upsampling
gen_model.add(tf.keras.layers.Conv2DTranspose(...)
gen_model.add(tf.keras.layers.LeakyReLU(...)
...
gen_model.add(tf.keras.layers.Reshape(...)
gen_model.add(tf.keras.layers.LeakyReLU(...)

# output layer
gen_model.add(tf.keras.layers.Conv2D(...))
```

The preceding code block involves the `Conv2D()` class and the `LeakyReLU()` class (similar to `ReLU`), but notice that there is max pooling code. Check online documentation for an explanation of upsampling and the purpose of the TensorFlow/Keras classes `LeakyReLU()` and `Conv2DTranspose()`.

## A High-Level View of GANs

In general, creating GANs involves the following high-level sequence of steps:

1) Select a dataset (ex: MNIST or cifar10).
2) Define and train the discriminator model.

3) Define and use the generator model.
4) Train the generator model.
5) Evaluate GAN model's performance.
6) Use the final generator model.

There are numerous types of GANs, such as DCGANs (deep convolutional GANs). Another detail to keep in mind is that GANs do differ from CNNs. First, the convolution often has a stride of (2, 2), which is to say that the convolutional filter moves two columns at a time, and then shifts downward two rows at a time. They do not contain a ReLU activation function nor do they perform max pooling. Another detail about GANs is the use of upscaling, which in a sense is like the opposite of downscaling (i.e., max pooling).

## The VAE-GAN Model

Another interesting model is the VAE-GAN model, which is a hybrid of a VAE and a GAN, and details about this model are here:

*https://towardsdatascience.com/gans-vs-autoencoders-comparison-of-deep-generative-models-985cf15936ea*

GANs are superior to VAEs, but they are also difficult to work with and require a lot of data and tuning. A GAN tutorial (by the same author) is available here:

*https://github.com/mrdragonbear/GAN-Tutorial*

## Summary

In this chapter, you learned about the architecture of an RNN, saw some tasks that you can solve due to its stateful architecture, and worked with a Keras-based code sample. Next you saw the architecture of an LSTM, as well as a basic code sample.

In addition, you saw a TensorFlow 1.x code sample for an LSTM cell whose output shows you the path of some of the internal calculations that are performed. In addition, you learned about variational autoencoders and some of their use cases.

Finally, you got an introduction to GANs, a high-level description of how to construct them, and how they are trained.

# *6*

# *ANGULAR AND TENSORFLOW.js*

T his chapter provides a very fast-paced introduction to TensorFlow. js. It includes various code samples that use TensorFlow.js and `tfjs-vis` for data visualization, along with a code sample that uses TensorFlow.js to perform linear regression in an Angular 10 application. After learning the basic sequence of steps for creating machine learning models in TensorFlow.js, you can learn how to create more complex models from online blog posts and tutorials. If you are familiar with TF 2/ `Keras`, then the TensorFlow.js code in this chapter should look familiar to you.

The first part of this chapter provides a quick introduction to TensorFlow.js, along with some of its features. You will learn about the TensorFlow.js APIs that are needed to create, compile, and train a machine learning model in TensorFlow.js, as well as an API for making predictions. You will see an example of how to use TensorFlow.js to perform linear regression in an HTML Web page.

The second part of this chapter contains examples of rendering various charts and graphs with `tfjs-vis`, including a line graph, bar chart, scatter plot, and a heat map. The third portion of this chapter contains a code sample that combines TensorFlow.js and `tfjs-vis` to perform linear regression in an HTML Web page. The final portion of this chapter shows you how to combine TensorFlow.js and `tfjs-vis` in an Angular application to perform linear regression, render the data points, and make a prediction.

Please keep in mind a few details before you read this chapter. First, you do need a basic understanding of HTML and JavaScript. You also need to be comfortable with the keywords `async` and `await` used in the code samples. This chapter does not provide any tutorial-like material for these topics, but you can easily find many online tutorials that explain HTML and JavaScript .

Second, we assume that you have read the material in earlier chapters pertaining to linear regression, as well as the Keras-related material in the appendix. Specifically, you need at least a basic understanding of activation functions, optimizers, MSE, SGD, loss functions, and metrics, all of which are discussed in Chapter 4.

Third, the code samples in this chapter are not product-ready code: you need to follow the best practices for TensorFlow.js. The description of each code sample is cursory, and a minimal set of TensorFlow.js APIs is discussed in this chapter. If you want to delve more deeply into TensorFlow.js, please visit the official website containing the TensorFlow.js APIs:

*https://js.tensorflow.org/api/latest/*

## What is TensorFlow.js?

TensorFlow.js is TensorFlow for modern browsers, which includes Chrome and Firefox, and most of the features of TensorFlow are available in TensorFlow.js. This chapter illustrates an example of TensorFlow.js in a stand-alone HTML Web page as well as how to use TensorFlow.js as part of an Angular application.

Before delving into more details about TensorFlow.js, please keep in mind that Google is in the process of releasing TensorFlow.js 2.x as this book goes to print. Additionally, Google is working on TensorFlow.js 3.x, but so far, a release date has not been announced. Google will publish release notes with complete details to perform the upgrade process.

Some of the modifications are straightforward. Specifically, the current version of TensorFlow.js uses this type of code:

```
import * as tf from @tensorflow/tfjs
```

TensorFlow.js 2.x uses the following code:

```
import {max, div, mul, depthToSpace} from @tensorflow/tjfs
```

TensorFlow.js leverages the power of WebGL to train models in a browser session. Some of the methods return a Promise, and some methods are synchronous.

In addition, there are two other important APIs: the `tf.tidy()` method and the `tf.dispose()` method. The `tf.tidy()` method essentially acts like a garbage collector, which is unavailable in WebGL. The `tf.dispose()` method performs a similar functionality for objects that contain tensors.

Incidentally, one convenient aspect of TensorFlow.js APIs is that there are package names that are parallel to the corresponding APIs in TensorFlow. For instance, the TensorFlow package `tf.keras.layers` corresponds to the TensorFlow.js package `tf.layers`. Hence, the TensorFlow.js API `tf.layers.dense` corresponds to the API `tf.keras.layers.Dense` in TensorFlow.

Although it's not necessary right now, it's worth your while to spend some time perusing the detailed list of the TensorFlow.js APIs at this URL:

*https://js.tensorflow.org/api/latest/*

## ML Models in TensorFlow.js

TensorFlow.js gives you several options for working with TensorFlow models in a browser:

- import trained models
- retrain models
- create models in a browser

If you already have a TensorFlow model, you can convert that model to the TensorFlow.js format and then use that model in a Web browser. The details of model conversion are here:

*https://www.tensorflow.org/js/guide/conversion*

Another possibility is to take advantage of transfer learning: you start with a previously trained model and then perform some (hopefully minimal) additional training with your own data.

| NOTE | *The code samples in this chapter involve models that have been developed in a browser (and tested in Firefox version 75.0.1).* |

## A Simple HTML Web Page with TensorFlow.js

Listing 6.1 shows the content of `tfjs-hello.html`, which illustrates how to reference the JavaScript code that pertains to TensorFlow.js and display a simple message.

**LISTING 6.1: tfjs-hello.html**

```
<html>
  <head>
    <!-- Load TensorFlow.js -->
    <script
       src="https://cdn.jsdelivr.net/npm/@tensorflow/tfjs/
dist/tf.min.js">
    </script>
  </head>
  <body>
      Hello
  </body>
</html
```

Listing 6.1 contains a `<script>` element that references the TensorFlow. js code, which does nothing in this example. The Web page displays the word `Hello` and nothing more.

# Working with Tensors in TensorFlow.js

TensorFlow.js provides several methods for working with tensors. The `tensor()` method supports multi-dimensional data points, but does not indicate the dimensionality of the data. However, TensorFlow.js provides dimension-specific APIs: the `tensor2d()` method is for 2D data points, the `tensor3d()` method is for 3D data points, and so forth, up to the `tensor6d()` method for data points of dimension 6.

For example, the following code snippet defines a 2D tensor that has a "shape" of 4x1:

```
const xs = tf.tensor2d([1, 2, 3, 4], [4, 1]);
```

The *shape* refers to the dimensionality of the elements in a tensor. Thus, the preceding code snippet specifies four samples, each of which contains a single value.

Returning to linear regression, you learned in the machine learning chapters that linear regression involves a set of data points and a set of labels.

For example, suppose we define the following array of input values:

```
var inputV = [[1,3], [2,6], [3,9]];
```

The corresponding tensor would be defined like the following:

```
const inputT = tf.tensor2d(inputV, [inputV.length, 1]);
```

Similarly, suppose that the corresponding labels are defined as follows:

```
var labelV = [[10], [20], [30]];
```

The corresponding tensor for the labels would be defined like the following:

```
const labelT = tf.tensor2d(labelV, [labelV.length, 1]);
```

As you can see in the definition of input and labelT, the first argument is the actual data and the second argument specifies the shape of the data.

## Machine Learning APIs in TensorFlow.js

This section contains some of the TensorFlow.js APIs for defining machine learning models in TensorFlow.js. As you learned from earlier chapters, there are several steps involved in training a machine learning model that are illustrated with Keras-based APIs in the appendix. In this section, we'll see an example of creating a very rudimentary model in TensorFlow. js that implements the sequence of steps that are shown below:

- define a model
- add one or more layers to the model
- compile the model
- initialize some data values
- fit (train) the model
- make some predictions

Let's see how to implement the preceding steps, starting with the simplest definition of a model in TensorFlow.js:

```
const model = tf.sequential();
```

The tf.sequential() API is for a model whose outputs from one layer are the inputs to the next adjacent layer (in a left-to-right direction). TensorFlow.js also supports another model via the tf.model() API, and you can learn about this model from the TensorFlow.js documentation.

Next, the following code snippet adds a dense (i.e., fully connected) layer to the defined model:

```
model.add(tf.layers.dense({units: 32, inputShape: [64]}));
```

The first layer (which is the preceding code snippet) *must* specify the input shape, which in this case is 64. TensorFlow.js uses automatic shape inference in order to determine the shape of subsequent layers in a model.

Now initialize the tensors xs and ys that represent the input and output values, respectively:

```
const xs = tf.tensor2d([1,2,3,4,5,6,7,8,],    [8,1]);
const ys = tf.tensor2d([3,6,9,12,15,18,21,24],[8,1]);
```

Now we can train this sequential model by invoking the fit() method, as shown here:

```
model.fit(xs, ys);
```

At this point, our model has been trained with the training data, so we can make a prediction with this code snippet:

```
model.predict(tf.tensor2d([10], [1, 1])).print()
```

You now know the basic sequence of steps that are necessary to create, compile, and train a model in TensorFlow.js, and also make predictions with that trained model.

Now let's look at an HTML Web page that uses TensorFlow.js to train a linear regression model and displays the result, which is the topic of the next section.

## Linear Regression with TensorFlow.js

Listing 6.2 shows the content of tfjs-linreg1.html, which illustrates how to perform a linear regression with TensorFlow.js.

*LISTING 6.2: tfjs-linreg1.html*

```
<html>
  <head>
    <script src="https://cdn.jsdelivr.net/npm/@tensorflow/
tfjs/dist/tf.min.js"> </script>
    <title>Hello from TensorFlowJS!</title>
  </head>

  <body>
    <h3>Linear Regression and Some Predictions</h3>
    <ul id="mylist">

    <script>
```

```
async function LinearRegression(){
    // 1) DEFINE THE MODEL:
    const model = tf.sequential();

    model.add(
        tf.layers.dense({
            units:1,
            inputShape:[1],
            bias: true
        })
    );

    // 2) COMPILE THE MODEL:
    // specify the loss, optimizer, and metrics:
    model.compile({
        loss:'meanSquaredError',
        optimizer: 'sgd',
        metrics: ['mse']
    });

    // 3) FIT/TRAIN THE MODEL:
    // y = 2*x+1 (relationship between xs and ys)
    const xs = tf.tensor1d([1,2,3,4,5,6,7,8,9,10]);
    const ys = tf.tensor1d([3,5,7,9,11,13,15,17,19,21]);
    await model.fit(xs, ys, {epochs:100});

    // 4) MAKE SOME PREDICTIONS
    // 4a) PREDICT Y for X=-30:
    var list1 = document.getElementById('mylist');
    var item1 = document.createElement('li');
        var pred1 = model.predict(tf.tensor1d([-30])).
dataSync();
  var data1=document.createTextNode("Predict(-30):"+pred1);
        item1.appendChild(data1);
        list1.appendChild(item1);

    // 4a) PREDICT Y for X=50:
    var item2 = document.createElement('li');
        var pred2 = model.predict(tf.tensor1d([50])).
dataSync();
   var data2=document.createTextNode("Predict(50):"+pred2);
        item2.appendChild(data2);
        list1.appendChild(item2);

    // 4c) PREDICT Y for X=100:
```

```
        var item3 = document.createElement('li');
            var pred3 = model.predict(tf.tensor1d([100])).
dataSync();
    var data3=document.createTextNode("Predict(100):"+pred3);
        item3.appendChild(data3);
        list1.appendChild(item3);
    }

    LinearRegression();
    </script>
  </body>
</html>
```

Listing 6.2 starts with a `<script>` element that references the TensorFlow. js code, followed by a `<body>` element that contains four main sections, as shown here:

```
// 1) DEFINE THE MODEL:
// 2) COMPILE THE MODEL:
// 3) FIT/TRAIN THE MODEL:
// 4) MAKE SOME PREDICTIONS
```

The first section defines the variable `model` as an instance of the TensorFlow.js `Sequential` model, which resembles `tf.keras.layers. Sequential` (discussed in the `Keras`-related appendix). Next, the `model` variable adds a single layer via the `dense` API in TensorFlow.js.

The second section specifies three parameter values, as shown here:

```
model.compile({
    loss:'meanSquaredError',
    optimizer: 'sgd',
    metrics: ['mse']
});
```

The purpose of these parameters has been discussed in previous chapters, and you can review that material if you need to refresh your memory.

The third section initializes the variables `xs` and `ys` and then invokes the `fit()` method of the model variable in order to train this model.

The fourth section contains three predictions for the value of `Y` when the value of `x` is -30, 50, and 100. The key idea is to invoke the `predict()` method of the model variable, once for each of the preceding values of `x`. For instance, this code snippet predicts the value of `Y` when the value of `x` is -30:

```
var pred1 = model.predict(tf.tensor1d([-30])).dataSync();
```

If need be, you can enhance the HTML code to create a more aesthetically pleasing effort (or you can simplify the code).

Launch this Web page in a browser and you will see the following output:

**Linear Regression and Some Predictions**

- Predict(-30):-61.6697998046875
- Predict(50):104.10870361328125
- Predict(100):207.7202606201172

According to the formula y = 2*x + 1, the correct values for -30, 50, and 100 are -59, 101, and 201, respectively. As you can see, the predictions are less accurate for larger positive (and negative) values of x.

Let's see how to combine TensorFlow.js with Angular, which is the topic of the next section.

## Angular, TensorFlow.js, and Linear Regression

This section contains an example of combining TensorFlow.js with Angular, and then training a model via linear regression. Copy the directory NGTFJSLinReg from the companion files into a convenient location. Listing 6.3 shows the content of app.component.ts, which uses a good portion of the code from the previous section.

### *LISTING 6.3: app.component.ts*

```
import { Component } from '@angular/core';
import * as tf       from '@tensorflow/tfjs';
// remember: npm install @tensorflow/tfjs --save

@Component({
  selector: 'app-root',
  styleUrls: ['./app.component.css'],
  template: '
    <h3>Prediction for Value 50:</h3>
    <div id="mydiv">
      {{predict}}
    </div>
  ',
})
export class AppComponent {
```

```
title = 'NGTFJSLinReg';
public predict = "";

constructor() {
  this.LinearRegression();
}

private async LinearRegression(){
  // 1) DEFINE THE MODEL:
  const model = tf.sequential();

  model.add(
    tf.layers.dense({
        units:1,
        inputShape:[1]
    })
  );

  // 2) COMPILE THE MODEL:
  // specify the loss, optimizer, and metrics:
  model.compile({
      loss:'meanSquaredError',
      optimizer: 'sgd',
      metrics: ['mse']
  });

  // 3) FIT/TRAIN THE MODEL:
  // y = 2*x+1 (relationship between xs and ys)
  const xs = tf.tensor1d([1,2,3,4,5,6,7,8,9,10]);
  const ys = tf.tensor1d([3,5,7,9,11,13,15,17,19,21]);
  await model.fit(xs, ys, {epochs:100});

  // 4) MAKE SOME PREDICTIONS
  // 4a) PREDICT Y for X=50:
  var mydiv = document.getElementById('mydiv');
  mydiv.innerText += model.predict(tf.tensor1d([50]));
}
}
```

Listing 6.3 contains the standard import statement, followed by a comment that contains the correct npm command to install TensorFlow.js in this Angular application. The next section contains boilerplate code, except for the template property, which includes an HTML <div> element that is populated with the output from the prediction (performed in step 4 below).

The next portion of Listing 6.3 defines an empty constructor that invokes a private method that contains all the TensorFlow-related functionality. Notice that the method `LinearRegression` (which is invoked in the constructor) is defined with the following signature:

```
private async LinearRegression(){. . .}
```

The preceding signature is slightly different from what you saw in the previous section, as shown here:

```
function async LinearRegression(){. . .}
```

The `LinearRegression` method has four main sections, as shown here:

```
// 1) DEFINE THE MODEL:
// 2) COMPILE THE MODEL:
// 3) FIT/TRAIN THE MODEL:
// 4) MAKE SOME PREDICTIONS
```

The first section defines the variable `model` as an instance of the TensorFlow. js `Sequential` model, which resembles `tf.keras.layers.Sequential` (discussed in the `Keras`-related appendix). Next, the `model` variable adds a single `tf.layers.dense` layer that specifies an input shape of size 1.

Notice that the `tf.layers.dense` API does not support the `bias` property that is specified in the code in the preceding section.

The second section specifies three parameter values, as shown here:

```
model.compile({
    loss:'meanSquaredError',
    optimizer: 'sgd',
    metrics: ['mse']
});
```

The purpose of these parameters has been discussed in previous chapters, and you can review that material if you need to refresh your memory.

The third section initializes the variables xs and ys and then invokes the `fit()` method of the model variable in order to train this model. The fourth section contains a prediction for the value of Y when the value of X is 50 by invoking the `predict()` method of the variable `model`. Now launch this Web page in a browser to see the following output.

**Prediction for Value 50:**
Tensor
[[104.7459564],]

According to the formula $y = 2*x + 1$, the correct value for 50 is 101, and the predicted value differs from the exact value by more than three.

Depending on the environment of your machine, you might encounter the following error during the compilation step:

```
ERROR in ../node_modules/@types/webgl2/index.d.ts:582:13 -
error TS2403: Subsequent variable declarations must have
the same type.   Variable 'WebGL2RenderingContext' must
be of type '{ new (): WebGL2RenderingContext; prototype:
WebGL2RenderingContext; readonly ACTIVE_ATTRIBUTES: num-
ber; readonly ACTIVE_TEXTURE: number; ... 556 more ...; rea-
donly WAIT_FAILED: number; }', but here has type '{ new ():
WebGL2RenderingContext; prototype: WebGL2RenderingContext;
readonly   ACTIVE_ATTRIBUTES:   number;   readonly   ACTIVE_
TEXTURE: number; ... 557 more ...; readonly MAX_CLIENT_
WAIT_TIMEOUT_WEBGL: number; }'.

582 declare var WebGL2RenderingContext: {
                ~~~~~~~~~~~~~~~~~~~~~~
    ../node_modules/typescript/lib/lib.dom.d.ts:16316:13
      16316 declare var WebGL2RenderingContext: {
                        ~~~~~~~~~~~~~~~~~~~~~~
      'WebGL2RenderingContext' was also declared here.
```

If you do see the preceding error, there are several ways to resolve this issue, one of which involves adding this snippet to `tsconfig.json` in the `src` subdirectory of your Angular application:

```
"skipLibCheck": true,
```

Now that you know how to create basic code samples with TensorFlow.js and also how to combine TensorFlow.js in an Angular application, let's look at `tfjs-vis`, which gives you the ability to display line graphs, bar charts, histograms, and so forth in an HTML Web page.

## Creating Line Graphs in tfjs-vis

Listing 6.4 shows the content of `tfjsvis-linegraph.js`, which contains the data for a line graph. Listing 6.5 shows the content of `tfjs-vis-linegraph.html`, which illustrates how to use `tfjs-vis` to display a line graph.

### LISTING 6.4: *tfjsvis-linegraph.js*

```
// define the data points
values = [
  [{x: 10, y: 20}, {x: 20, y: 30}, {x: 30, y: 5},  {x: 40,
y: 12}],
  [{x: 10, y: 40}, {x: 20, y: 0},  {x: 30, y: 50}, {x: 40,
y: -5}]
];

// legend-related information
let series = ['Dataset1', 'Dataset2'];

// render the line graph
tfvis.render.linechart(document.getElementById('plot1'),
{values, series}, {
  xLabel: 'x-axis',
  yLabel: 'y-axis'
});
```

Listing 6.4 defines the variables `values` with data points and the variable series that contains the strings to display in a legend. The final portion of Listing 6.4 invokes the `tfvis` API for rendering a line graph in the HTML `<div>` element whose `class` value is `plot`.

### LISTING 6.5: *tfjsvis-linegraph.html*

```
<html>
  <head>
    <script src="https://cdn.jsdelivr.net/npm/@tensorflow/
tfjs@latest"> </script>
    <script src="https://cdn.jsdelivr.net/npm/@tensorflow/
tfjs-vis@latest"> </script>

    <style>
      .plot {
        display: inline-block;
        width: 50%;
        margin: 10px;
      }
    </style>
  </head>
```

```
<body>
  <div class="plot" id="plot1"></div>
</body>

<script src="tfjsvis-barchart.js"> </script>
</html>
```

Listing 6.5 contains a <head> element with two <script> elements that reference the necessary tfjs-vis JavaScript code for rendering charts and graphs. The <style> element specifies some properties for layout purposes.

The next portion of Listing 6.5 defines a <div> element where the line graph is rendered, and the final code snippet in Listing 6.5 is a <script> element that references the code in tfjsvis-barchart.js.

Figure 6.1 shows the line graph that is displayed when you launch the code in Listing 6.5.

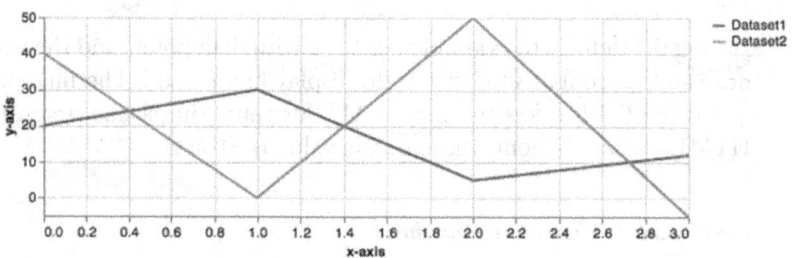

*FIGURE 6.1* A line graph

## Creating Bar Charts in tfjs-vis

Listing 6.6 shows the content of tfjsvis-barchart.js, which contains the data for a bar chart. Listing 6.7 shows the content of tfjsvis-bar-chart.html, which illustrates how to use tfjs-vis to display a bar chart.

### *LISTING 6.6: tfjsvis-barchart.js*

```
// define the data points
const data = [
    {index: 'foo', value: 1}, {index: 'bar', value: 7},
    {index: 3, value: 3}, {index: 5, value: 6}];

// render the bar chart
```

```
tfvis.render.barchart(document.getElementById('plot1'),
data, {
  yLabel: 'y-axis',
  width:  400
});
```

Listing 6.6 defines the variables `values` with data points and the `data` series that contains the strings to display in a legend. The final portion of Listing 6.6 invokes the `tfvis.render.barchart` API for rendering a bar chart in the HTML `<div>` element whose `class` value is `plot`.

### LISTING 6.7: *tfjsvis-barchart.html*

```
<html>
  <head>
    <script src="https://cdn.jsdelivr.net/npm/@tensorflow/
tfjs@latest"> </script>
    <script src="https://cdn.jsdelivr.net/npm/@tensorflow/
tfjs-vis@latest"> </script>

    <style>
      .plot {
        display: inline-block;
        width: 50%;
        margin: 10px;
      }
    </style>
  </head>

  <body>
    <div class="plot" id="plot1"></div>
  </body>

  <script src="tfjsvis-barchart.js"> </script>
</html>
```

Listing 6.7 contains a `<head>` element with two `<script>` elements that reference the necessary `tfjs-vis` JavaScript code for rendering charts and graphs. The `<style>` element specifies some properties for layout purposes.

The next portion of Listing 6.7 defines a `<div>` element where the line graph is rendered, and the final code snippet in Listing 6.7 is a `<script>` element that references the code in `tfjsvis-barchart.js`.

Figure 6.2 shows the bar chart that is displayed when you launch the code in Listing 6.7.

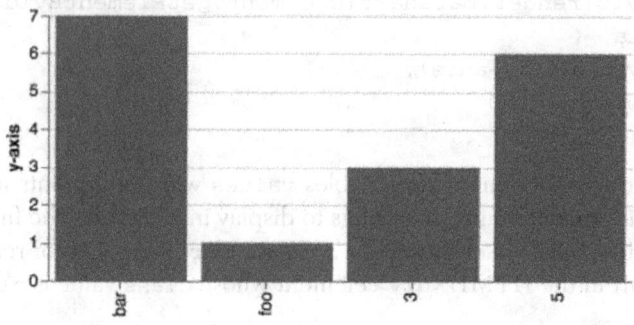

**FIGURE 6.2** A bar chart

## Creating Scatter Plots in tfjs-vis

Listing 6.8 shows the content of `tfjsvis-scatterplot.js`, which contains the data for a scatter plot. Listing 6.9 shows the content of the HTML Web page `tfjsvis-scatterplot.html`, which illustrates how to use `tfjs-vis` to display a scatter plot.

### LISTING 6.8: tfjsvis-scatterplot.js

```
// define the data points
const data = [
    {index: 'foo', value: 1}, {index: 'bar', value: 7},
    {index: 3, value: 3}, {index: 5, value: 6}];

// render the bar chart
tfvis.render.barchart(document.getElementById('plot1'),
data, {
  yLabel: 'y-axis',
  width:  400
});
```

Listing 6.8 defines the variables `values` with data points and the `data` series that contains the strings to display in a legend. The final portion of Listing 6.8 invokes the `tfvis.render.barchart` API for rendering a bar chart in the HTML `<div>` element whose `class` value is `plot`.

### LISTING 6.9: tfjsvis-scatterplot.html

```
<html>
  <head>
```

```
    <script src="https://cdn.jsdelivr.net/npm/@tensorflow/
tfjs@latest"> </script>
    <script src="https://cdn.jsdelivr.net/npm/@tensorflow/
tfjs-vis@latest"> </script>
    <style>
      .plot {
        display: inline-block;
        width: 50%;
        margin: 10px;
      }
    </style>
  </head>

  <body>
    <div class="plot" id="plot1"></div>
  </body>

  <script src="tfjsvis-barchart.js"> </script>
</html>
```

Listing 6.9 contains a <head> element with two <script> elements that reference the necessary tfjs-vis JavaScript code for rendering charts and graphs. The <style> element specifies some properties for layout purposes.

The next portion of Listing 6.9 defines a <div> element where the scatter plot is rendered, and the final code snippet in Listing 6.8 is a <script> element that references the code in tfjsvis-scatterplot.js.

Figure 6.3 shows the scatter plot that is displayed when you launch the code in Listing 6.9.

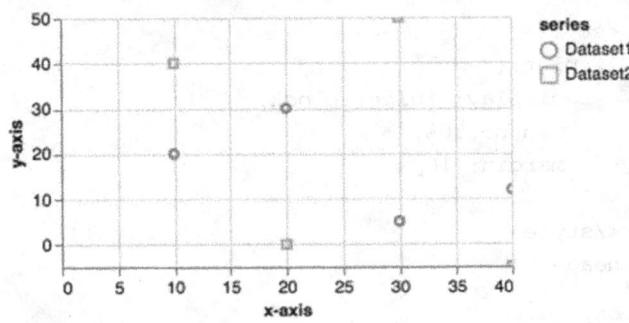

*FIGURE 6.3* A scatter plot

## Creating Histograms in tfjs-vis

Listing 6.10 shows the content of tfjsvis-histogram.js, which contains the data for a histogram. Listing 6.11 shows the content of the HTML Web page tfjsvis-histogram.html, which illustrates how to use tfjs-vis to display a histogram.

### LISTING 6.10: tfjsvis-histogram.js

```
// define the data points
data = [1, 5, 12, 12, 5, 10, -2, -8];

// render the histogram
tfvis.render.histogram(document.getElementById('plot1'),
data, {
  maxBins: 5,
  width: 400
});
```

Listing 6.10 defines the variables values with data points and the data series that contains the strings to display in a legend. The final portion of Listing 6.10 invokes the tfvis.render.histogram API for rendering a histogram in the HTML <div> element whose class value is plot.

### LISTING 6.11: tfjsvis-histogram.html

```
<html>
  <head>
    <script src="https://cdn.jsdelivr.net/npm/@tensorflow/
tfjs@latest"> </script>
    <script src="https://cdn.jsdelivr.net/npm/@tensorflow/
tfjs-vis@latest"> </script>

    <style>
      .plot {
        display: inline-block;
        width: 50%;
        margin: 10px;
      }
    </style>
  </head>

  <body>
    <div class="plot" id="plot1"></div>
  </body>
```

```
<script src="tfjsvis-histogram.js"> </script>
</html>
```

Listing 6.11 contains a <head> element with two <script> elements that reference the necessary tfjs-vis JavaScript code for rendering charts and graphs. The <style> element specifies some properties for layout purposes.

The next portion of Listing 6.11 defines a <div> element where the histogram is rendered, and the final code snippet in Listing 6.10 is a <script> element that references the code in tfjsvis-histogram.js.

Figure 6.4 shows the histogram that is displayed when you launch the code in Listing 6.11.

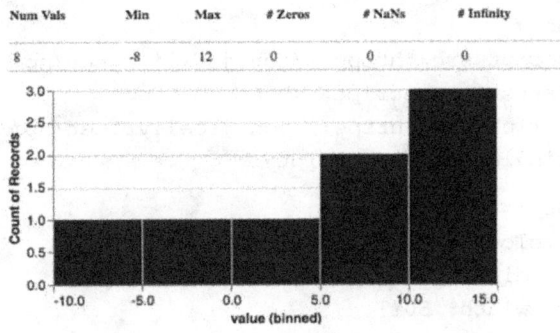

**FIGURE 6.4**  A histogram

## Creating Heat Maps in tfjs-vis

Listing 6.12 shows the content of tfjsvis-heatmap.js, which contains the data for a histogram. Listing 6.13 shows the content of the HTML Web page tfjsvis-heatmap.html, which illustrates how to use tfjs-vis to display a heat map.

### LISTING 6.12: tfjsvis-heatmap.js

```
// render the heat map
tfvis.render.heatmap(document.getElementById('plot1'), {
    values: [[1,0,0], [0,0.5,0.8], [0,0.8,0.5]],
    xTickLabels: ['Tall', 'Medium', 'Short'],
    yTickLabels: ['Tall', 'Medium', 'Short']
}, {
```

```
  width:  500,
  height: 500,
  xLabel: 'TypeA',
  yLabel: 'TypeB',
  colorMap: 'reds'
});
```

Listing 6.12 defines the variable `values` with data points and two strings to display in the horizontal and vertical axes of the heat map. The final portion of Listing 6.12 invokes the `tfvis.render.heatmap` API for rendering a heat map in the HTML `<div>` element whose `class` value is `plot`.

### LISTING 6.13: tfjsvis-heatmap.html

```html
<html>
  <head>
    <script src="https://cdn.jsdelivr.net/npm/@tensorflow/
tfjs@latest"> </script>
    <script src="https://cdn.jsdelivr.net/npm/@tensorflow/
tfjs-vis@latest"> </script>

    <style>
      .plot {
        display: inline-block;
        width: 50%;
        margin: 10px;
      }

    </style>
  </head>

  <body>
    <div class="plot" id="plot1"></div>
  </body>

  <script src="tfjsvis-heatmap.js"> </script>
</html>
```

Listing 6.13 contains a `<head>` element with two `<script>` elements that reference the necessary `tfjs-vis` JavaScript code for rendering charts and graphs. The `<style>` element specifies some properties for layout purposes.

The next portion of Listing 6.13 defines a `<div>` element where the heat map is rendered, and the final code snippet in Listing 6.13 is a `<script>` element that references the code in `tfjsvis-heatmap.js`.

Figure 6.5 shows the heat map that is displayed when you launch the code in Listing 6.13.

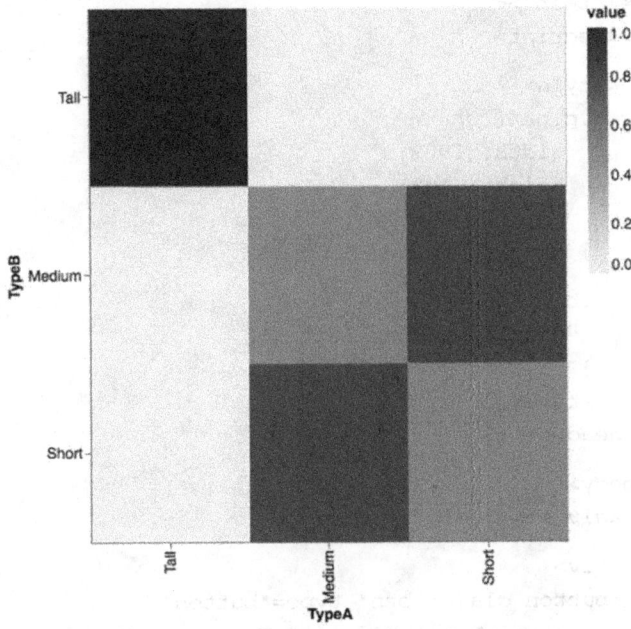

**FIGURE 6.5**   A heat map

This concludes the portion of the chapter pertaining to some of the data visualization functionality that is available in `tfjs-vis`. The next portion of the chapter contains a code sample that combines TensorFlow.js and `tfjs-vis` in an Angular application that performs linear regression.

## TensorFlow.js, tfjs-vis, and Linear Regression

Listing 6.14 shows the content of `tfjs-vis-linreg1.html`, which illustrates how to generate a set of random-like values and then use machine learning and linear regression to determine the best-fitting line.

*LISTING 6.14: tfjs-vis-linreg1.html*

```
<html>
  <head>
    <script src="https://cdn.jsdelivr.net/npm/@tensorflow/
tfjs@latest">
```

```
      </script>
      <script
        src="https://cdn.jsdelivr.net/npm/@tensorflow/tfjs-
   vis@latest">
      </script>

      <style>
        .plot {
          width: 100%;
          height: 40%;
          margin: 4px;
        }

        .btn {
          display: float-left;
        }
      </style>
   </head>

   <body>
     <div id="mydiv"></div>

     <div>
     <button class="btn" type="button"
   onclick="trainLinearModel()">Train the Model</button>
     </div>
     <!-- the scatterplot is displayed here: -->
     <div class="plot" id="plot1"></div>
   </body>

   <script>
    async function trainLinearModel() {
       //-----------------------------------
       // define a simple model that has:
       // 1) a single input (numeric value)
       // 3) a connection to the output layer
       // 4) an output layer of one neuron
       //-----------------------------------

       const model = tf.sequential();
         model.add(tf.layers.dense({units: 1, inputShape:
   [1]}));
       model.compile({
         loss: 'meanSquaredError',
         optimizer: 'sgd'
```

```
    });

    var epochs  = 100
    var maxRand = 30
    var count   = 100
    items1 = []
    itemsX = []
    itemsY = []
    values = []

    // define the data points
    for(var i=0; i<count; i++) {
      x = i
      y = 2*x + 1 + Math.random()*maxRand

      items1.push({"x":x, "y":y})
      itemsX.push(x)
      itemsY.push(y)
    }

    values.push(items1)

    const xs = tf.tensor1d([1,2,3,4,5,6,7,8,9,10]);
    const ys = tf.tensor1d([3,5,7,9,11,13,15,17,19,21]);

    // legend-related information
    let series1 = ['Dataset1', 'Dataset2'];

    // render the scatter plot in the 'plot1' element:
          tfvis.render.scatterplot(document.getElementBy-
  Id('plot1'), {values,series1}, {
      width: 600,
      xLabel: 'x-axis',
      yLabel: 'y-axis'
    })

    // train the model:
    await model.fit(xs, ys, {epochs: epochs});

    // predict the value of y when x = 52.5:
    var mydiv = document.getElementById('mydiv');
    mydiv.innerText += "Prediction for 52.5: "+
                  model.predict(tf.tensor1d([50]));
    }
  </script>
</html>
```

Listing 6.14 contains a `<head>` element with `<script>` elements that reference the necessary `tfjs-vis` JavaScript code for rendering charts and graphs and for the TensorFlow.js code. The `<style>` element specifies some properties for layout purposes.

The next portion of Listing 6.14 defines a `<div>` element that contains a `<button>` element for invoking the training process. Another `<div>` element specifies where the scatter plot is rendered for the data points in this example.

The next portion of Listing 6.14 contains a `<script>` element with the function `trainLinearModel()`, which contains all the code to perform linear regression. The next block of code defines the variable model, adds a single layer, and then compiles the model, just like you have seen in previous code samples.

Before we can train the model via the `fit()` method, we need to generate some data values. In this example, a `for` loop iterates through the x values, which are the integers from 1 to 100, and then calculates the corresponding y values, as shown here:

```
// define the data points
for(var i=0; i<count; i++) {
    x = i
    y = 2*x + 1 + Math.random()*maxRand

    items1.push({"x":x, "y":y})
    itemsX.push(x)
    itemsY.push(y)
}
```

The arrays `itemsX` and `itemsY` contain the x values and y values, respectively, and the array `items1` contains the value pairs `(x,y)`.

The next portion of Listing 6.14 contains the code for rendering a scatter plot, which is virtually identical to the code that you saw in an earlier example.

The next code snippet trains the model via the `fit()` method, in exactly the same way as previous code samples, as shown here:

```
await model.fit(xs, ys, {epochs: epochs});
```

Finally, the last portion of Listing 6.14 invokes the `predict()` method of the variable model to predict the value of y when the value of x is 52.5, and then populates this value in the appropriate `<div>` element, as shown here:

```
// predict the value of y when x = 52.5:
var mydiv = document.getElementById('mydiv');
mydiv.innerText += "Prediction for 52.5: "+
                    model.predict(tf.tensor1d([50]));
```

Figure 6.6 shows the contents of the Web page after you launch the code in Listing 6.14 and you click on the top-most button.

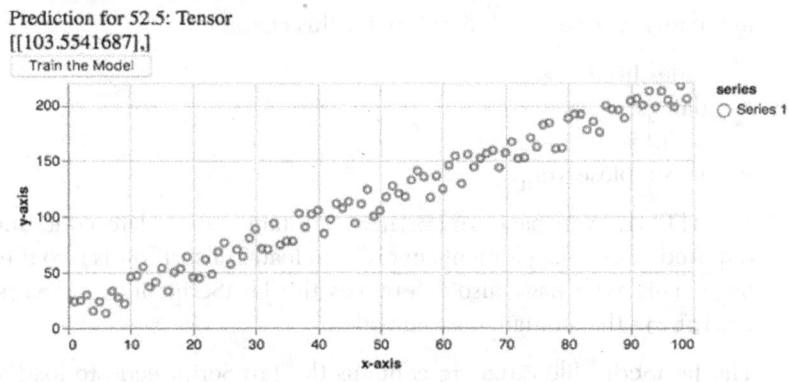

**FIGURE 6.6** A machine learning prediction

## The MNIST Dataset

In a subsequent section, you will learn how to train a deep learning model in TensorFlow.js using the MNIST dataset. In fact, this dataset is frequently one of the first datasets that people encounter when they begin their study of deep learning.

The MNIST (Modified NIST) dataset contains 70,000 greyscale images of handwritten digits (0 through 9, inclusive), where each image has dimensions 28x28. Hence, each image consists of 784 pixels values, and a pixel value is a number between 0 and 255, inclusive, which corresponds to the range of numbers in each component of the (R,G,B) color model.

Every image in the MNIST dataset has a label that corresponds to the digit that is displayed in each image. Hence, the images that display the digit 0 will have the label 0, the images that display the digit 1 will have the label 1, and so forth. Since there are 10 possible digits, there are 10 distinct labels, and roughly 10% of the dataset belongs to each of the 10 labels. Keep in mind that the images in the MNIST dataset contain a single digit (i.e., no images contain multiple digits).

## Displaying MNIST Images

This section contains a minimalistic example of displaying some MNIST images in an HTML Web page. The necessary files are from the following online tutorial:

*https://www.tensorflow.org/js/tutorials/training/handwritten_digit_cnn*

There are three files that you need in this section, all of which are included in the mnistimages subdirectory for this chapter:

- index.html
- data.js
- script.js
- mysimpleserver.py

The HTML Web page index.html contains boilerplate code and the required <script> elements in order to load TensorFlow.js into the Web page. This Web page also references the JavaScript files data.js and script.js that contain custom code.

The JavaScript file data.js contains the JavaScript code to load a randomly selected subset of 20 images from the MNIST dataset.

The JavaScript file script.js contains the JavaScript code that renders the randomly selected images in the HTML Web page.

Listing 6.15 shows the content of mysimpleserver.py, which acts as a simple web server for Python 3.x.

### LISTING 6.15: mysimpleserver.py (for Python 3.x)

```python
import http.server
import socketserver

PORT = 8080
Handler = http.server.SimpleHTTPRequestHandler

with socketserver.TCPServer(("", PORT), Handler) as httpd:
    print("serving at port", PORT)
    httpd.serve_forever()
```

Now open a command shell, navigate to the directory that contains the Python script mysimpleserver.py, and enter the following command:

```
python mysimpleserver.py
```

The preceding command launches a Web server on port 8080, which is the value of the `port` variable in the Python script. If need be, you can change the value of the `port` variable to a different number.

**NOTE** *Python 2.x provides `SimpleHTTPServer`, whereas Python 3.x provides the http.server module.*

**Important:** Firefox has a CORS (Cross Origin Resource Sharing) restriction whereby `file:///` requests result in the following error:

```
Cross-Origin Request Blocked: The Same Origin Policy dis-
allows reading the remote resource at file:///Users/owner/
mercury-learning/Ang10DL/manuscript/ch6-tfjs/mnistimages/
data.js. (Reason: CORS request not http).
```

If you want to see more details regarding Firefox and CORS issues, visit

*https://developer.mozilla.org/en-US/docs/Web/HTTP/CORS/Errors/ CORSRequestNotHttp*

The simplest solution for the preceding CORS error is to launch index. html in Safari and then disable the CORS restriction by navigating from the menu bar as follows:

```
Developer > Disable Cross Origin Restrictions
```

Now open a browser session and navigate to the following URL:

```
http://localhost:8080/index.html
```

Wait a few moments to see a set of images (these are shown in Figure 6.7).

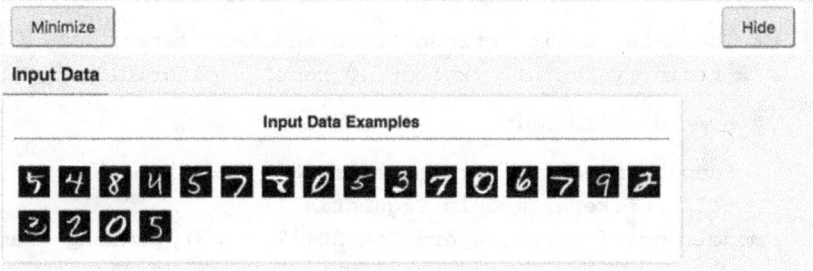

**FIGURE 6.7** MNIST images

For your convenience, the next (optional) section is a quick review of a `Keras`-based code sample that defines a model for training on the

CIFAR10 dataset. Feel free to skip this section if you are ready for the code sample that involves TensorFlow.js and the MNIST dataset.

## Training a Model with the CIFAR10 Dataset (optional)

In Chapter 5, you learned about CNNs (Convolutional Networks) and Appendix A contains the code sample keras_cnn_cifar10.py, which trains a CNN with the cifar10 dataset.

The code for training a neural network on the CIFAR10 dataset is similar to training on an MNIST dataset that you will see in the next section. However, the Keras-based code is somewhat more compact than the corresponding TensorFlow.js code, so it's useful to keep this code in mind when you look at the TensorFlow.js code.

Listing 6.16 shows a portion of the code from the Python script keras_cifar10_cnn.py, located in Appendix A.

### LISTING 6.16: keras_cifar10_block.py

```
// NOTE: THE COMPLETE FILE IS LISTING A-5 in Appendix A
import tensorflow as tf

batch_size = 32
num_classes = 10
epochs = 100
num_predictions = 20

cifar10 = tf.keras.datasets.cifar10

# The data, split between train and test sets:
(x_train, y_train), (x_test, y_test) = cifar10.load_data()

# some details omitted

# keep in mind the structure of this code block:
model = tf.keras.models.Sequential()
model.add(tf.keras.layers.Conv2D(32, (3,3), padding='same',
                 input_shape=x_train.shape[1:]))
model.add(tf.keras.layers.Activation('relu'))
model.add(tf.keras.layers.Conv2D(32, (3, 3)))
model.add(tf.keras.layers.Activation('relu'))
model.add(tf.keras.layers.MaxPooling2D(pool_size=(2, 2)))
model.add(tf.keras.layers.Dropout(0.25))
```

```
model.add(tf.keras.layers.Dense(num_classes))
model.add(tf.keras.layers.Activation('softmax'))

# use RMSprop optimizer to train the model
model.compile(loss='categorical_crossentropy',
              optimizer=opt,
              metrics=['accuracy'])

# some details omitted

model.fit(x_train, y_train,
          batch_size=batch_size,
          epochs=epochs,
          validation_data=(x_test, y_test),
          shuffle=True)

# evaluate and display results from test data
scores = model.evaluate(x_test, y_test, verbose=1)
print('Test loss:', scores[0])
print('Test accuracy:', scores[1])
```

Note that a "vanilla" CNN involves a convolutional layer, followed by the ReLU activation function, and a max pooling layer. In addition, the final layer of the Keras model is the softmax activation function, which converts the 10 numeric values in the fully connected layer to a set of 10 non-negative numbers between 0 and 1, whose sum equals 1 (this gives us a probability distribution).

Now let's proceed to the next section that shows you how to use TensorFlow.js to define and train a neural network on the MNIST dataset.

## Deep Learning and the MNIST Dataset

In Chapter 5, you learned about CNNs and how to create a Keras-based model for a CNN. In this section, we'll create and train such a model on the MNIST dataset by performing the following steps:

- Step 1: Load the data from the MNIST dataset
- Step 2: Create a deep learning model using TensorFlow.js
- Step 3: Train the deep learning model
- Step 4: Use the trained model for inferencing on new MNIST images

There are four files that you need in this section, all of which are included in the mnistimages2 subdirectory for this chapter:

- index.html
- data.js
- script.js
- mysimpleserver.py (same code as previous section)

The details for Step 1 are discussed in an earlier section of this chapter, so we don't need to duplicate those details.

Step 2 is performed in the JavaScript file `script.js`, whose first portion is the same as the script.js file in the previous section. The code for creating a model consists of the following steps that are listed as a comment block in `script.js`:

```
// the getModel() function creates a model:
// 1) define the variable model of type tf.sequential()
// 2) add a conv2d layer
// 3) add a max pooling layer
// 4) add a conv2d layer
// 5) add a max pooling layer
// 6) add a flatten layer
// 7) add a dense layer
// 8) compile the model with an 'adam' optimizer
```

Step 3 is performed by the JavaScript `train()` function that is defined in the JavaScript file `script.js`.

**Important:** If you haven't already done so, please read the previous section regarding the CORS (Cross Origin Resource Sharing) restriction in Firefox and how to use Safari instead of Firefox.

Now open a command shell, navigate to the directory that contains the Python script `mysimpleserver.py`, and enter the following command:

```
python mysimpleserver.py
```

The preceding command launches a Web server on port 8080. If need be, you can change the value of the `port` variable to a different port number in the Python script.

**NOTE**

*Python 2.x provides* `SimpleHTTPServer`, *whereas Python 3.x provides the* `http.server` *module.*

Next, open a (Safari) browser session and enter the following URL:

```
http://localhost:8080/index.html
```

Figure 6.8 shows the first of three images for this example, and it displays the model architecture that is defined in the JavaScript file script.js.

Input Data     Visor

| Model Architecture | | | |
|---|---|---|---|
| Layer Name | Output Shape | # Of Params | Trainable |
| conv2d_Conv2D1 | [batch,24,24,8] | 208 | true |
| max_pooling2d_MaxPooling2D1 | [batch,12,12,8] | 0 | true |
| conv2d_Conv2D2 | [batch,8,8,16] | 3,216 | true |
| max_pooling2d_MaxPooling2D2 | [batch,4,4,16] | 0 | true |
| flatten_Flatten1 | [batch,256] | 0 | true |
| dense_Dense1 | [batch,10] | 2,570 | true |

*FIGURE 6.8*  Model architecture

Figure 6.9 shows the second of three images for this example, and it displays a graph with the loss values and the accuracy values at the end of each batch of data.

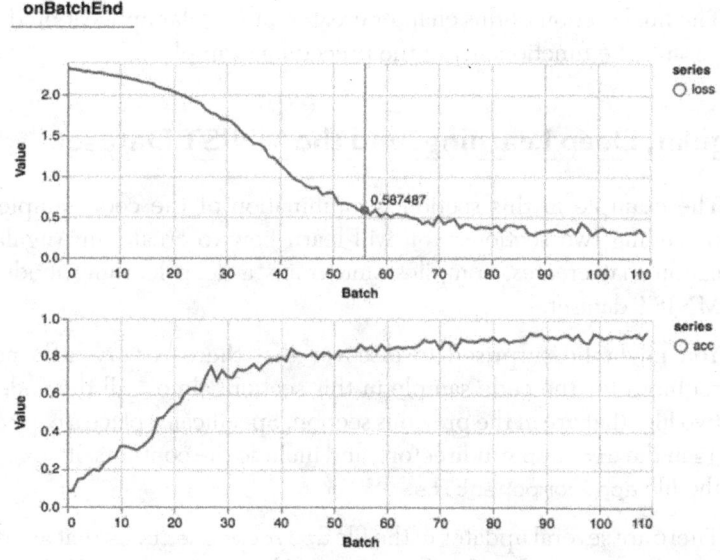

*FIGURE 6.9*  Loss and accuracy graph

Figure 6.10 shows the third of three images for this example, and it displays a graph with the loss values and the accuracy values at the end of each epoch.

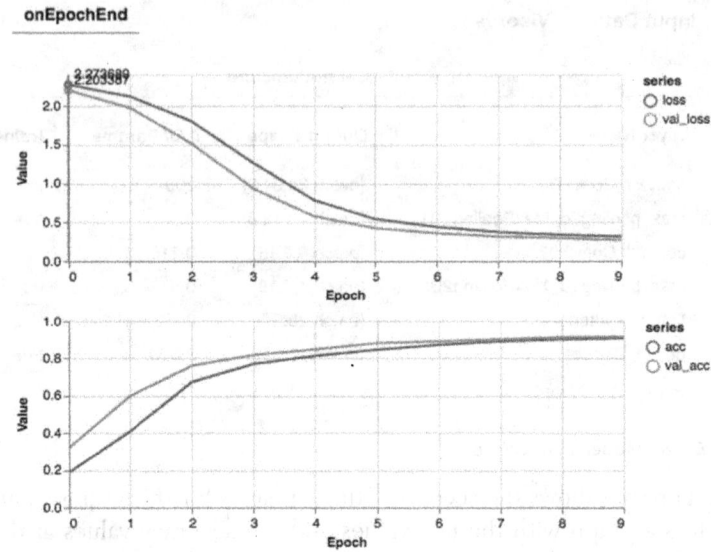

**FIGURE 6.10** Loss and accuracy values for each epoch

The final section of this chapter creates an Angular application that incorporates the functionality of the preceding example.

## Angular, Deep Learning, and the MNIST Dataset

The example in this section is culmination of the code samples in the preceding two sections: you will learn how to create an Angular application that creates, compiles, and trains a deep learning model on the MNIST dataset.

You might be surprised to discover that there is very little new code required for the code sample in this section: almost all the code is from two files that are in the previous section. Specifically, place a copy of data. js in the src/app subdirectory, and include the contents of script.js in the file app.component.ts.

There are several updates in the file app.component.ts that are required, as well as one update for the data.js file, as summarized below.

Step 1: Include the following code block at the top of app.component.ts:

```
import { Component } from '@angular/core';
import * as tf        from '@tensorflow/tfjs';
```

```
import * as tfvis     from '@tensorflow/tfjs-vis';
import {MnistData}    from './data.js';
```

Step 2: Remember to invoke the following pair of npm commands:

```
// remember: npm install @tensorflow/tfjs --save
// remember: npm install @tensorflow/tfjs-vis --save
```

Step 3: Update the constructor with the following code snippet:

```
constructor() {
    this.run();
}
```

Step 4: Remove the `addEventListener` code snippet (at the bottom of `script.js`).

Step 5: Remove the "function" keyword from the following functions:

```
async function showExamples(data)
async function run()
function getModel()
async function train(model, data)
```

Step 6: Include the "this" keyword in the following code snippets:

```
await this.showExamples(data);
const model = this.getModel();
await this.train(model, data);
```

Step 7: You also need to add the following code snippet at the top of the file data.js, and make sure it's placed above the copyright notice:

```
import * as tf from '@tensorflow/tfjs';
```

Now copy the directory NGTFJSCNN from the companion files into a convenient location. Listing 6.16 shows the initial portion of the file app. component.ts that trains a CNN in TensorFlow.js.

### LISTING 6.16: app.component.ts

```
import { Component } from '@angular/core';
import * as tf       from '@tensorflow/tfjs';
import * as tfvis    from '@tensorflow/tfjs-vis';
import {MnistData}   from './data.js';

// remember: npm install @tensorflow/tfjs --save
// remember: npm install @tensorflow/tfjs-vis --save

@Component({
```

```
    selector: 'app-root',
    styleUrls: ['./app.component.css'],
    template: '
      <h2>Train a CNN with TensorFlow.js</h2>
    ',
})
export class AppComponent {
    title = 'NGTFJSCNN';

    constructor() {
      this.run();
    }

    // the remaining code is from script.js
    // the required changes are listed above
    // the full code is in the companion files
}
```

Listing 6.16 contains a small portion of app.component.ts, with some of the required changes shown in bold.

Next, open a browser session and enter the following URL:

```
http://localhost:8080/index.html
```

After a few moments, you will see the same output as you saw in the previous section, which are shown in Figure 6.8, Figure 6.9, and Figure 6.10.

## Possible Compilation Error

During the compilation step for this Angular application, you might encounter the following error message:

```
ERROR in node_modules/@types/webgl2/index.d.ts:582:13 -
error TS2403: Subsequent variable declarations must have
the same type. Variable 'WebGL2RenderingContext' must
be of type '{ new (): WebGL2RenderingContext; prototype:
WebGL2RenderingContext; readonly ACTIVE_ATTRIBUTES: num-
ber; readonly ACTIVE_TEXTURE: number; ... 556 more ...; rea-
donly WAIT_FAILED: number; }', but here has type '{ new ():
WebGL2RenderingContext; prototype: WebGL2RenderingContext;
readonly ACTIVE_ATTRIBUTES: number; readonly ACTIVE_
TEXTURE: number; ... 557 more ...; readonly MAX_CLIENT_
WAIT_TIMEOUT_WEBGL: number; }'.
```

```
582 declare var WebGL2RenderingContext: {
        ~~~~~~~~~~~~~~~~~~~~~~

    node_modules/typescript/lib/lib.dom.d.ts:16535:13
      16535 declare var WebGL2RenderingContext: {
                        ~~~~~~~~~~~~~~~~~~~~~~

      'WebGL2RenderingContext' was also declared here.
```

One solution for the preceding error is to update the section labeled compilerOptions in the file tsconfig.json with the following code snippet:

```
"skipLibCheck": true,
```

Additional information is available here:

*https://www.tensorflow.org/js/tutorials/setup#typescript*

## Summary

This chapter started with a quick overview of TensorFlow.js, along with an example of performing linear regression in an HTML Web page with TensorFlow.js.

Next, you saw an assortment of examples of charts and graphs using tfjs-vis, including a line graph, a bar chart, a scatter plot, and a heat map.

In addition, you learned how to combine TensorFlow.js and tfjs-vis to perform linear regression in an HTML Web page. Then you saw how to display MNIST images in an HTML Web page, followed by an example of training a neural network on the MNIST dataset.

Finally, you learned how to create an Angular application that uses TensorFlow.js to create, compile, and train a deep learning model on the MNIST dataset, along with graphs that display the values of the loss and accuracy during each batch of every epoch.

# INTRODUCTION TO KERAS

This appendix introduces you to Keras, along with code samples that illustrate how to define basic neural networks and deep neural networks with various datasets with as MNIST and Cifar10.

The first part of this appendix briefly discusses some of the important namespaces (such as tf.keras.layers) and their contents, as well as a simple Keras-based model.

The second section contains an example of performing linear regression with Keras and a simple CSV file. It includes Keras-based MLP neural network that is trained on the MNIST dataset.

The third section contains a simple example of training a neural network with the cifar10 dataset. This code sample is similar to training a neural network on the MNIST dataset and requires a very small code change.

The final section contains two examples of Keras-based models that perform early stopping, which is convenient when the model exhibits minimal improvement (that is specified by you) during the training process.

## What is Keras?

If you are already comfortable with Keras, you can skim this section to learn about the new namespaces and what they contain, and then proceed to the next section that contains details for creating a Keras-based model.

If you are new to Keras, you might be wondering why this section is included in this appendix. First, Keras is well-integrated into TF 2, and it's in the tf.keras namespace. Second, Keras is well-suited for defining models to solve a myriad of tasks, such as linear regression and logistic regression, as well as deep learning tasks involving CNNs, RNNs, and LSTMs that are discussed in the Appendix.

The next sub-sections contain lists of bullet items for various Keras-related namespaces, and they will be very familiar if you have worked with TF 1.x. If you are new to TF 2, you'll see examples of some of the classes in subsequent code samples.

## Working with **Keras** Namespaces in TF 2

TF 2 provides the tf.keras namespace, which in turn contains the following namespaces:

- tf.keras.layers
- tf.keras.models
- tf.keras.optimizers
- tf.keras.utils
- tf.keras.regularizers

The preceding namespaces contain various layers in Keras models, different types of Keras models, optimizers (Adam et al), utility classes, and regularizers (such as L1 and L2), respectively.

Currently there are three ways to create Keras-based models:

- The Sequential API
- The Functional API
- The Model API

The Keras-based code samples in this book use primarily the Sequential API (it's the most intuitive and straightforward). The Sequential API enables you to specify a list of layers, most of which are available in the tf.keras.layers namespace (discussed later).

The Keras-based models that use the functional API involve specifying layers that are passed as function-like elements in a pipeline-like fashion. Although the functional API provides some additional flexibility, you will probably use the Sequential API to define Keras-based models if you are a TF 2 beginner.

The model-based API provides the greatest flexibility, and it involves defining a Python class that encapsulates the semantics of your Keras model. This class is a subclass of the tf.model.Model class, and you must implement the two methods __init__ and call to define a Keras model in this subclass.

Perform an online search for more details regarding the Functional API and the Model API.

### Working with the tf.keras.layers Namespace

The most common (and also the simplest) Keras-based model is the Sequential() class that is in the tf.keras.models namespace. This model is comprised of various layers that belong to the tf.keras.layers namespace, as shown here:

- tf.keras.layers.Conv2D()
- tf.keras.layers.MaxPooling2D()
- tf.keras.layers.Flatten()
- tf.keras.layers.Dense()
- tf.keras.layers.Dropout()
- tf.keras.layers.BatchNormalization()
- tf.keras.layers.embedding()
- tf.keras.layers.RNN()
- tf.keras.layers.LSTM()
- tf.keras.layers.Bidirectional (ex: BERT)

The Conv2D() and MaxPooling2D() classes are used in Keras-based models for CNNs, which are discussed in Chapter 5. Generally speaking, the next six classes in the preceding list can appear in models for CNNs as well as models for machine learning. The RNN() class is for simple RNNS and the LSTM class is for LSTM-based models. The Bidirectional() class is a bi-directional LSTM that you will often see in models for solving NLP (Natural Language Processing) tasks. One very important NLP model is BERT (from Google), which is based on the Transformer architecture (also from Google).

### Working with the tf.keras.activations Namespace

Machine learning and deep learning models require activation functions. For Keras-based models, the activation functions are in the tf.keras.activations namespace, some of which are listed here:

- tf.keras.activations.relu
- tf.keras.activations.selu
- tf.keras.activations.linear

- `tf.keras.activations.elu`
- `tf.keras.activations.sigmoid`
- `tf.keras.activations.softmax`
- `tf.keras.activations.softplus`
- `tf.keras.activations.tanh`

The ReLU/SELU/ELU functions are closely related, and they often appear in ANNs (Artificial Neural Networks) and CNNs. Before the `ReLU()` function became popular, the `sigmoid()` and `tanh()` functions were used in ANNs and CNNs. However, they are still important and they are used in various gates in GRUs and LSTMs. The `softmax()` function is typically used in the pair of layers consisting of the right-most hidden layer and the output layer.

## Working with the keras.tf.datasets Namespace

For your convenience, TF 2 provides a set of built-in datasets in the `tf.keras.datasets` namespace, some of which are listed here:

- `tf.keras.datasets.boston_housing`
- `tf.keras.datasets.cifar10`
- `tf.keras.datasets.cifar100`
- `tf.keras.datasets.fashion_mnist`
- `tf.keras.datasets.imdb`
- `tf.keras.datasets.mnist`
- `tf.keras.datasets.reuters`

The preceding datasets are popular for training models with small datasets. The `mnist` dataset and `fashion_mnist` dataset are both popular when training CNNs, whereas the `boston_housing` dataset is popular for linear regression. The `Titanic` dataset is also popular for linear regression, but it's not currently supported as a default dataset in the `tf.keras.datasets` namespace.

## Working with the tf.keras.experimental Namespace

The `contrib` namespace in TF 1.x has been deprecated in TF 2, and it's successor is the `tf.keras.experimental` namespace, which contains the following classes (among others):

- `tf.keras.experimental.CosineDecay`
- `tf.keras.experimental.CosineDecayRestarts`

- `tf.keras.experimental.LinearCosineDecay`
- `tf.keras.experimental.NoisyLinearCosineDecay`
- `tf.keras.experimental.PeepholeLSTMCell`

If you are a beginner, you probably won't use any of the classes in the preceding list. Although the `PeepholeLSTMCell` class is a variation of the LSTM class, there are limited use cases for this class.

## Working with Other tf.keras Namespaces

TF 2 provides a number of other namespaces that contain useful classes, some of which are listed here:

- `tf.keras.callbacks`      (early stopping)
- `tf.keras.optimizers`     (Adam et al)
- `tf.keras.regularizers`   (L1 and L2)
- `tf.keras.utils`          (to_categorical)

The `tf.keras.callbacks` namespace contains a class that you can use for *early stopping*, which is to say that it's possible to terminate the training process if there is an insufficient reduction in the cost function in two successive iterations.

The `tf.keras.optimizers` namespace contains the various optimizers that are available for working in conjunction with cost functions, which includes the popular `Adam` optimizer.

The `tf.keras.regularizers` namespace contains two popular regularizers: the L1 regularizer (also called LASSO in machine learning) and the L2 regularizer (also called the Ridge regularizer in machine learning). L1 is for the MAE (Mean Absolute Error) and L2 is for the MSE (Mean Squared Error). Both of these regularizers act as penalty terms that are added to the chosen cost function to reduce the influence of the features in a machine learning model. Note that LASSO can drive values to zero, with the result that features are actually eliminated from a model, and hence it is related to the feature selection in machine learning.

The `tf.keras.utils` namespace contains an assortment of functions, including the `to_categorical()` function for converting a class vector into a binary class.

Although there are other namespaces in TF 2, the classes listed in all the preceding subsections will probably suffice for the majority of your tasks if you are a beginner in TF 2 and machine learning.

## TF 2 Keras versus "Standalone" Keras

The original Keras is actually a specification, with various backend frameworks such as TensorFlow, Theano, and CNTK. Currently, standalone Keras does not support TF 2, whereas the implementation of Keras in tf.keras has been optimized for performance.

Standalone Keras lives in perpetuity in the keras.io package, which is discussed in detail at the Keras website: *keras.io*.

Now that you have a high-level view of the TF 2 namespaces for Keras and the classes that they contain, let's find out how to create a Keras-based model, which is the subject of the next section.

# Creating a Keras-Based Model

The following list of steps describes the high-level sequence involved in creating, training, and testing a Keras model:

Step 1: Determine a model architecture (the number of hidden layers, various activation functions, and so forth).

Step 2: Invoke the compile() method

Step 3: Invoke the fit() method to train the model

Step 4: Invoke the evaluate() method to evaluate the trained model

Step 5: Invoke the predict() method to make predictions

Step 1 involves determining the values of a number of hyperparameters, including

- The number of hidden layers
- The number of neurons in each hidden layer
- The initial values of the weights of edges
- The cost function
- The optimizer
- The learning rate
- The dropout rate
- The activation function(s)

Steps 2 through 4 involve the training data, whereas Step 5 involves the test data, which are included in the following more detailed sequence of steps for the preceding list:

- Specify a dataset (if necessary, convert data to numeric data).
- Split the dataset into training data and test data (usually 80/20 split).
- Define the Keras model (such as the tf.keras.models.Sequential() API).
- Compile the Keras model (the compile() API).
- Train (fit) the Keras model (the fit() API).
- Make a prediction (the prediction() API).

Note that the preceding bullet items skip some steps that are part of a real Keras model, such as evaluating the Keras model on the test data, as well as dealing with issues such as overfitting.

The first bulleted item states that you need a dataset, which can be as simple as a CSV file with 100 rows of data and just 3 columns (or even smaller). In general, a dataset is substantially larger: it can be a file with 1,000,000 rows of data and 10,000 columns in each row. We'll look at a concrete dataset in a subsequent section.

A Keras model is in the tf.keras.models namespace, and the simplest (and also very common) Keras model is tf.keras.models.Sequential. In general, a Keras model contains layers that are in the tf.keras.layers namespace, such as tf.keras.Dense (which means that two adjacent layers are completely connected).

The activation functions that are referenced in Keras layers are in the tf.nn namespace, such as the tf.nn.ReLU for the ReLU activation function.

Here's a code block of the Keras model that's described in the preceding paragraphs (which covers the first four bullet points):

```
import tensorflow as tf

model = tf.keras.models.Sequential([
  tf.keras.layers.Dense(512, activation=tf.nn.relu),
])
```

We have three more bulleted items to discuss, starting with the compilation step. Keras provides a compile() API for this step, an example of which is here:

```
model.compile(optimizer='adam',
              loss='sparse_categorical_crossentropy',
              metrics=['accuracy'])
```

Next we need to specify a training step, and Keras provides the fit()
API (as you can see, it's not called train()), an example of which is here:

```
model.fit(x_train, y_train, epochs=5)
```

The final step is the prediction that is performed via the predict() API,
an example of which is here:

```
pred = model.predict(x)
```

Keep in mind that the evaluate() method is used for evaluating an
trained model, and the output of this method is accuracy or loss. The
predict() method makes predictions from the input data.

Listing A.1 shows the content of tf2_basic_keras.py, which combines
the code blocks in the preceding steps into a single code sample.

### LISTING A.1: *tf2_basic*_keras.*py*

```
import tensorflow as tf

# NOTE: we need the train data and test data

model = tf.keras.models.Sequential([
  tf.keras.layers.Dense(1, activation=tf.nn.relu),
])

model.compile(optimizer='adam',
              loss='sparse_categorical_crossentropy',
              metrics=['accuracy'])

model.fit(x_train, y_train, epochs=5)
model.evaluate(x_test, y_test)
```

Listing A.1 contains no new code, and we've essentially glossed over some
of the terms such as the *optimizer* (an algorithm that is used in conjunction with a cost function), the *loss* (the type of loss function), and the
*metrics* (how to evaluate the efficacy of a model).

The explanations for these details cannot be condensed into a few paragraphs (alas), but the good news is that you can find a plethora of detailed
online blog posts that discuss these terms.

## Keras and Linear Regression

This section contains a simple example of creating a Keras-based model
in order to solve a task involving linear regression: given a positive number
representing kilograms of pasta, predict its corresponding price. Listing

A.2 shows the content of pasta.csv and Listing A.3 shows the content of keras_pasta.py that perform this task.

***LISTING A.2: pasta.csv***

```
weight,price
5,30
10,45
15,70
20,80
25,105
30,120
35,130
40,140
50,150
```

***LISTING A.3: keras_pasta.py***

```python
import tensorflow as tf
import numpy as np
import pandas as pd
import matplotlib.pyplot as plt

# price of pasta per kilogram
df = pd.read_csv("pasta.csv")

weight = df['weight']
price  = df['price']

model = tf.keras.models.Sequential([
    tf.keras.layers.Dense(units=1,input_shape=[1])
])

# MSE loss function and Adam optimizer
model.compile(loss='mean_squared_error',
              optimizer=tf.keras.optimizers.Adam(0.1))

# train the model
history = model.fit(weight, price, epochs=100, verbose=False)

# graph the # of epochs versus the loss
plt.xlabel('Number of Epochs')
plt.ylabel("Loss Values")
plt.plot(history.history['loss'])
plt.show()

print("Cost for 11kg:",model.predict([11.0]))
print("Cost for 45kg:",model.predict([45.0]))
```

Listing A.3 initializes the Pandas Dataframe df with the contents of the CSV file pasta.csv, and then initializes the variables weight and cost with the first and second columns, respectively, of df.

The next portion of Listing A.3 defines a Keras-based model that consists of a single Dense layer. This model is compiled and trained, and then a graph is displayed that shows the "number of epochs" on the horizontal axis and the corresponding value of the loss function for the vertical axis. Launch the code in Listing A.3 to see the following output:

```
Cost for 11kg: [[41.727108]]
Cost for 45kg: [[159.02121]]
```

Figure A.1 displays a graph of epochs versus loss during the training process.

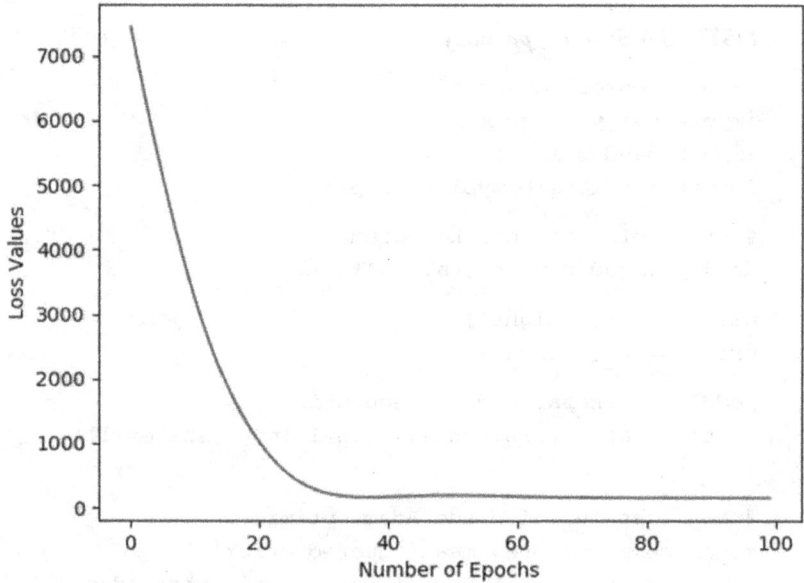

*FIGURE A.1*   A graph of epochs versus loss

## Keras, MLPs, and MNIST

This section contains a simple example of creating a Keras-based MLP neural network that will be trained with the MNIST dataset. Listing A.4 shows the content of keras_mlp_mnist.py that performs this task.

*LISTING A.4: keras_mlp_mnist.py*

```
import tensorflow as tf
import numpy as np

# instantiate mnist and load data:
mnist = tf.keras.datasets.mnist
(x_train, y_train), (x_test, y_test) = mnist.load_data()

# one-hot encoding for all labels to create 1x10
# vectors that are compared with the final layer:
y_train = tf.keras.utils.to_categorical(y_train)
y_test  = tf.keras.utils.to_categorical(y_test)

image_size = x_train.shape[1]
input_size = image_size * image_size

# resize and normalize the 28x28 images:
x_train = np.reshape(x_train, [-1, input_size])
x_train = x_train.astype('float32') / 255
x_test  = np.reshape(x_test, [-1, input_size])
x_test  = x_test.astype('float32') / 255

# initialize some hyper-parameters:
batch_size = 128
hidden_units = 128
dropout_ratea = 0.20

# define a Keras-based model:
model = tf.keras.models.Sequential()
model.add(tf.keras.layers.Dense(hidden_units,
input_dim=input_size))
model.add(tf.keras.layers.Activation('relu'))
model.add(tf.keras.layers.Dropout(dropout_rate))
model.add(tf.keras.layers.Dense(hidden_units))
model.add(tf.keras.layers.Activation('relu'))
model.add(tf.keras.layers.Dense(10))
model.add(tf.keras.layers.Activation('softmax'))

model.summary()

model.compile(loss='categorical_crossentropy',
              optimizer='adam',
              metrics=['accuracy'])
```

```
# train the network on the training data:
model.fit(x_train, y_train, epochs=10,
batch_size=batch_size)

# calculate and then display the accuracy:
loss, acc = model.evaluate(x_test, y_test,
batch_size=batch_size)
print("\nTest accuracy: %.1f%%" % (100.0 * acc))
```

Listing A.4 contains the usual import statements and then initializes the variable mnist as a reference to the MNIST dataset. The next portion of Listing A.4 contains some typical code that populates the training dataset and the test dataset and converts the labels to numeric values via the technique known as "one-hot" encoding.

Next, several hyperparameters are initialized, and a Keras-based model is defined that specifies three Dense layers and the ReLu activation function. This model is compiled and trained, and the accuracy on the test dataset is computed and then displayed. Launch the code in Listing A.4 to see the following output:

```
Model: "sequential"
```

| Layer (type) | Output Shape | Param # |
| --- | --- | --- |
| dense (Dense) | (None, 256) | 200960 |
| activation (Activation) | (None, 256) | 0 |
| dropout (Dropout) | (None, 256) | 0 |
| dense_1 (Dense) | (None, 256) | 65792 |
| activation_1 (Activation) | (None, 256) | 0 |
| dropout_1 (Dropout) | (None, 256) | 0 |
| dense_2 (Dense) | (None, 10) | 2570 |
| activation_2 (Activation) | (None, 10) | 0 |

```
Total params: 269,322
Trainable params: 269,322
Non-trainable params: 0

Train on 60000 samples
Epoch 1/10
60000/60000 [=====================] - 4s 74us/sample - loss:
0.4281 - accuracy: 0.8683
Epoch 2/10
60000/60000 [=====================] - 4s 66us/sample - loss:
0.1967 - accuracy: 0.9417
```

```
Epoch 3/10
60000/60000 [====================] - 4s 63us/sample - loss:
0.1507 - accuracy: 0.9547
Epoch 4/10
60000/60000 [====================] - 4s 63us/sample - loss:
0.1298 - accuracy: 0.9600
Epoch 5/10
60000/60000 [====================] - 4s 60us/sample - loss:
0.1141 - accuracy: 0.9651
Epoch 6/10
60000/60000 [====================] - 4s 66us/sample - loss:
0.1037 - accuracy: 0.9677
Epoch 7/10
60000/60000 [====================] - 4s 61us/sample - loss:
0.0940 - accuracy: 0.9702
Epoch 8/10
60000/60000 [====================] - 4s 61us/sample - loss:
0.0897 - accuracy: 0.9718
Epoch 9/10
60000/60000 [====================] - 4s 62us/sample - loss:
0.0830 - accuracy: 0.9747
Epoch 10/10
60000/60000 [====================] - 4s 64us/sample - loss:
0.0805 - accuracy: 0.9748
10000/10000 [====================] - 0s 39us/sample - loss:
0.0654 - accuracy: 0.9797

Test accuracy: 98.0%
```

## Keras, CNNs, and cifar10

This section contains a simple example of training a neural network with the cifar10 dataset. This code sample is similar to training a neural network on the MNIST dataset, and requires a very small code change.

Keep in mind that images in MNIST have the dimensions 28x28, whereas images in cifar10 have the dimensions 32x32. Always ensure that images have the same dimensions in a dataset, otherwise the results can be unpredictable.

**NOTE** *Make sure that the images in your dataset have the same dimensions*

Listing A.5 shows the content of `keras_cnn_cifar10.py`, which trains a CNN with the `cifar10` dataset.

*LISTING A.5: keras_cnn_cifar10.py*

```
import tensorflow as tf

batch_size = 32
num_classes = 10
epochs = 100
num_predictions = 20

cifar10 = tf.keras.datasets.cifar10

# The data, split between train and test sets:
(x_train, y_train), (x_test, y_test) = cifar10.load_data()
print('x_train shape:', x_train.shape)
print(x_train.shape[0], 'train samples')
print(x_test.shape[0], 'test samples')

# Convert class vectors to binary class matrices
y_train       =       tf.keras.utils.to_categorical(y_train,
num_classes)
y_test = tf.keras.utils.to_categorical(y_test, num_classes)

model = tf.keras.models.Sequential()
model.add(tf.keras.layers.Conv2D(32, (3, 3), padding='same',
                  input_shape=x_train.shape[1:]))
model.add(tf.keras.layers.Activation('relu'))
model.add(tf.keras.layers.Conv2D(32, (3, 3)))
model.add(tf.keras.layers.Activation('relu'))
model.add(tf.keras.layers.MaxPooling2D(pool_size=(2, 2)))
model.add(tf.keras.layers.Dropout(0.25))

# you can also duplicate the preceding code block here

model.add(tf.keras.layers.Flatten())
model.add(tf.keras.layers.Dense(512))
model.add(tf.keras.layers.Activation('relu'))
model.add(tf.keras.layers.Dropout(0.5))
model.add(tf.keras.layers.Dense(num_classes))
model.add(tf.keras.layers.Activation('softmax'))

# use RMSprop optimizer to train the model
model.compile(loss='categorical_crossentropy',
```

```
                optimizer=opt,
                metrics=['accuracy'])
x_train = x_train.astype('float32')
x_test = x_test.astype('float32')
x_train /= 255
x_test /= 255

model.fit(x_train, y_train,
          batch_size=batch_size,
          epochs=epochs,
          validation_data=(x_test, y_test),
          shuffle=True)
# evaluate and display results from test data
scores = model.evaluate(x_test, y_test, verbose=1)
print('Test loss:', scores[0])
print('Test accuracy:', scores[1])
```

Listing A.5 contains the usual import statement and then initializes the variable cifar10 as a reference to the cifar10 dataset. The next section of code is similar to the contents of Listing A.4: the main difference is that this Keras-based model defines a CNN instead of an MLP. Hence, the first layer is a convolutional layer, as shown here:

```
model.add(tf.keras.layers.Conv2D(32, (3, 3), padding='same',
                input_shape=x_train.shape[1:]))
```

Note that a "vanilla" CNN involves a convolutional layer (which is the purpose of the preceding code snippet), followed by the ReLU activation function, and a max pooling layer, both of which are displayed in Listing A.5. In addition, the final layer of the Keras model is the softmax activation function, which converts the 10 numeric values in the "fully connected" layer to a set of 10 non-negative numbers between 0 and 1, whose sum equals 1 (this gives us a probability distribution).

This model is compiled and trained, and then evaluated on the test dataset. The last portion of Listing A.5 shows the value of the test-related loss and accuracy, both of which are calculated during the preceding evaluation step. Launch the code in Listing A.5 to see the following output (note that the code was stopped after partially completing the second epoch):

```
x_train shape: (50000, 32, 32, 3)
50000 train samples
10000 test samples
```

```
Epoch 1/100
50000/50000 [==============================] - 285s 6ms/
sample - loss: 1.7187 - accuracy: 0.3802 - val_loss: 1.4294
- val_accuracy: 0.4926
Epoch 2/100
 1888/50000 [>.............................] - ETA: 4:39 -
loss: 1.4722 - accuracy: 0.4635
```

## Resizing Images in Keras

Listing A.6 shows the content of keras_resize_image.py, which illustrates how to resize an image in Keras.

### LISTING A.6: keras_resize_image.py

```
import tensorflow as tf
import numpy as np
import imageio
import matplotlib.pyplot as plt

# use any image that has 3 channels
inp = tf.keras.layers.Input(shape=(None, None, 3))
out = tf.keras.layers.Lambda(lambda image: tf.image.
resize(image, (128, 128)))(inp)

model = tf.keras.Model(inputs=inp, outputs=out)
model.summary()

# read the contents of a PNG or JPG
X = imageio.imread('sample3.png')

out = model.predict(X[np.newaxis, ...])
fig, axes = plt.subplots(nrows=1, ncols=2)
axes[0].imshow(X)
axes[1].imshow(np.int8(out[0,...]))

plt.show()
```

Listing A.6 contains the usual import statements and then initializes the variable inp so that it can accommodate a color image, followed by the variable out that is the result of resizing inp so that it has dimensions 28x23. Next, inp and out are specified as the values of inputs and outputs, respectively, for the Keras model, as shown in this code snippet:

```
model = tf.keras.Model(inputs=inp, outputs=out)
```

Next, the variable X is initialized as a reference to the result of reading the contents of the image `sample3.png`. The remainder of Listing A.6 involves displaying two images: the original image and the resized image. Launch the code in Listing A.6 to see a graph of an image and its resized image as shown in Figure A.2.

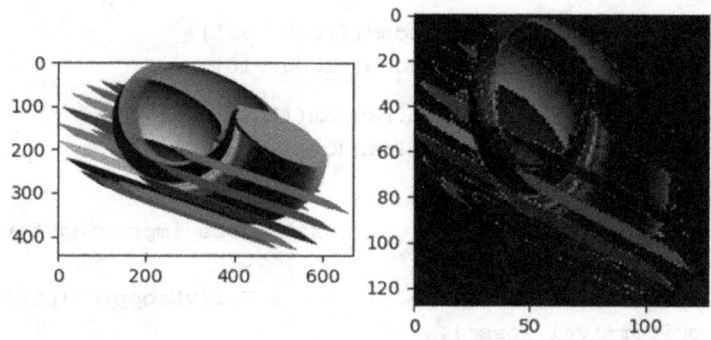

*FIGURE A.2* A graph of an image and its resized image

# Keras and Early Stopping (1)

After specifying the training set and the test set from a dataset, you also decide on the number of training epochs. A value that's too large can lead to overfitting, whereas a value that's too small can lead to underfitting. Moreover, model improvement can diminish and subsequent training iterations become redundant.

Early stopping is a technique that allows you to specify a large value for the number of epochs, and yet the training stops if the model performance improvement drops below a threshold value.

There are several ways that you can specify early stopping, and they involve the concept of a callback function. Listing A.7 shows the content of `tf2_keras_callback.py`, which performs early stopping via a callback mechanism.

*LISTING A.7: tf2_keras_callback.py*

```
import tensorflow as tf
import numpy as np
```

```
model = tf.keras.Sequential()
model.add(tf.keras.layers.Dense(64, activation='relu'))
model.add(tf.keras.layers.Dense(64, activation='relu'))
model.add(tf.keras.layers.Dense(10, activation='softmax'))

model.compile(optimizer=tf.keras.optimizers.Adam(0.01),
              loss='mse',        # mean squared error
              metrics=['mae'])   # mean absolute error

data   = np.random.random((1000, 32))
labels = np.random.random((1000, 10))

val_data   = np.random.random((100, 32))
val_labels = np.random.random((100, 10))

callbacks = [
  # stop training if "val_loss" stops improving for over 2
epochs
              tf.keras.callbacks.EarlyStopping(patience=2,
monitor='val_loss'),
  # write TensorBoard logs to the ./logs directory
  tf.keras.callbacks.TensorBoard(log_dir='./logs')
]

model.fit(data, labels, batch_size=32, epochs=50,
callbacks=callbacks,
          validation_data=(val_data, val_labels))

model.evaluate(data, labels, batch_size=32)
```

Listing A.7 defines a Keras-based model with three hidden layers and then compiles the model. The next portion of Listing A.7 uses the np.random. random function to initialize the variables data, labels, val_data, and val_labels.

The interesting code involves the definition of the callbacks variable that specifies tf.keras.callbacks.EarlyStopping class with a value of 2 for patience, which means that the model stops training if there is an insufficient reduction in the value of val_loss. The callbacks variable includes the tf.keras.callbacks.TensorBoard class to specify the logs subdirectory as the location for the TensorBoard files.

Next, the model.fit() method is invoked with a value of 50 for the epochs (shown in bold), followed by the model.evaluate() method. Launch the code in Listing A.7 to see the following output:

```
Epoch 1/50
1000/1000 [================] -  0s  354us/sample  -  loss:
0.2452 - mae: 0.4127 - val_loss: 0.2517 - val_mae: 0.4205
Epoch 2/50
1000/1000 [================] - 0s 63us/sample - loss: 0.2447
- mae: 0.4125 - val_loss: 0.2515 - val_mae: 0.4204
Epoch 3/50
1000/1000 [================]- 0s 63us/sample - loss: 0.2445
- mae: 0.4124 - val_loss: 0.2520 - val_mae: 0.4209
Epoch 4/50
1000/1000 [================] - 0s 68us/sample - loss: 0.2444
- mae: 0.4123 - val_loss: 0.2519 - val_mae: 0.4205
1000/1000 [================] - 0s 37us/sample - loss: 0.2437
- mae: 0.4119
(1000, 10)
```

Notice that the code stopped training after four epochs, even though 50 epochs are specified in the code.

## Keras and Early Stopping (2)

The previous section contains a code sample with minimalistic functionality with respect to the use of callback functions in Keras. However, you can also define a custom class that provides finer-grained functionality that uses a callback mechanism.

Listing A.8 shows the content of tf2_keras_callback2.py, which performs early stopping via a callback mechanism (the new code is shown in bold).

### LISTING A.8: tf2_keras_callback2.py

```
import tensorflow as tf
import numpy as np

model = tf.keras.Sequential()
model.add(tf.keras.layers.Dense(64, activation='relu'))
model.add(tf.keras.layers.Dense(64, activation='relu'))
model.add(tf.keras.layers.Dense(10, activation='softmax'))

model.compile(optimizer=tf.keras.optimizers.Adam(0.01),
              loss='mse',          # mean squared error
              metrics=['mae'])    # mean absolute error
```

```
data    = np.random.random((1000, 32))
labels = np.random.random((1000, 10))

val_data    = np.random.random((100, 32))
val_labels = np.random.random((100, 10))
class MyCallback(tf.keras.callbacks.Callback):
  def on_train_begin(self, logs={}):
    print("on_train_begin")

  def on_train_end(self, logs={}):
    print("on_train_begin")
    return

  def on_epoch_begin(self, epoch, logs={}):
    print("on_train_begin")
    return

  def on_epoch_end(self, epoch, logs={}):
    print("on_epoch_end")
    return

  def on_batch_begin(self, batch, logs={}):
    print("on_batch_begin")
    return

  def on_batch_end(self, batch, logs={}):
    print("on_batch_end")
    return

callbacks = [MyCallback()]
model.fit(data, labels, batch_size=32, epochs=50,
callbacks=callbacks,
          validation_data=(val_data, val_labels))

model.evaluate(data, labels, batch_size=32)
```

The new code in Listing A.8 differs from Listing A.7. It is limited to the code block that is displayed in bold. This new code defines a custom Python class with several methods, each of which is invoked during the appropriate point during the Keras lifecycle execution. The six methods consist of three pairs of methods for the start event and end event associated with training, epochs, and batches, as listed here:

- `def on_train_begin()`
- `def on_train_end()`
- `def on_epoch_begin()`

- def on_epoch_end()
- def on_batch_begin()
- def on_batch_end()

The preceding methods contain just a print() statement in Listing A.8, and you can insert any code you wish in any of these methods. Launch the code in Listing A.8 to see the following output:

```
on_train_begin
on_train_begin
Epoch 1/50
on_batch_begin
on_batch_end
   32/1000 [..................] - ETA: 4s - loss: 0.2489 -
mae: 0.4170on_batch_begin
on_batch_end
on_batch_begin on_batch_end
// details omitted for brevity
on_batch_begin
on_batch_end
on_batch_begin
on_batch_end
992/1000 [===================>.] - ETA: 0s - loss: 0.2468 -
mae: 0.4138on_batch_begin
on_batch_end
on_epoch_end
1000/1000 [=====================] - 0s 335us/sample - loss:
0.2466 - mae: 0.4136 - val_loss: 0.2445 - val_mae: 0.4126
on_train_begin
Epoch 2/50
on_batch_begin
on_batch_end
 32/1000 [............................] - ETA: 0s - loss:
0.2465 - mae: 0.4133on_batch_begin
on_batch_end
on_batch_begin
on_batch_end
// details omitted for brevity
on_batch_end
on_epoch_end
1000/1000 [=====================] - 0s 51us/sample - loss:
0.2328 - mae: 0.4084 - val_loss: 0.2579 - val_mae: 0.4241
on_train_begin
```

```
 32/1000 [.....................] - ETA: 0s - loss: 0.2295 -
mae: 0.4030
1000/1000 [=====================] - 0s 22us/sample - loss:
0.2313 - mae: 0.4077
(1000, 10)
```

## Keras and Metrics

Many Keras-based models only specify accuracy as the metric for evaluating a trained model, as shown here:

```
model.compile(optimizer='adam',
              loss='sparse_categorical_crossentropy',
              metrics=['accuracy'])
```

However, there are many other built-in metrics available, each of which is encapsulated in a Keras class in the tf.keras.metrics namespace. Some of these metrics are as follows:

- class Accuracy: how often predictions match labels
- class BinaryAccuracy: how often predictions match labels
- class CategoricalAccuracy: how often predictions match labels
- class FalseNegatives: the number of false negatives
- class FalsePositives: the number of false positives
- class Mean: the (weighted) mean of the given values
- class Precision: the precision of the predictions with respect to the labels
- class Recall: the recall of the predictions with respect to the labels
- class TrueNegatives: the number of true negatives
- class TruePositives: the number of true positives

Earlier in this chapter, you learned about the confusion matrix that provides numeric values for TP, TN, FP, and FN, and each of these values has a corresponding Keras class: TruePositive, TrueNegative, FalsePositive, and FalseNegative, respectively. Perform an online search for code samples that use the metrics in the preceding list.

## Saving and Restoring Keras Models

Listing A.9 shows the content of tf2_keras_save_model.py, which creates, trains, and saves a Keras-based model, and then creates a new model that is populated with the data from the saved model.

**LISTING A.8: tf2_keras_save_model.py**

```python
import tensorflow as tf
import os
def create_model():
  model = tf.keras.models.Sequential([
    tf.keras.layers.Flatten(input_shape=(28, 28)),
    tf.keras.layers.Dense(512, activation=tf.nn.relu),
    tf.keras.layers.Dropout(0.2),
    tf.keras.layers.Dense(10, activation=tf.nn.softmax)
  ])

  model.compile(optimizer=tf.keras.optimizers.Adam(),
     loss=tf.keras.losses.sparse_categorical_crossentropy,
                metrics=['accuracy'])

  return model

# Create a basic model instance
model = create_model()
model.summary()

checkpoint_path = "checkpoint/cp.ckpt"
checkpoint_dir = os.path.dirname(checkpoint_path)

# Create checkpoint callback
cp_callback = tf.keras.callbacks.
ModelCheckpoint(checkpoint_path,
save_weights_only=True, verbose=1)

# => model #1: create the first model
model = create_model()

mnist = tf.keras.datasets.mnist
(X_train, y_train),(X_test, y_test) = mnist.load_data()

X_train, X_test = X_train / 255.0, X_test / 255.0
print("X_train.shape:",X_train.shape)

model.fit(X_train, y_train,  epochs = 2,
          validation_data = (X_test,y_test),
             callbacks = [cp_callback])  # pass callback to
training

# => model #2: create a new model and load saved model
model = create_model()
loss, acc = model.evaluate(X_test, y_test)
```

```
print("Untrainedmodel, accuracy: {:5.2f}%".format(100*acc))

model.load_weights(checkpoint_path)
loss,acc = model.evaluate(X_test, y_test)
print("Restored model, accuracy: {:5.2f}%".format(100*acc))
```

Listing A.8 starts with the `create_model()` Python function that creates and compiles a Keras-based model. The next portion of Listing A.8 defines the location of the file that will be saved as well as the checkpoint callback, as shown here:

```
checkpoint_path = "checkpoint/cp.ckpt"
checkpoint_dir = os.path.dirname(checkpoint_path)

# Create checkpoint callback
cp_callback = tf.keras.callbacks.
ModelCheckpoint(checkpoint_path,
save_weights_only=True, verbose=1)
```

The next portion of Listing A.8 trains the current model using the MNIST dataset, and also specifies `cp_callback` so that the model can be saved.

The final code block in Listing A.8 creates a new Keras-based model by invoking the Python method `create_model()` again, evaluating this new model on the test-related data, and displaying the value of the accuracy. Next, the model is loaded with the saved model weights via the `load_weights()` API. The relevant code block is reproduced here:

```
model = create_model()
loss, acc = model.evaluate(X_test, y_test)
print("Untrainedmodel, accuracy: {:5.2f}%".format(100*acc))

model.load_weights(checkpoint_path)
loss,acc = model.evaluate(X_test, y_test)
print("Restored model, accuracy: {:5.2f}%".format(100*acc))
```

Now launch the code in Listing A.8 to see the following output:

```
on_train_begin
Model: "sequential"
```

| Layer (type | Output Shape | Param # |
| --- | --- | --- |
| flatten (Flatten) | (None, 784) | 0 |
| dense (Dense) | (None, 512) | 401920 |

| dropout (Dropout) | (None, 512) | 0 |
|---|---|---|
| dense_1 (Dense) | (None, 10) | 5130 |

```
Total params: 407,050
Trainable params: 407,050
Non-trainable params: 0

Train on 60000 samples, validate on 10000 samples
Epoch 1/2
59840/60000 [===============>.] - ETA: 0s - loss: 0.2173 -
accuracy: 0.9351
Epoch 00001: saving model to checkpoint/cp.ckpt
60000/60000 [==================] - 10s 168us/sample - loss:
0.2170 - accuracy: 0.9352 - val_loss: 0.0980 - val_accu-
racy: 0.9696
Epoch 2/2
59936/60000 [===============>.] - ETA: 0s - loss: 0.0960 -
accuracy: 0.9707
Epoch 00002: saving model to checkpoint/cp.ckpt
60000/60000 [============] - 10s 174us/sample - loss:
0.0959 - accuracy: 0.9707 - val_loss: 0.0735 - val_accu-
racy: 0.9761
10000/10000 [==================] - 1s 86us/sample - loss:
2.3986 - accuracy: 0.0777
Untrained model, accuracy:  7.77%
10000/10000 [=============================] - 1s 67us/
sample - loss: 0.0735 - accuracy: 0.9761
Restored model, accuracy: 97.61%
```

Th directory where you launched this code sample contains a new subdirectory called checkpoint, whose contents are shown here:

```
-rw-r--r-- 1 owner  staff   1222 Aug 17 14:34 cp.ckpt.index
-rw-r--r-- 1 owner  staff  4886716 Aug 17 14:34 cp.ckpt.
data-00000-of-00001
-rw-r--r-- 1 owner  staff       71 Aug 17 14:34 checkpoint
```

## Summary

This appendix introduced you to some of the features of Keras and an assortment of Keras-based code samples involving basic neural networks with the MNIST and Cifar10 datasets. You learned about some of the important namespaces (such as `tf.keras.layers`) and their contents.

Next, you saw an example of performing linear regression with `Keras` and a simple CSV file. Then, you learned how to create a `Keras`-based MLP neural network that is trained on the MNIST dataset.

In addition, you saw examples of `Keras`-based models that perform early stopping, which is convenient when the model exhibits minimal improvement (that is specified by you) during the training process.

# INTRODUCTION TO *TF 2*

Welcome to TensorFlow 2! This chapter introduces you to various features of TensorFlow 2 (abbreviated as TF 2), as well as some of the TF 2 tools and projects that are covered under the TF 2 umbrella. This appendix includes TF 2 code samples that illustrate new TF 2 features (such as tf.GradientTape and the @tf.function decorator), plus code samples that show how to write code "the TF 2 way."

Despite the simplicity of many topics in this chapter, they provide you with a foundation for TF 2. You can think of this appendix appendix as your starting point for learning about T 2, in conjunction with the appendix that discusses Keras.

Keep in mind that the TensorFlow 1.x releases are considered legacy code after the production release of TF 2. Google will provide only security-related updates for TF 1.x (i.e., no new code development), and support TensorFlow 1.x for at least another year beyond the initial production release of TF 2. For your convenience, TensorFlow provides a conversion script to facilitate the automatic conversion of TensorFlow 1.x code to TF 2 code in many cases (details provided later in this chapter).

This appendix contains several sections regarding TF 1.x, all of which are placed near the end of this appendix. If you do not have TF 1.x code, these sections are optional (and they are labeled as such).

The first part of this appendix briefly discusses some TF 2 features and some of the tools that are included under the TF 2 umbrella. The second section of this appendix shows you how to write TF 2 code involving TF constants and TF variables.

The third section digresses a bit: you will learn about the new TF 2 Python function decorator @tf.function that is used in many code samples in this appendix. Although this decorator is not always required, it's important to become comfortable with this feature, and there are some non-intuitive caveats regarding its use that are discussed in this section.

The fourth section of this appendix shows you how to perform typical arithmetic operations in TF 2, how to use some of the built-in TF 2 functions, and how to calculate trigonometric values. If you need to perform scientific calculations, see the code samples that pertain to the type of precision that you can achieve with floating point numbers in TF 2. This section also shows you how to use for loops and how to calculate exponential values.

The fifth section contains TF 2 code samples involving arrays, such as creating an identity matrix, a constant matrix, a random uniform matrix, and a truncated normal matrix, along with an explanation about the difference between a truncated matrix and a random matrix. This section also shows you how to multiply $2^{nd}$ order tensors in TF 2 and how to convert Python arrays to $2^{nd}$ order tensors in TF 2. The sixth section contains code samples that illustrate how to use some of the new features of TF 2, such as tf.GradientTape.

Although the TF 2 code samples in this book use Python 3.x, it's possible to modify the code samples to run under Python 2.7. Also make note of the following convention in this book (and only this book): TF 1.x files have a "tf" prefix and TF 2 files have a "tf2" prefix.

With all that in mind, the next section discusses a few details of TF 2, its architecture, and some of its features.

## What is TF 2?

TF 2 is an open source framework from Google that is the newest version of TensorFlow. The TF 2 framework is a modern framework that's well-suited for machine learning (ML) and deep learning (DL), and it's available through an Apache license. Interestingly, TensorFlow surprised many people, perhaps even members of the TF team, in terms of the creativity and plethora of use cases for TF in areas such as art, music, and medicine. For a variety of reasons, the TensorFlow team created TF 2 with the goal of consolidating the TF APIs, eliminating duplication of APIs, enabling rapid prototyping, and making debugging an easier experience.

There is good news if you are a fan of Keras: improvements in TF 2 are partially due to the adoption of Keras as part of the core functionality of

TF 2. In fact, TF 2 extends and optimizes Keras so that it can take advantage of all the advanced features in TF 2.

If you work primarily with deep learning models (CNNs, RNNs, LSTMs, and so forth), you'll probably use some of the classes in the tf.keras namespace, which is the implementation of Keras in TF 2. Moreover, tf.keras.layers provides several standard layers for neural networks. As you'll see later, there are several ways to define Keras-based models, via the tf.keras.Sequential class, a functional style definition, and via a subclassing technique. Alternatively, you can still use lower-level operations and automatic differentiation if you wish to do so.

Furthermore, TF 2 removes duplicate functionality, provides a more intuitive syntax across APIs, and also compatibility throughout the TF 2 ecosystem. TF 2 even provides a backward compatibility module called tf.compat.v1 (which does not include tf.contrib), and a conversion script tf_upgrade_v2 to help users migrate from TF 1.x to TF 2.

Another significant change in TF 2 is eager execution as the default mode (not deferred execution), with new features such as the @tf.function decorator and TF 2 privacy-related features. Here is a condensed list of some TF 2 features and related technologies:

- support for tf.keras: a specification for high-level code for ML and DL
- tensorflow.js v1.0: TF in modern browsers
- TensorFlow Federated: an open source framework for ML and decentralized data
- Ragged Tensors: nested variable-length ("uneven") lists
- TensorFlow Probability: probabilistic models combined with deep learning
- Tensor2Tensor: a library of DL models and datasets

TF 2 also supports a variety of programming languages and hardware platforms, including

- Support for Python, Java, C++
- Desktop, server, mobile device (TF Lite)
- CPU/GPU/TPU support
- Linux and Mac OS X support
- VM for Windows

Navigate to the TF 2 home page, where you will find links to many resources for TF 2: *https://www.tensorflow.org*

## TF 2 Use Cases

TF 2 is designed to solve tasks that arise in a plethora of use cases, some of which are listed here:

- Image recognition
- Computer vision
- Voice/sound recognition
- Time series analysis
- Language detection
- Language translation
- Text-based processing
- Handwriting Recognition

The preceding list of use cases can be solved in TF 1.x as well as TF 2, and in the latter case, the code tends to be simpler and cleaner compared to their TF 1.x counterpart.

## TF 2 Architecture: The Short Version

TF 2 is written in C++ and supports operations involving primitive values and tensors (discussed later). The default execution mode for TF 1.x is *deferred execution* whereas TF 2 uses *eager execution* (think "immediate mode"). Although TF 1.4 introduced eager execution, the vast majority of TF 1.x code samples that you find online use deferred execution.

TF 2 supports arithmetic operations on tensors (i.e., multi-dimensional arrays with enhancements) as well as conditional logic, for loops, and while loops. Although it's possible to switch between eager execution mode and deferred mode in TF 2, all the code samples in this book use eager execution mode.

Data visualization is handled via TensorBoard (discussed in Chapter 2) that is included as part of TF 2. As you will see in the code samples in this book, TF 2 APIs are available in Python and can therefore be embedded in Python scripts.

Let's learn how to install TF 2, which is the topic of the next section.

## TF 2 Installation

Install TensorFlow by issuing the following command from the command line:

```
pip install tensorflow==2.0.0-beta1
```

When a production release of TF 2 is available, you can issue the following command from the command line (which will be the most current version of TF 2):

```
pip install --upgrade tensorflow
```

If you want to install a specific version (let's say version 1.13.1) of TensorFlow, type the following command:

```
pip install --upgrade tensorflow==1.13.1
```

You can also downgrade the installed version of TensorFlow. For example, if you have installed version 1.13.1 and you want to install version 1.10, specify the value 1.10 in the preceding code snippet. TensorFlow will uninstall your current version and install the version that you specified (i.e., 1.10).

As a sanity check, create a Python script with the following three lines of code to determine the version number of TF that is installed on your machine:

```
import tensorflow as tf
print("TF Version:",tf.__version__)
print("eager execution:",tf.executing_eagerly())
```

Launch the preceding code to see something similar to the following output:

```
TF version: 2.3.0
eager execution: True
```

As a simple example of TF 2 code, place this code snippet in a text file:

```
import tensorflow as tf
print("1 + 2 + 3 + 4 =", tf.reduce_sum([1, 2, 3, 4]))
```

Launch the preceding code from the command line to see the following output:

```
1 + 2 + 3 + 4 = tf.Tensor(10, shape=(), dtype=int32)
```

## TF 2 and the Python REPL

In case you aren't already familiar with the Python REPL (read-eval-print-loop), it's accessible by opening a command shell and then typing the following command:

```
python
```

As a simple illustration, access TF 2-related functionality in the REPL by importing the TF 2 library as follows:

```
>>> import tensorflow as tf
```

Now check the version of TF 2 that is installed on your machine with this command:

```
>>> print('TF version:',tf.__version__)
```

The output of the preceding code snippet is shown here (the number that you see depends on which version of TF 2 that you installed):

```
TF version: 2.0.0-beta1
```

Although the REPL is useful for short code blocks, the TF 2 code samples in this book are Python scripts that you can launch with the Python executable.

## Other TF 2-based Toolkits

In addition to providing support for TF 2-based code on multiple devices, TF 2 provides the following toolkits:

- TensorBoard for visualization (included as part of TensorFlow)
- TensorFlow Serving (hosting on a server)
- TensorFlow Hub
- TensorFlow Lite (for mobile applications)
- Tensorflow.js (for Web pages and NodeJS)

*TensorBoard* is a graph visualization tool that runs in a browser. Launch TensorBoard from the command line as follows: open a command shell and type the following command to access a saved TF graph in the subdirectory /tmp/abc (or a directory of your choice):

```
tensorboard -logdir /tmp/abc
```

Note that there are two consecutive dashes ("-") that precede the logdir parameter in the preceding command. Now launch a browser session and navigate to this URL: localhost:6006

After a few moments you will see a visualization of the TF 2 graph that was created in your code and then saved in the directory /tmp/abc.

*TensorFlow Serving* is a cloud-based flexible, high-performance serving system for ML models that is designed for production environments. TensorFlow Serving makes it easy to deploy new algorithms and experiments, while keeping the same server architecture and APIs. More information is here: *https://www.TF 2.org/serving/*

*TensorFlow Lite* was specifically created for mobile development (both Android and iOS). Please keep in mind that TensorFlow Lite supersedes TF 2 Mobile, which was an earlier SDK for developing mobile applications. TensorFlow Lite (which also exists for TF 1.x) supports on-device ML inference with low latency and a small binary size. Moreover, TensorFlow Lite supports hardware acceleration with the Android Neural Networks API. More information about TensorFlow Lite is here:

```
https://www.tensorflow.org/lite/
```

A more recent addition is `tensorflow.js`, which provides JavaScript APIs to access TensorFlow in a Web page. The `tensorflow.js` toolkit was previously called `deeplearning.js`. You can also use `tensorflow.js` with NodeJS. More information about `tensorflow.js` is here:

*https://js.tensorflow.org*

## TF 2 Eager Execution

TF 2 eager execution mode makes TF 2 code much easier to write compared to TF 1.x code (which used deferred execution mode). You might be surprised to discover that TF introduced eager execution as an alternative to deferred execution in version 1.4.1, but this feature was vastly underutilized. With TF 1.x code, TensorFlow creates a dataflow graph that consists of 1) a set of `tf.Operation` objects that represent units of computation and 2) `tf.Tensor` objects that represent the units of data that flow between operations.

TF 2 evaluates operations immediately without instantiating a session object or a creating a graph. Operations return concrete values instead of creating a computational graph. TF 2 eager execution is based on the Python control flow instead of graph control flow. Arithmetic operations are simpler and intuitive, as you will see in code samples later in this chapter. Moreover, TF 2 eager execution mode simplifies the debugging process. However, keep in mind that there isn't a 1:1 relationship between a graph and eager execution.

## TF 2 Tensors, Data Types, and Primitive Types

In simplified terms, a TF 2 tensor is an n-dimensional array that is similar to a `NumPy ndarray`. A TF 2 tensor is defined by its dimensionality, as illustrated here:

```
scalar number:      a zeroth-order tensor
vector:             a first-order tensor
```

```
matrix:              a second-order tensor
3-dimensional array: a 3rd order tensor
```

The next section discusses some of the data types that are available in TF 2, followed by a section that discusses TF 2 primitive types.

## TF 2 Data Types

TF 2 supports the following data types (similar to the supported data types in TensorFlow 1.x):

- `tf.float32`
- `tf.float64`
- `tf.int8`
- `tf.int16`
- `tf.int32`
- `tf.int64`
- `tf.uint8`
- `tf.string`
- `tf.bool`

The data types in the preceding list are self-explanatory: two floating point types, four integer types, one unsigned integer type, one string type, and one Boolean type. As you can see, there is a 32-bit and a 64-bit floating point type, and integer types that range from 8-bit through 64-bit.

## TF 2 Primitive Types

TF 2 supports `tf.constant()` and `tf.Variable()` as primitive types. Notice the capital "V" in `tf.Variable()`: this indicates a TF 2 class (which is not the case for a lowercase initial letter, such as `tf.constant()`).

A TF 2 *constant* is an immutable value, and a simple example is shown here:

```
aconst = tf.constant(3.0)
```

A TF 2 *variable* is a trainable value in a TF 2 graph. For example, the slope m and y-intercept b of a best-fitting line for a dataset consisting of points in the Euclidean plane are two examples of trainable values. Some examples of TF variables are shown here:

```
b = tf.Variable(3, name="b")
x = tf.Variable(2, name="x")
z = tf.Variable(5*x, name="z")
```

```
W = tf.Variable(20)
lm = tf.Variable(W*x + b, name="lm")
```

Notice that b, x, and z are defined as TF variables. In addition, b and x are initialized with numeric values, whereas the value of the variable z is an expression that depends on the value of x (which equals 2).

## Constants in TF 2

Here is a short list of some properties of TF 2 constants:

- initialized during their definition
- cannot change their value ("immutable")
- can specify their name (optional)
- the type is required (ex: tf.float32)
- are not modified during training

Listing B.1 shows the content of tf2_constants1.py, which illustrates how to assign and print the values of some TF 2 constants.

### LISTING B.1: tf2_constants1.py

```
import tensorflow as tf

scalar = tf.constant(10)
vector = tf.constant([1,2,3,4,5])
matrix = tf.constant([[1,2,3],[4,5,6]])
cube   =
tf.constant([[[1],[2],[3]],[[4],[5],[6]],[[7],[8],[9]]])

print(scalar.get_shape())
print(vector.get_shape())
print(matrix.get_shape())
print(cube.get_shape())
```

Listing B.1 contains four tf.constant() statements that define TF 2 tensors of dimension 0, 1, 2, and 3, respectively. The second part of Listing B.1 contains four print() statements that display the shape of the four TF 2 constants that are defined in the first section of Listing B.1. The output from Listing B.1 is here:

```
()
(5,)
(2, 3)
(3, 3, 1)
```

Listing B.2 shows the content of `tf2_constants2.py`, which illustrates how to assign values to TF 2 constants and then print those values.

### LISTING B.2: tf2_constants2.py

```
import tensorflow as tf

x = tf.constant(5,name="x")
y = tf.constant(8,name="y")

@tf.function
def calc_prod(x, y):
  z = 2*x + 3*y
  return z

result = calc_prod(x, y)
print('result =',result)
```

Listing B.2 defines a decorated (shown in bold) Python function `calc_prod()` with TF 2 code that would otherwise be included in a TF 1.x `tf.Session()` code block. Specifically, z would be included in a `sess.run()` statement, along with a `feed_dict` that provides values for x and y. Fortunately, a decorated Python function in TF 2 makes the code look like normal Python code.

## Variables in TF 2

TF 2.0 eliminates global collections and their associated APIs, such as `tf.get_variable`, `tf.variable_scope`, and `tf.initializers.global_variables`. Whenever you need a `tf.Variable` in TF 2, construct and initialize it directly, as shown here:

```
tf.Variable(tf.random.normal([2, 4])
```

Listing B.3 shows the content of `tf2_variables.py`, which illustrates how to compute values involving TF constants and variables in a `with` code block.

### LISTING B.3: tf2_variables.py

```
import tensorflow as tf

v = tf.Variable([[1., 2., 3.], [4., 5., 6.]])
print("v.value():", v.value())
print("")
```

```
print("v.numpy():", v.numpy())
print("")

v.assign(2 * v)
v[0, 1].assign(42)
v[1].assign([7., 8., 9.])
print("v:",v)
print("")

try:
  v[1] = [7., 8., 9.]
except TypeError as ex:
  print(ex)
```

Listing B.3 defines a TF 2 variable v and prints its value. The next portion of Listing B.3 updates the value of v and prints its new value. The last portion of Listing B.3 contains a try/except block that attempts to update the value of v[1]. The output from Listing B.3 is here:

```
v.value(): tf.Tensor(
[[1. 2. 3.]
 [4. 5. 6.]], shape=(2, 3), dtype=float32)

v.numpy(): [[1. 2. 3.]
 [4. 5. 6.]]

v: <tf.Variable 'Variable:0' shape=(2, 3) dtype=float32,
numpy=
array([[ 2., 42.,  6.],
       [ 7.,  8.,  9.]], dtype=float32)>

'ResourceVariable' object does not support item assignment
```

This concludes the quick tour involving TF 2 code that contains various combinations of TF constants and TF variables. The next few sections delve into more details regarding the TF primitive types that you saw in the preceding sections.

## The tf.rank() API

The *rank* of a TF 2 tensor is the dimensionality of the tensor, whereas the *shape* of a tensor is the number of elements in each dimension. Listing B.4 shows the content of tf2_rank.py, which illustrates how to find the rank of TF 2 tensors.

**LISTING B.4: tf2_rank.py**

```
import tensorflow as tf # tf2_rank.py

A = tf.constant(3.0)
B = tf.fill([2,3], 5.0)
C = tf.constant([3.0, 4.0])

@tf.function
def show_rank(x):
  return tf.rank(x)

print('A:',show_rank(A))
print('B:',show_rank(B))
print('C:',show_rank(C))
```

Listing B.4 contains familiar code for defining the TF constant A, followed by the TF tensor B, which is a 2x3 tensor in which every element has the value 5. The TF tensor C is a 1x2 tensor with the values 3.0 and 4.0.

The next code block defines the decorated Python function show_rank() that returns the rank of its input variable. The final section invokes show_rank() with A and then with B. The output from Listing B.4 is here:

```
A: tf.Tensor(0, shape=(), dtype=int32)
B: tf.Tensor(2, shape=(), dtype=int32)
C: tf.Tensor(1, shape=(), dtype=int32)
```

# The tf.shape() API

The *shape* of a TF 2 tensor is the number of elements in each dimension of a given tensor.

Listing B.5 shows the content of tf2_getshape.py, which illustrates how to find the shape of TF 2 tensors.

**LISTING B.5: tf2_getshape.py**

```
import tensorflow as tf

a = tf.constant(3.0)
print("a shape:",a.get_shape())

b = tf.fill([2,3], 5.0)
print("b shape:",b.get_shape())
```

```
c = tf.constant([[1.0,2.0,3.0], [4.0,5.0,6.0]])
print("c shape:",c.get_shape())
```

Listing B.5 contains the definition of the TF constant a whose value is 3.0. Next, the TF variable b is initialized as a 1x2 vector with the values [[2,3], 5.0], followed by the constant c, whose values are [[1.0,2.0,3.0],[4.0,5.0,6.0]]. The three print() statements display the values of a, b, and c. The output from Listing B.5 is here:

```
a shape: ()
b shape: (2, 3)
c shape: (2, 3)
```

Shapes that specify a 0-D Tensor (scalar) are numbers (9, -5, 2.34, and so forth), [], and (). As another example, Listing B.6 shows the content of tf2_shapes.py, which contains an assortment of tensors and their shapes.

### LISTING B.6: tf2_shapes.py

```
import tensorflow as tf

list_0 = []
tuple_0 = ()
print("list_0:",list_0)
print("tuple_0:",tuple_0)

list_1 = [3]
tuple_1 = (3)
print("list_1:",list_1)
print("tuple_1:",tuple_1)

list_2 = [3, 7]
tuple_2 = (3, 7)
print("list_2:",list_2)
print("tuple_2:",tuple_2)

any_list1 = [None]
any_tuple1 = (None)
print("any_list1:",any_list1)
print("any_tuple1:",any_tuple1)

any_list2 = [7,None]
any_list3 = [7,None,None]
print("any_list2:",any_list2)
print("any_list3:",any_list3)
```

Listing B.6 contains simple lists and tuples of various dimensions to illustrate the difference between these two types. The output from Listing B.6 is probably what you would expect, and it's shown here:

```
list_0: []
tuple_0: ()
list_1: [3]
tuple_1: 3
list_2: [3, 7]
tuple_2: (3, 7)
any_list1: [None]
any_tuple1: None
any_list2: [7, None]
any_list3: [7, None, None]
```

## Variables in TF 2 (Revisited)

TF 2 variables can be updated during backward error propagation. TF 2 variables can also be saved and then restored at a later point in time. The following list contains some properties of TF 2 variables:

- initial value is optional
- must be initialized before graph execution
- updated during training
- constantly recomputed
- they hold values for weights and biases
- in-memory buffer (saved/restored from disk)

Here are some simple examples of TF 2 variables:

```
b = tf.Variable(3, name='b')
x = tf.Variable(2, name='x')
z = tf.Variable(5*x, name="z")

W = tf.Variable(20)
lm = tf.Variable(W*x + b, name="lm")
```

Notice that the variables b, x, and W specify constant values, whereas the variables z and lm specify expressions that are defined in terms of other variables. If you are familiar with linear regression, you undoubtedly noticed that the variable lm (linear model) defines a line in the Euclidean plane. Other properties of TF 2 variables are listed below:

- a tensor that's updateable via operations
- exist outside the context of session.run

- like a "regular" variable
- holds the learned model parameters
- variables can be shared (or non-trainable)
- used for storing/maintaining state
- internally stores a persistent tensor
- you can read/modify the values of the tensor
- multiple workers see the same values for `tf.Variables`
- the best way to represent shared, persistent state manipulated by your program

TF 2 also provides the method `tf.assign()` to modify values of TF 2 variables; be sure to read the relevant code sample later in this chapter so that you learn how to use this API correctly.

### TF 2 Variables versus Tensors

Keep in mind the following distinction between TF variables and TF tensors: TF *variables* represent your model's trainable parameters (ex: weights and biases of a neural network), whereas TF *tensors* represents the data fed into your model and the intermediate representations of that data as it passes through your model.

In the next section, you will learn about the `@tf.function` "decorator" for Python functions and how it can improve performance.

## What is `@tf.function` in TF 2?

TF 2 introduced the `@tf.function` "decorator" for Python functions that defines a graph and performs session execution: it's sort of a successor to `tf.Session()` in TF 1.x. Since graphs can still be useful, `@tf.function` transparently converts Python functions into functions that are backed by graphs. This decorator also converts tensor-dependent Python control flow into the TF control flow and also adds control dependencies to order read and write operations to the TF 2 state. Remember that `@tf.function` works best with TF 2 operations instead of NumPy operations or Python primitives.

In general, you won't need to decorate functions with `@tf.function`; use it to decorate high-level computations, such as one step of training or the forward pass of a model.

Although TF 2 eager execution mode facilitates a more intuitive user interface, this ease-of-use can be at the expense of the performance (the performance decreases). Fortunately, the `@tf.function` decorator is a technique for generating graphs in TF 2 code that execute more quickly than eager execution mode.

The performance benefit depends on the type of operations that are performed: matrix multiplication does not benefit from the use of `@tf.function`, whereas optimizing a deep neural network can benefit from `@tf.function`.

## How Does `@tf.function` Work?

Whenever you decorate a Python function with `@tf.function`, TF 2 automatically builds the function in graph mode. If a Python function that is decorated with `@tf.function` invokes other Python functions that are not decorated with `@tf.function`, then the code in those "non-decorated" Python functions is also included in the generated graph.

Another point to keep in mind is that a `tf.Variable` in eager mode is actually a "plain" Python object: this object is destroyed when it's out of scope. A `tf.Variable` object defines a persistent object if the function is decorated via `@tf.function`. In this scenario, eager mode is disabled and the `tf.Variable` object defines a node in a persistent TF 2 graph. Consequently, a function that works in eager mode without annotation can fail when it is decorated with `@tf.function`.

## A Caveat about `@tf.function` in TF 2

If constants are defined *before* the definition of a decorated Python function, you can print their values inside the function using the Python `print()` function. If constants are defined *inside* the definition of a decorated Python function, you can print their values inside the function using the TF 2 `tf.print()` function. Consider this code block:

```
import tensorflow as tf

a = tf.add(4, 2)

@tf.function
def compute_values():
  print(a) # 6

compute_values()
```

```
# output:
# tf.Tensor(6, shape=(), dtype=int32)
```

The correct result is displayed (shown in bold). However, if you define constants *inside* a decorated Python function, the output contains types and attributes but *not* the execution of the addition operation. Consider the following code block:

```
import tensorflow as tf

@tf.function
def compute_values():
  a = tf.add(4, 2)
  print(a)

compute_values()
```

```
# output:
# Tensor("Add:0", shape=(), dtype=int32)
```

The zero in the preceding output is part of the tensor name and not an outputted value. Specifically, Add:0 is output zero of the tf.add() operation. Any additional invocation of compute_values() prints nothing. If you want actual results, one solution is to return a value from the function, as shown here:

```
import tensorflow as tf

@tf.function
def compute_values():
  a = tf.add(4, 2)
  return a

result = compute_values()
print("result:", result)
```

The output from the preceding code block is here:

```
result: tf.Tensor(6, shape=(), dtype=int32)
```

A second solution involves the TF tf.print() function instead of the Python print() function, as shown in bold in this code block:

```
@tf.function
def compute_values():
  a = tf.add(4, 2)
  tf.print(a)
```

A third solution is to cast the numeric values to Tensors if they do not affect the shape of the generated graph, as shown here:

```
import tensorflow as tf

@tf.function
def compute_values():
  a = tf.add(tf.constant(4), tf.constant(2))
  return a

result = compute_values()
print("result:", result)
```

### The tf.print() Function and Standard Error

There is one more detail to remember: the Python print() function sends output to the standard output that is associated with a file descriptor whose value is 1; on the other hand, tf.print() sends output to the standard error that is associated with a file descriptor whose value is 2. In programming languages such as C, only errors are sent to the standard error, so keep in mind that the behavior of tf.print() differs from the convention regarding standard out and standard error. The following code snippets illustrate this difference:

```
python3 file_with_print.py    1>print_output
python3 file_with_tf.print.py 2>tf.print_output
```

If your Python file contains both print() and tf.print(), you can capture the output as follows:

```
python3 both_prints.py 1>print_output 2>tf.print_output
```

However, keep in mind that the preceding code snippet might also redirect *real* error messages to the file tf.print_output.

## Working with With @tf.function in TF 2

The preceding section explained how the output differs depending on whether you use the Python print() function or the tf.print() function in TF 2 code, where the latter function also sends output to the standard error instead of the standard output.

This section contains several examples of the @tf.function decorator in TF 2 to show you some nuances in behavior that depend on where you define constants and whether you use the tf.print() function or the

Python print() function. Also keep in mind the comments in the previous section regarding @tf.function, as well as the fact that you don't need to use @tf.function in all your Python functions.

## An Example Without @tf.function

Listing B.7 shows the content of tf2_simple_function.py, which illustrates how to define a Python function with TF 2 code.

*LISTING B.7: tf2_simple_function.py*

```
import tensorflow as tf

def func():
    a = tf.constant([[10,10],[11.,1.]])
    b = tf.constant([[1.,0.],[0.,1.]])
    c = tf.matmul(a, b)
    return c

print(func().numpy())
```

The code in Listing B.7 is straightforward: a Python function func() defines two TF 2 constants, computes their product, and returns that value.

Since TF 2 works in eager mode by default, the Python function func() is treated as a "normal" function. Launch the code to see the following output:

```
[[20. 30.]
 [22. 3.]]
```

## An Example With @tf.function

Listing B.8 shows the content of tf2_at_function.py, which illustrates how to define a decorated Python function with TF code.

*LISTING B.8: tf2_at_function.py*

```
import tensorflow as tf

@tf.function
def func():
    a = tf.constant([[10,10],[11.,1.]])
    b = tf.constant([[1.,0.],[0.,1.]])
```

```
  c = tf.matmul(a, b)
  return c
print(func().numpy())
```

Listing B.8 defines a decorated Python function: the rest of the code is identical to Listing B.7. However, because of the `@tf.function` annotation, the Python `func()` function is wrapped in a `tensorflow.python.eager.def_function.Function` object. The Python function is assigned to the `.python_function` property of the object.

When `func()` is invoked, the graph construction begins. Only the Python code is executed, and the behavior of the function is traced so that TF 2 can collect the required data to construct the graph. The output is shown here:

```
[[20. 30.]
 [22.  3.]]
```

## Overloading Functions With `@tf.function`

If you have worked with programming languages such as Java and C++, you are already familiar with the concept of *overloading* a function. If this term is new to you, the idea is simple: an *overloaded function* is a function that can be invoked with different data types. For example, you can define an overloaded "add" function that can add two numbers as well as "add" (i.e., concatenate) two strings.

If you're curious, overloaded functions in various programming languages are implemented via *name mangling*, which means that the signature (the parameters and their data types for the function) are appended to the function name to generate a unique function name. (This happens "under the hood," which means that you don't need to worry about the implementation details.)

Listing B.9 shows the content of `tf2_overload.py`, which illustrates how to define a decorated Python function that can be invoked with different data types.

### LISTING B.9: *tf2_overload.py*

```
import tensorflow as tf

@tf.function
def add(a):
  return a + a
```

```
print("Add 1:            ", add(1))
print("Add 2.3:          ", add(2.3))
print("Add string tensor:", add(tf.constant("abc")))

c   =   add.get_concrete_function(tf.TensorSpec(shape=None,
dtype=tf.string))
c(a=tf.constant("a"))
```

Listing B.9 defines a decorated Python function add() that is preceded by a @tf.function decorator. This function can be invoked by passing an integer, a decimal value, or a TF 2 tensor, and the correct result is calculated. Launch the code to see the following output:

```
Add 1:     tf.Tensor(2, shape=(), dtype=int32)
Add 2.3:   tf.Tensor(4.6, shape=(), dtype=float32)
Add string tensor:  tf.Tensor(b'abcabc', shape=(),
                     dtype=string)
c:  <tensorflow.python.eager.function.ConcreteFunction
    object at 0x1209576a0>
```

## What is AutoGraph in TF 2?

AutoGraph refers to the conversion from Python code to its graph representation, which is a significant new feature in TF 2. AutoGraph is automatically applied to functions that are decorated with @tf.function; this decorator creates callable graphs from Python functions.

AutoGraph transforms a subset of Python syntax into its portable, high-performance and language agnostic graph representation, thereby bridging the gap between TF 1.x and TF 2.0. In fact, autograph allows you to inspect its auto-generated code with this code snippet. For example, if you define a Python function called my_product(), you can inspect its auto-generated code with this snippet:

```
print(tf.autograph.to_code(my_product))
```

In particular, the Python for/while construct in implemented in TF 2 via tf.while_loop (break and continue are also supported). The Python if construct is implemented in TF 2 via tf.cond. The "for _ in dataset" is implemented in TF 2 via dataset.reduce.

AutoGraph also has some rules for converting loops. A for loop is converted if the iterable in the loop is a Tensor, and a while loop is converted if the while condition depends on a Tensor. If a loop is converted, it is dynamically unrolled with tf.while_loop, as well as the special case of a for x in tf.data.Dataset (the latter is transformed into tf.data. Dataset.reduce). If a loop is not converted, it is statically unrolled.

AutoGraph supports the control flow that is nested arbitrarily deep, so you can implement many types of ML programs.

## Arithmetic Operations in TF 2

Listing B.10 shows the content of tf2_arithmetic.py, which illustrates how to perform arithmetic operations in a TF 2.

### LISTING B.10: tf2_arithmetic.py

```
import tensorflow as tf

@tf.function # replace print() with tf.print()
def compute_values():
  a = tf.add(4, 2)
  b = tf.subtract(8, 6)
  c = tf.multiply(a, 3)
  d = tf.math.divide(a, 6)

  print(a) # 6
  print(b) # 2
  print(c) # 18
  print(d) # 1

compute_values()
```

Listing B.10 defines the decorated Python function compute_values() with simple code for computing the sum, difference, product, and quotient of two numbers via the tf.add(), tf.subtract(), tf.multiply(), and the tf.math.divide() APIs, respectively. The four print() statements display the values of a, b, c, and d. The output from Listing B.10 is here:

```
tf.Tensor(6,   shape=(), dtype=int32)
tf.Tensor(2,   shape=(), dtype=int32)
tf.Tensor(18,  shape=(), dtype=int32)
tf.Tensor(1.0, shape=(), dtype=float64)
```

## Caveats for Arithmetic Operations in TF 2

You can also perform arithmetic operations involving TF 2 constants and variables. Listing B.11 shows the content of tf2_const_var.py, which illustrates how to perform arithmetic operations involving a TF 2 constant and a variable.

***LISTING B.11: tf2_const_var.py***

```
import tensorflow as tf

v1 = tf.Variable([4.0, 4.0])
c1 = tf.constant([1.0, 2.0])

diff = tf.subtract(v1,c1)
print("diff:",diff)
```

Listing B.11 computes the difference of the TF variable v1 and the TF constant c1, and the output is shown here:

```
diff: tf.Tensor([3. 2.], shape=(2,), dtype=float32)
```

However, if you update the value of v1 and then print the value of diff, it will *not* change. You must reset the value of diff, just as you would in other imperative programming languages.

Listing B.12 shows the content of tf2_const_var2.py, which illustrates how to perform arithmetic operations involving a TF 2 constant and a variable.

***LISTING B.12: tf2_const_var2.py***

```
import tensorflow as tf

v1 = tf.Variable([4.0, 4.0])
c1 = tf.constant([1.0, 2.0])

diff = tf.subtract(v1,c1)
print("diff1:",diff.numpy())

# diff is NOT updated:
v1.assign([10.0, 20.0])
print("diff2:",diff.numpy())

# diff is updated correctly:
diff = tf.subtract(v1,c1)
print("diff3:",diff.numpy())
```

Listing B.12 re-computes the value of diff in the final portion of Listing B.11, after which it has the correct value. The output is shown here:

```
diff1: [3. 2.]
diff2: [3. 2.]
diff3: [9. 18.]
```

## TF 2 and Built-in Functions

Listing B.13 shows the content of tf2_math_ops.py, which illustrates how to perform additional arithmetic operations in a TF graph.

*LISTING B.13: tf2_math_ops.py*

```
import tensorflow as tf

PI = 3.141592

@tf.function # replace print() with tf.print()
def math_values():
  print(tf.math.divide(12,8))
  print(tf.math.floordiv(20.0,8.0))
  print(tf.sin(PI))
  print(tf.cos(PI))
  print(tf.math.divide(tf.sin(PI/4.), tf.cos(PI/4.)))

math_values()
```

Listing B.13 contains a hard-coded approximation for PI, followed by the decorated Python function math_values() with five print() statements that display various arithmetic results. Note in particular the third output value is a very small number (the correct value is zero). The output from Listing B.13 is here:

```
1.5
tf.Tensor(2.0,            shape=(), dtype=float32)
tf.Tensor(6.2783295e-07,  shape=(), dtype=float32)
tf.Tensor(-1.0,           shape=(), dtype=float32)
tf.Tensor(0.99999964,     shape=(), dtype=float32)
```

Listing B.14 shows the content of tf2_math-ops_pi.py, which illustrates how to perform arithmetic operations in TF 2.

*LISTING B.14: tf2_math_ops_pi.py*

```
import tensorflow as tf
import math as m

PI = tf.constant(m.pi)

@tf.function # replace print() with tf.print()
def math_values():
  print(tf.math.divide(12,8))
```

```
print(tf.math.floordiv(20.0,8.0))
print(tf.sin(PI))
print(tf.cos(PI))
print(tf.math.divide(tf.sin(PI/4.), tf.cos(PI/4.)))

math_values()
```

Listing B.14 is almost identical to the code in Listing B.13: the only difference is that Listing B.14 specifies a hard-coded value for PI, whereas Listing B.14 assigns m.pi to the value of PI. As a result, the approximated value is one decimal place closer to the correct value of zero. The output from Listing B.14 is here. Notice how the output format differs from Listing B.13 due to the Python print() function:

```
1.5
tf.Tensor(2.0,          shape=(), dtype=float32)
tf.Tensor(-8.742278e-08, shape=(), dtype=float32)
tf.Tensor(-1.0,          shape=(), dtype=float32)
tf.Tensor(1.0,           shape=(), dtype=float32)
```

## Calculating Trigonometric Values in TF 2

Listing B.15 shows the content of tf2_trig_values.py, which illustrates how to compute values involving trigonometric functions in TF 2.

### LISTING B.15: tf2_trig_values.py

```
import tensorflow as tf
import math as m

PI = tf.constant(m.pi)

a = tf.cos(PI/3.)
b = tf.sin(PI/3.)
c = 1.0/a # sec(60)
d = 1.0/tf.tan(PI/3.) # cot(60)

@tf.function # this decorator is okay
def math_values():
  print("a:",a)
  print("b:",b)
  print("c:",c)
  print("d:",d)

math_values()
```

Listing B.14 is straightforward: there are several of the same TF 2 APIs that you saw in Listing B.13. In addition, Listing B.14 contains the tf.tan() API, which computes the tangent of a number (in radians). The output from Listing B.14 is here:

```
a: tf.Tensor(0.49999997, shape=(), dtype=float32)
b: tf.Tensor(0.86602545, shape=(), dtype=float32)
c: tf.Tensor(2.0000002,  shape=(), dtype=float32)
d: tf.Tensor(0.57735026, shape=(), dtype=float32)
```

## Calculating Exponential Values in TF 2

Listing B.15 shows the content of tf2_exp_values.py, which illustrates how to compute values involving additional trigonometric functions in TF 2.

### LISTING B.15: tf2_exp_values.py

```
import tensorflow as tf

a  = tf.exp(1.0)
b  = tf.exp(-2.0)
s1 = tf.sigmoid(2.0)
s2 = 1.0/(1.0 + b)
t2 = tf.tanh(2.0)

@tf.function # this decorator is okay
def math_values():
  print('a: ', a)
  print('b: ', b)
  print('s1:', s1)
  print('s2:', s2)
  print('t2:', t2)

math_values()
```

Listing B.15 starts with the TF 2 APIs tf.exp(), tf.sigmoid(), and tf.tanh() that compute the exponential value of a number, the sigmoid value of a number, and the hyperbolic tangent of a number, respectively. The output from Listing B.15 is here:

```
a:  tf.Tensor(2.7182817,  shape=(), dtype=float32)
b:  tf.Tensor(0.13533528, shape=(), dtype=float32)
s1: tf.Tensor(0.880797,   shape=(), dtype=float32)
s2: tf.Tensor(0.880797,   shape=(), dtype=float32)
t2: tf.Tensor(0.9640276,  shape=(), dtype=float32)
```

## Working with Strings in TF 2

Listing B.16 shows the content of tf2_strings.py, which illustrates how to work with strings in TF 2.

***LISTING B.16: tf2_strings.py***

```
import tensorflow as tf

x1 = tf.constant("cafã")
print("x1:",x1)
tf.strings.length(x1)
print("")

len1 = tf.strings.length(x1, unit="UTF8_CHAR")
len2 = tf.strings.unicode_decode(x1, "UTF8")

print("len1:",len1.numpy())
print("len2:",len2.numpy())
print("")

# String arrays
x2 = tf.constant(["Cafã", "Coffee", "caffè", "咖啡"])
print("x2:",x2)
print("")

len3 = tf.strings.length(x2, unit="UTF8_CHAR")
print("len2:",len3.numpy())
print("")

r = tf.strings.unicode_decode(x2, "UTF8")
print("r:",r)
```

Listing B.16 defines the TF 2 constant x1 as a string that contains an accent mark. The first print() statement displays the first three characters of x1, followed by a pair of hexadecimal values that represent the accented "e" character. The second and third print() statements display the number of characters in x1, followed by the UTF8 sequence for the string x1.

The next portion of Listing B.16 defines the TF 2 constant x2 as a 1st order TF 2 tensor that contains four strings. The next print() statement displays the contents of x2, using UTF8 values for characters that contain accent marks.

The final portion of Listing B.16 defines r as the Unicode values for the characters in the string x2. The output from Listing B.14 is here:

```
x1: tf.Tensor(b'caf\xc3\xa9', shape=(), dtype=string)
```

```
len1: 4
len2: [ 99  97 102 233]

x2:  tf.Tensor([b'Caf\xc3\xa9'  b'Coffee'  b'caff\xc3\xa8'
b'\xe5\x92\x96\xe5\x95\xa1'], shape=(4,), dtype=string)

len2: [4 6 5 2]

r: <tf.RaggedTensor [[67, 97, 102, 233], [67, 111, 102,
102, 101, 101], [99, 97, 102, 102, 232], [21654, 21857]]>
```

Chapter 2 contains a complete code sample with more examples of a RaggedTensor in TF 2.

## Working with Tensors and Operations in TF 2

Listing B.17 shows the content of tf2_tensors_operations.py, which illustrates how to use various operators with tensors in TF 2.

### LISTING B.17: tf2_tensors_operations.py

```
import tensorflow as tf

x = tf.constant([[1., 2., 3.], [4., 5., 6.]])

print("x:", x)
print("")
print("x.shape:", x.shape)
print("")
print("x.dtype:", x.dtype)
print("")
print("x[:, 1:]:", x[:, 1:])
print("")
print("x[..., 1, tf.newaxis]:", x[..., 1, tf.newaxis])
print("")
print("x + 10:", x + 10)
print("")
print("tf.square(x):", tf.square(x))
print("")
print("x @ tf.transpose(x):", x @ tf.transpose(x))

m1 = tf.constant([[1., 2., 4.], [3., 6., 12.]])
print("m1:                ", m1 + 50)
print("m1 + 50:           ", m1 + 50)
```

```
print("m1 * 2:              ", m1 * 2)
print("tf.square(m1):    ", tf.square(m1))
```

Listing B.17 defines the TF tensor x that contains a 2x3 array of real numbers. The bulk of the code in Listing B.17 illustrates how to display properties of x by invoking x.shape and x.dtype, as well as the TF function tf.square(x). The output from Listing B.17 is here:

```
x: tf.Tensor(
[[1. 2. 3.]
 [4. 5. 6.]], shape=(2, 3), dtype=float32)

x.shape: (2, 3)

x.dtype: <dtype: 'float32'>

x[:, 1:]: tf.Tensor(
[[2. 3.]
 [5. 6.]], shape=(2, 2), dtype=float32)

x[..., 1, tf.newaxis]: tf.Tensor(
[[2.]
 [5.]], shape=(2, 1), dtype=float32)

x + 10: tf.Tensor(
[[11. 12. 13.]
 [14. 15. 16.]], shape=(2, 3), dtype=float32)

tf.square(x): tf.Tensor(
[[ 1.  4.  9.]
 [16. 25. 36.]], shape=(2, 3), dtype=float32)

x @ tf.transpose(x): tf.Tensor(
[[14. 32.]
 [32. 77.]], shape=(2, 2), dtype=float32)

m1:              tf.Tensor(
[[51. 52. 54.]
 [53. 56. 62.]], shape=(2, 3), dtype=float32)

m1 + 50:          tf.Tensor(
[[51. 52. 54.]
 [53. 56. 62.]], shape=(2, 3), dtype=float32)

m1 * 2:          tf.Tensor(
[[ 2.  4.  8.]
 [ 6. 12. 24.]], shape=(2, 3), dtype=float32)
```

```
tf.square(m1):      tf.Tensor(
[[  1.   4.  16.]
 [  9.  36. 144.]], shape=(2, 3), dtype=float32)
```

## 2nd Order Tensors in TF 2 (1)

Listing B.18 shows the content of tf2_elem2.py, which illustrates how to define a 2nd order TF tensor and access elements in that tensor.

### LISTING B.18: tf2_elem2.py

```
import tensorflow as tf

arr2 = tf.constant([[1,2],[2,3]])

@tf.function
def compute_values():
  print('arr2: ',arr2)
  print('[0]:  ',arr2[0])
  print('[1]:  ',arr2[1])

compute_values()
```

Listing B.18 contains the TF constant arr1 that is initialized with the values [[1,2],[2,3]]. The three print() statements display the value of arr1, the value of the element whose index is 1, and the value of the element whose index is [1,1]. The output from Listing B.18 is here:

```
arr2:    tf.Tensor(
[[1 2]
 [2 3]], shape=(2, 2), dtype=int32)
[0]:    tf.Tensor([1 2], shape=(2,), dtype=int32)
[1]:    tf.Tensor([2 3], shape=(2,), dtype=int32)
```

## 2nd Order Tensors in TF 2 (2)

Listing B.19 shows the content of tf2_elem3.py, which illustrates how to define a 2nd order TF 2 tensor and access elements in that tensor.

### LISTING B.19: tf2_elem3.py

```
import tensorflow as tf

arr3 = tf.constant([[[1,2],[2,3]],[[3,4],[5,6]]])
```

```
@tf.function # replace print() with tf.print()
def compute_values():
  print('arr3:    ',arr3)
  print('[1]:     ',arr3[1])
  print('[1,1]:   ',arr3[1,1])
  print('[1,1,0]:',arr3[1,1,0])

compute_values()
```

Listing B.19 contains the TF constant `arr3` that is initialized with the values `[[[1,2],[2,3]],[[3,4],[5,6]]]`. The four `print()` statements display the value of `arr3`, the value of the element whose index is 1, the value of the element whose index is `[1,1]`, and the value of the element whose index is `[1,1,0]`. The output from Listing B.19 (adjusted slightly for display purposes) is here:

```
arr3:     tf.Tensor(
[[[1 2]
  [2 3]]

 [[3 4]
  [5 6]]], shape=(2, 2, 2), dtype=int32)
[1]:      tf.Tensor(
[[3 4]
 [5 6]], shape=(2, 2), dtype=int32)
[1,1]:    tf.Tensor([5 6], shape=(2,), dtype=int32)
[1,1,0]: tf.Tensor(5, shape=(), dtype=int32)
```

## Multiplying Two 2nd Order Tensors in TF

Listing B.20 shows the content of `tf2_mult.py`, which illustrates how to multiply 2nd order tensors in TF 2.

### LISTING B.20: tf2_mult.py

```
import tensorflow as tf

m1 = tf.constant([[3., 3.]])    # 1x2
m2 = tf.constant([[2.],[2.]])   # 2x1
p1 = tf.matmul(m1, m2)          # 1x1

@tf.function
def compute_values():
  print('m1:',m1)
```

```
    print('m2:',m2)
    print('p1:',p1)
```

```
compute_values()
```

Listing B.20 contains two TF constant m1 and m2 that are initialized with the values [[3., 3.]] and [[2.],[2.]]. Due to the nested square brackets, m1 has shape 1x2, whereas m2 has shape 2x1. Hence, the product of m1 and m2 has shape (1,1).

The three print() statements display the value of m1, m2, and p1. The output from Listing B.20 is here:

```
m1: tf.Tensor([[3. 3.]], shape=(1, 2), dtype=float32)
m2: tf.Tensor(
[[2.]
 [2.]], shape=(2, 1), dtype=float32)
p1: tf.Tensor([[12.]], shape=(1, 1), dtype=float32)
```

## Convert Python Arrays to TF Tensors

Listing B.21 shows the content of tf2_convert_tensors.py, which illustrates how to convert a Python array to a TF 2 tensor.

### LISTING B.21: tf2_convert_tensors.py

```
import tensorflow as tf
import numpy as np

x1 = np.array([[1.,2.],[3.,4.]])
x2 = tf.convert_to_tensor(value=x1, dtype=tf.float32)

print ('x1:',x1)
print ('x2:',x2)
```

Listing B.21 is straightforward, starting with an import statement for TensorFlow and one for NumPy. Next, the x_data variable is a NumPy array, and x is a TF tensor that is the result of converting x_data to a TF tensor. The output from Listing B.21 is here:

```
x1: [[1. 2.]
 [3. 4.]]
x2: tf.Tensor(
[[1. 2.]
 [3. 4.]], shape=(2, 2), dtype=float32)
```

## Conflicting Types in TF 2

Listing B.22 shows the content of tf2_conflict_types.py, which illustrates what happens when you try to combine incompatible tensors in TF 2.

### LISTING B.22: tf2_conflict_types.py

```
import tensorflow as tf

try:
  tf.constant(1) + tf.constant(1.0)
except tf.errors.InvalidArgumentError as ex:
  print(ex)

try:
  tf.constant(1.0, dtype=tf.float64) + tf.constant(1.0)
except tf.errors.InvalidArgumentError as ex:
print(ex)
```

Listing B.22 contains two try/except blocks. The first block adds two constants 1 and 1.0, which are compatible. The second block attempts to add the value 1.0 that's declared as a tf.float64 with 1.0, which are not compatible tensors. The output from Listing B.22 is here:

```
cannot compute Add as input #1(zero-based) was expected to
be a int32 tensor but is a float tensor [Op:Add] name: add/
cannot compute Add as input #1(zero-based) was expected to
be a double tensor but is a float tensor [Op:Add] name: add/
```

# Differentiation and `tf.GradientTape` in TF 2

Automatic differentiation (i.e., calculating derivatives) is useful for implementing ML algorithms, such as back propagation, for training various types of NNs (Neural Networks). During eager execution, the TF 2 context manager `tf.GradientTape` traces the operations for computing gradients. This context manager provides a `watch()` method for specifying a tensor that is differentiated (in the mathematical sense of the word).

The `tf.GradientTape` context manager records all forward-pass operations on a tape. Next, it computes the gradient by playing the tape backward, and then discards the tape after a single gradient computation. Thus, a `tf.GradientTape` can only compute one gradient: subsequent invocations throw a runtime error. Keep in mind that the tf.Gradient-Tape context manager only exists in eager mode.

Why do we need the tf.GradientTape context manager? Consider deferred execution mode, where we have a graph in which we know how nodes are connected. The gradient computation of a function is performed in two steps: 1) backtracking from the output to the input of the graph and 2) computing the gradient to obtain the result.

By contrast, in eager execution, the only way to compute the gradient of a function using automatic differentiation is to construct a graph. After constructing the graph of the operations executed within the tf.Gradient-Tape context manager on some watchable element (such as a variable), we can instruct the tape to compute the required gradient. If you want a more detailed explanation, the tf.GradientTape documentation page contains an example that explains how and why tapes are needed.

The default behavior for tf.GradientTape is to "play once and then discard." However, it's possible to specify a persistent tape, which means that the values are persistant and therefore the tape can be played multiple times. The next section contains several examples of tf.GradientTape, including an example of a persistent tape.

## Examples of tf.GradientTape

Listing B.23 shows the content of tf2_gradient_tape1.py, which illustrates how to invoke tf.GradientTape in TF 2. This example is one of the simplest examples of using tf.GradientTape in TF 2.

*LISTING B.23: tf2_gradient_tape1.py*

```
import tensorflow as tf

w = tf.Variable([[1.0]])

with tf.GradientTape() as tape:
  loss = w * w

grad = tape.gradient(loss, w)
print("grad:",grad)
```

Listing B.23 defines the variable w, followed by a with statement that initializes the variable loss with expression w*w. Next, the variable grad is initialized with the derivative that is returned by the tape, and then evaluated with the current value of w.

As a reminder, if we define the function z = w*w, then the first derivative of z is the term 2*w , and when this term is evaluated with the value of 1.0 for w, the result is 2.0. Launch the code in Listing B.23 to see the following output:

```
grad: tf.Tensor([[2.]], shape=(1, 1), dtype=float32)
```

## Using the `watch()` Method of `tf.GradientTape`

Listing B.24 shows the content of tf2_gradient_tape2.py, which also illustrates the use of tf.GradientTape with the watch() method in TF 2.

*LISTING B.24: tf2_gradient_tape2.py*

```
import tensorflow as tf

x = tf.constant(3.0)

with tf.GradientTape() as g:
  g.watch(x)
  y = 4 * x * x
dy_dx = g.gradient(y, x)
```

Listing B.24 contains a similar with statement as Listing B.23, but this time, a watch() method is also invoked to watch the tensor x. As you saw in the previous section, if we define the function y = 4*x*x, then the first derivative of y is the term 8*x; when the latter term is evaluated with the value 3.0, the result is 24.0.

Launch the code in Listing B.24 to see the following output:

```
dy_dx: tf.Tensor(24.0, shape=(), dtype=float32)
```

## Using Nested Loops with `tf.GradientTape`

Listing B.25 shows the content of tf2_gradient_tape3.py, which illustrates how to define nested loops with tf.GradientTape to calculate the first and the second derivative of a tensor in TF 2.

*LISTING B.25: tf2_gradient_tape3.py*

```
import tensorflow as tf

x = tf.constant(4.0)
with tf.GradientTape() as t1:
```

```
  with tf.GradientTape() as t2:
    t1.watch(x)
    t2.watch(x)
    z = x * x * x
  dz_dx = t2.gradient(z, x)
d2z_dx2 = t1.gradient(dz_dx, x)

print("First  dz_dx:  ",dz_dx)
print("Second d2z_dx2:",d2z_dx2)

x = tf.Variable(4.0)
with tf.GradientTape() as t1:
  with tf.GradientTape() as t2:
    z = x * x * x
  dz_dx = t2.gradient(z, x)
d2z_dx2 = t1.gradient(dz_dx, x)

print("First  dz_dx:  ",dz_dx)
print("Second d2z_dx2:",d2z_dx2)
```

The first portion of Listing B.25 contains a nested loop, where the outer loop calculates the first derivative and the inner loop calculates the second derivative of the term x*x*x when x equals 4. The second portion of Listing B.25 contains another nested loop that produces the same output with a slightly different syntax.

In case you're a bit rusty regarding derivatives, the next code block shows you a function z, its first derivative z', and its second derivative z'':

```
z   = x*x*x
z'  = 3*x*x
z'' = 6*x
```

When we evaluate z, z', and z'' with the value 4.0 for x, the result is 64.0, 48.0, and 24.0, respectively. Launch the code in Listing B.25 to see the following output:

```
First  dz_dx:    tf.Tensor(48.0, shape=(), dtype=float32)
Second d2z_dx2:  tf.Tensor(24.0, shape=(), dtype=float32)
First  dz_dx:    tf.Tensor(48.0, shape=(), dtype=float32)
Second d2z_dx2:  tf.Tensor(24.0, shape=(), dtype=float32)
```

## Other Tensors with `tf.GradientTape`

Listing B.26 shows the content of `tf2_gradient_tape4.py`, which illustrates how to use `tf.GradientTape` to calculate the first derivative of an expression that depends on a 2x2 tensor in TF 2.

*LISTING B.26: tf2_gradient_tape4.py*

```
import tensorflow as tf

x = tf.ones((3, 3))

with tf.GradientTape() as t:
  t.watch(x)
  y = tf.reduce_sum(x)
  print("y:",y)
  z = tf.multiply(y, y)
  print("z:",z)
  z = tf.multiply(z, y)
  print("z:",z)

# the derivative of z with respect to y
dz_dy = t.gradient(z, y)
print("dz_dy:",dz_dy)
```

In Listing B.26, y equals the sum of the elements in the 3x3 tensor x, which is 9.

Next, z is assigned the term y*y and then multiplied again by y, so the final expression for z (and its derivative) is here:

```
z  = y*y*y
z' = 3*y*y
```

When z' is evaluated with the value 9 for y, the result is 3*9*9, which equals 243. Launch the code in Listing B.26 to see the following output (slightly reformatted for readability):

```
y: tf.Tensor(9.0,      shape=(), dtype=float32)
z: tf.Tensor(81.0,     shape=(), dtype=float32)
z: tf.Tensor(729.0,    shape=(), dtype=float32)
dz_dy: tf.Tensor(243.0, shape=(), dtype=float32)
```

## A Persistent Gradient Tape

Listing B.27 shows the content of tf2_gradient_tape5.py, which illustrates how to define a persistent gradient tape with tf.GradientTape to calculate the first derivative of a tensor in TF 2.

*LISTING B.27: tf2_gradient_tape5.py*

```
import tensorflow as tf

x = tf.ones((3, 3))
```

```
with tf.GradientTape(persistent=True) as t:
    t.watch(x)
    y = tf.reduce_sum(x)
    print("y:",y)
    w = tf.multiply(y, y)
    print("w:",w)
    z = tf.multiply(y, y)
    print("z:",z)
    z = tf.multiply(z, y)
    print("z:",z)

# the derivative of z with respect to y
dz_dy = t.gradient(z, y)
print("dz_dy:",dz_dy)
dw_dy = t.gradient(w, y)
print("dw_dy:",dw_dy)
```

Listing B.27 is almost the same as Listing B.26: the new sections are displayed in bold. Note that w is the term y*y, and therefore the first derivative w' is 2*y. Hence, the values for w and w' are 81 and 18, respectively, when they are evaluated with the value 9.0. Launch the code in Listing B.27 to see the following output (slightly reformatted for readability), where the new output is shown in bold:

```
y: tf.Tensor(9.0,      shape=(), dtype=float32)
w: tf.Tensor(81.0,     shape=(), dtype=float32)
z: tf.Tensor(81.0,     shape=(), dtype=float32)
z: tf.Tensor(729.0,    shape=(), dtype=float32)
dz_dy: tf.Tensor(243.0, shape=(), dtype=float32)
dw_dy: tf.Tensor(18.0,  shape=(), dtype=float32)
```

# Google Colaboratory

Depending on the hardware, GPU-based TF 2 code can sometimes be about 15 times faster than CPU-based TF 2 code. However, the cost of a good GPU can be a significant factor. Although NVIDIA provides GPUs, those consumer-based GPUs are not optimized for multi-GPU support (which *is* supported by TF 2).

Fortunately, Google Colaboratory is an affordable alternative that provides free GPU and TPU support, and also runs as a Jupyter notebook environment. In addition, Google Colaboratory executes your code in the cloud and involves zero configuration, and it's available here:

*https://colab.research.google.com/notebooks/welcome.ipynb*

This `Jupyter` notebook is suitable for training simple models and testing ideas quickly. Google Colaboratory makes it easy to upload local files, install software in `Jupyter` notebooks, and even connect Google Colaboratory to a `Jupyter` runtime on your local machine.

Some of the supported features of Colaboratory include TF 2 execution with GPUs, visualization using Matplotlib, and the ability to save a copy of your Google Colaboratory notebook to Github by using `File > Save a copy to GitHub`.

Moreover, you can load any .ipynb on GitHub by just adding the path to the URL `colab.research.google.com/github/` (see the Colaboratory website for details).

Google Colaboratory has support for other technologies, such as HTML and SVG, enabling you to render SVG-based graphics in notebooks that are in Google Colaboratory. One point to keep in mind: any software that you install in a Google Colaboratory notebook is only available on a per-session basis. If you log out and log in again, you need to perform the same installation steps that you performed during your earlier Google Colaboratory session.

As mentioned earlier, there is one other *very* nice feature of Google Colaboratory: you can execute code on a GPU for up to twelve hours per day for free. This free GPU support is extremely useful for people who don't have a suitable GPU on their local machine (which is probably the majority of users). Now they can launch TF 2 code to train neural networks in less than 20 or 30 minutes, which would otherwise require multiple hours of CPU-based execution time.

You can launch Tensorboard inside a Google Colaboratory notebook with the following command (replace the specified directory with your own location):

```
%tensorboard --logdir /logs/images
```

Keep in mind the following details about Google Colaboratory. First, whenever you connect to a server in Google Colaboratory, you start what's known as a *session*. You can execute the code in a session with a GPU or a TPU, and you can execute your code without any time limit for your session. However, if you select the GPU option for your session, only the first 12 hours of GPU execution time are free. Any additional GPU time during that same session incurs a small charge (see the website for those details).

The other point to keep in mind is that any software that you install in a Jupyter notebook during a given session will *not* be saved when you exit that session. For example, the following code snippet installs TFLearn in a Jupyter notebook:

```
!pip install tflearn
```

When you exit the current session and later start a new session, you need to install TFLearn again, as well as any other software (such as Github repositories) that you also installed in any previous sessions.

Incidentally, you can run TF 2 code and TensorBoard in Google Colaboratory, with support for CPUs and GPUs (and support for TPUs will be available later). The following link has more information:

```
https://www.tensorflow.org/tensorboard/r2/tensorboard_in_
notebooks
```

## Other Cloud Platforms

GCP (Google Cloud Platform) is a cloud-based service that enables you to train TF 2 code in the cloud. GCP provides deep learning images (similar in concept to Amazon AMIs) that are available here:

*https://cloud.google.com/deep-learning-vm/docs*

The preceding link provides documentation and a link to DL images based on different technologies, including TF 2 and PyTorch, with GPU and CPU versions of those images. Along with support for multiple versions of Python, you can work in a browser session or from the command line.

### GCP SDK

Install GCloud SDK on a Mac-based laptop by downloading the software at this link: *https://cloud.google.com/sdk/docs/quickstart-macos*

You should receive $300 worth of credit (over one year) if you have never used Google cloud.

## Summary

This appendix introduced you to TF 2, a very brief view of its architecture, and some of the tools that are part of the TF 2 family. Then you learned how to write basic Python scripts containing TF 2 code with TF constants and variables. You also learned how to perform arithmetic operations and also some built-in TF functions.

Next, you learned how to calculate trigonometric values, how to use `for` loops, and how to calculate exponential values. You also saw how to perform various operations on $2^{nd}$ order TF 2 tensors. In addition, you saw code samples that illustrate how to use some of the new features of TF 2, such as the `@tf.function` decorator and `tf.GradientTape`.

Then you got an introduction to Google Colaboratory, which is a cloud-based environment for machine learning and deep learning. This environment is based on Jupyter notebooks, with support for Python and various other languages. Google Colaboratory also provides up to 12 hours of free GPU use on a daily basis, which is a very nice feature.

# C

# TF 2 DATASETS

This appendix discusses the TF 2 tf.data.Dataset namespace and the classes therein that support a rich set of operators for processing very large datasets (i.e., datasets that are too large to fit in memory). This chapter includes lazy operators (such as filter() and map()) that you can invoke via method chaining to extract a desired subset of data from a dataset. In addition, you'll learn about TF 2 Estimators (in the tf.estimator namespace) and TF 2 layers (in the tf.keras. layers namespace).

Please note that a *dataset* in this appendix refers to a TF 2 class in the tf.data.Dataset namespace. Such a dataset acts as a wrapper for actual data, where the latter can be a CSV file or some other data source. This appendix does not cover TF 2 built-in datasets of "pure" data, such as MNIST, CIFAR, and IRIS, except for cases in which they are part of code samples that involve TF 2 lazy operators.

Familiarity with lambda expressions (discussed later) and Functional Reactive Programming are helpful for this appendix. The code samples appendix here are straightforward if you already have experience with Observables in RxJS, RxAndroid, RxJava, or some other environment that involves lazy execution.

The first part of this appendix briefly introduces you to TF 2 Datasets and lambda expressions, along with some simple code samples. You will learn about iterators that work with TF 1.x tf.data.Datasets and TF 2 *generators* (which are Python functions with a @tf.function decorator).

The second part of this appendix discusses TextLineDatasets, which are convenient for working with text files. As explained previously, the

TF 2 code samples in this section use TF 2 generators instead of iterators (which work with TF 1.x).

The third part of this appendix discusses various lazy operators, such as `filter()`, `map()`, and `batch()` operators, and also briefly describes how they work (and when you might need to use them). You'll also learn *method chaining* for combining these operators, which results in powerful code combinations that can significantly reduce the complexity of your TF 2 code.

The final portion of the appendix briefly discusses TF 2 estimators in the `tf.estimator` namespace (which are a layer of abstraction above `tf.keras.layers`), as well as TF 2 `layers` that provide an assortment of classes for DNNs (Dense Neural Networks) and CNNs (Convolutional Neural Networks) that are discussed in Chapter 5.

# The TF 2 `tf.data.Datasets`

Before we delve into this topic, we need to make sure that the following distinction is clear: a dataset contains rows of data (often in a flat file), where the columns are called *features* and the rows represent an *instance* of the dataset. In contrast, a TF 2 `Dataset` refers to a class in the `tf.data.Dataset` namespace that acts like a wrapper around a "regular" dataset that contains rows of data.

You can also think of a TF 2 `Dataset` as being analogous to a `Pandas DataFrame`. Again, if you are familiar with `Observables` in Angular (or something similar), you can perform a quick knowledge transfer as you learn about TF 2 `Datasets`.

TF 2 `tf.data.Datasets` are well-suited for creating asynchronous and optimized data pipelines. In brief, the TF 2 `Dataset` API loads data from the disk (both images and text), applies optimized transformations, creates batches, and sends the batches to the GPU. In fact, the TF 2 `Dataset` API is well-suited for better GPU utilization. In addition, use `tf.functions` in TF 2.0 to fully utilize dataset asynchronous prefetching/streaming features.

According to the TF 2 documentation, "a dataset can be used to represent an input pipeline as a collection of elements (nested structures of tensors) and a logical plan of transformations that act on those elements."

A TF 2 `tf.data.Dataset` is designed to handle very large datasets. A TF 2 `Dataset` can also represent an input pipeline as a collection of elements (i.e., a nested structure of tensors), along with a logical plan of transformations that act on those elements. For example, you can define a TF 2 Dataset that initially contains the lines of text in a text file, then extract the lines of text that start with a "#" character, and then display only the first three matching lines. Creating this pipeline is easy: create a TF 2 Dataset and then chain the lazy operators filter() and take(), which is similar to an example that you will see later in this appendix.

## Creating a Pipeline

Think of a dataset as a pipeline that starts with a source, which can be a NumPy array, tensors in memory, or some other source. If the source involves tensors, use tf.data.Dataset.from_tensors() to combine the input, otherwise use tf.data.Dataset.from_tensor_slices() if you want a separate row for each input tensor. On the other hand, if the input data is located on disk in a TFRecord format (which is recommended), construct a tf.data.TFRecordDataset.

The difference between the first two APIs is shown below:

```
#combine the input into one element => [[1, 2], [3, 4]]
t1 = tf.constant([[1, 2], [3, 4]])
ds1 = tf.data.Dataset.from_tensors(t1)

#a separate element for each item: [1, 2], [3, 4]
t2 = tf.constant([[1, 2], [3, 4]])
ds2 = tf.data.Dataset.from_tensor_slices(t2)
for item in ds1:
  print("1item:",item)

print("--------------")

for item in ds2:
  print("2item:",item)
```

The output from the preceding code block is here:

```
1item: tf.Tensor(
[[1 2]
 [3 4]], shape=(2, 2), dtype=int32)
--------------
2item: tf.Tensor([1 2], shape=(2,), dtype=int32)
2item: tf.Tensor([3 4], shape=(2,), dtype=int32)
```

The TF 2 `from_tensors()` API also requires compatible dimensions, which means that the following code snippet causes an error:

```
# exception: ValueError: Dimensions 10 and 9 are not
compatible
ds1 = tf.data.Dataset.from_tensor_slices(
    (tf.random_uniform([10, 4]), tf.random_uniform([9])))
```

On the other hand, the TF 2 from_tensor_slices() API does not have a compatibility restriction, so the following code snippet works correctly:

```
ds2 = tf.data.Dataset.from_tensors(
    (tf.random_uniform([10, 4]), tf.random_uniform([9])))
```

Another situation in which there are differences in these two APIs involves the use of lists, as shown here:

```
ds1 = tf.data.Dataset.from_tensor_slices(
    [tf.random_uniform([2, 3]), tf.random_uniform([2, 3])])

ds2 = tf.data.Dataset.from_tensors(
    [tf.random_uniform([2, 3]), tf.random_uniform([2, 3])])

print(ds1) # shapes: (2, 3)
print(ds2) # shapes: (2, 2, 3)
```

In the preceding code block, the TF 2 `from_tensors()` API creates a 3D tensor whose shape is (2,2,3), whereas the TF 2 `from_tensor_slices()` API merges the input tensor and produces a tensor whose shape is (2,3).

As a further illustration of these two APIs, consider the following code block:

```
import tensorflow as tf

ds1 = tf.data.Dataset.from_tensor_slices(
    (tf.random.uniform([3, 2]), tf.random.uniform([3])))

ds2 = tf.data.Dataset.from_tensors(
    (tf.random.uniform([3, 2]), tf.random.uniform([3])))

print('-----------------------------')
for i, item in enumerate(ds1):
  print('elem1: ' + str(i + 1), item[0], item[1])

print('-----------------------------')
for i, item in enumerate(ds2):
  print('elem2: ' + str(i + 1), item[0], item[1])
print('-----------------------------')
```

Launch the preceding code to see the following output:

```
----------------------------
elem1: 1 tf.Tensor([0.965013 0.8327141], shape=(2,), dtype=-
float32) tf.Tensor(0.03369963, shape=(), dtype=float32)
elem1: 2 tf.Tensor([0.2875235  0.11409616], shape=(2,),
dtype=float32) tf.Tensor(0.05131495, shape=(),
dtype=float32)
elem1:  3  tf.Tensor([0.08330548  0.13498652],  shape=(2,),
dtype=float32) tf.Tensor(0.3145547, shape=(), dtype=float32)
----------------------------

elem2: 1 tf.Tensor(
[[0.9139079  0.13430142]
 [0.9585271  0.58751714]
 [0.4501326  0.8380357 ]], shape=(3, 2), dtype=float32)
tf.Tensor([0.00776255 0.2655964  0.61935973], shape=(3,),
dtype=float32)
----------------------------
```

## Basic Steps for TF 2 `Datasets`

Perform the following three steps to create and process the contents of a
TF 2 `Dataset`:

1) Create or import data.
2) Define a generator (Python function).
3) Consume the data.

There are many ways to populate a TF 2 `Dataset` from multiple sources.
For simplicity, the code samples in the first part of this appendix perform
the following steps: start by creating a TF 2 `Dataset` instance with an
initialized NumPy array of data; second, define a Python function to iterate
through the TF 2 `Dataset`; and third, access the elements of the dataset
(and in some cases, supply those elements to a TF 2 model).

As a side note: keep in mind that TF 1.x combines `Datasets` with *iterators*, whereas TF 2 uses *generators* with `Datasets`. TF 2 uses generators
because eager execution (the default execution mode for TF 2) does not
support iterators.

## A Simple TF 2 `tf.data.Dataset`

Listing C.3.1 shows the content of tf2_numpy_dataset.py, which illustrates how to create a very basic TF 2 tf.data.Dataset from a NumPy

array of numbers. Although this code sample is minimalistic, it's the initial code block that appears in other code samples in this appendix.

**LISTING C.3.1: tf2_numpy_dataset.py**

```
import tensorflow as tf
import numpy as np

x = np.arange(0, 10)

# make a dataset from a numpy array
ds = tf.data.Dataset.from_tensor_slices(x)
```

Listing C.3.1 contains two familiar `import` statements and then initializes the variable `x` as a `NumPy` array with the integers from 0 through 9, inclusive. The variable `ds` is initialized as a TF 2 `Dataset` that's based on the contents of the variable `x`.

Note that nothing else happens in Listing C.3.1, and no output is generated. Later, you will see more meaningful code samples involving TF 2 `Datasets`.

## What are Lambda Expressions?

In brief, a *lambda expression* is an anonymous function. Use lambda expressions to define local functions that can be passed as arguments, returned as the value of function calls, or used as "one-off" function definitions.

Informally, a lambda expression takes an input variable and performs some type of operation (specified by you) on that variable. For example, here's a "bare bones" lambda expression that adds the number 1 to an input variable x:

```
lambda x: x + 1
```

The term on the left of the ":" is x, and it's just a formal variable name that acts as the input (you can replace x with another string that's convenient for you). The term on the right of the ":" is x+1, which simply increments the value of the input x.

As another example, the following lambda expression doubles the value of the input parameter:

```
lambda x: 2*x
```

You can also define a lambda expression in a valid TF 2 code snippet, as shown here (ds is a TF 2 Dataset that is defined elsewhere):

```
ds.map(lambda x: x + 1)
```

Even if you are unfamiliar with TF 2 Datasets or the map() operator, you can still understand the preceding code snippet. Later in this appendix, you'll see other examples of lambda expressions that are used in conjunction with lazy operators.

The next section contains a complete TF 2 code sample that illustrates how to define a generator (which is a Python function) that adds the number 1 to the elements of a TF 2 Dataset.

# Working with Generators in TF 2

Listing C.3.2 shows the content of tf2_plusone.py, which illustrates how to use a lambda expression to add the number 1 to the elements of a TF 2 Dataset.

### LISTING C.3.2: tf2_plusone.py

```
import tensorflow as tf
import numpy as np

x = np.arange(0, 10)
def gener():
  for i in x:
    yield (i+1)

ds = tf.data.Dataset.from_generator(gener, (tf.int64))

#for value in ds.take(len(x)):
for value in ds:
  print("1value:",value)

for value in ds.take(2*len(x)):
  print("2value:",value)
```

Listing C.3.2 initializes the variable x as a NumPy array consisting of the integers from 0 through 9, inclusive. Next, the variable ds is initialized as a TF 2 Dataset that is created from the Python function gener(), which returns the input value incremented by 1. Notice that the Python function gener() does *not* have a @tf.function() decorator: even so, this function is treated as a generator because it's specified as such in the from_generator() API.

The next portion of Listing C.3.2 contains two for loops that iterate through the elements of ds and displays their values. Since the first for loop does not specify the number of elements in ds, that for loop will process all the numbers in ds.

Here's an important detail regarding generators in TF 2: they only emit a single value when they are invoked. This means that the for loop in the Python gener() function does *not* execute 10 times: it executes only *once* when it is invoked, and then it "waits" until the gener() function is invoked again.

In case it's helpful, you can think of the gener() function as a "writer" that prints a single value to a pipe, and elsewhere there is some code that acts like a "reader" that reads a data value from the pipe. The code that acts as a reader is the first for loop that is reproduced here:

```
for value in ds:
    print("1value:",value)
```

How does the preceding code block invoke the gener() function when it doesn't even appear in the code? The answer is simple: the preceding code block indirectly invokes the gener() function because it's specified in the definition of ds, as shown here in bold:

```
ds = tf.data.Dataset.from_generator(gener, (tf.int64))
```

To summarize, each time that the preceding for loop executes, it invokes the Python gener() function, which in turn prints a value and then waits until it is invoked again.

The second for loop also acts as a reader, and this time the code invokes the take() operator (it takes data from the dataset) that specifies *twice* the length of the NumPy array x. Why would anyone specify a length that is greater than the number of elements in the underlying array? There may be various reasons (perhaps it was accidental), so it's good to know what happens in this situation (see if you can correctly guess the result). The output from launching the code in Listing C.3.2 is here:

```
1value: tf.Tensor(1,   shape=(), dtype=int64)
1value: tf.Tensor(2,   shape=(), dtype=int64)
1value: tf.Tensor(3,   shape=(), dtype=int64)
1value: tf.Tensor(4,   shape=(), dtype=int64)
1value: tf.Tensor(5,   shape=(), dtype=int64)
```

```
1value: tf.Tensor(6,   shape=(), dtype=int64)
1value: tf.Tensor(7,   shape=(), dtype=int64)
1value: tf.Tensor(8,   shape=(), dtype=int64)
1value: tf.Tensor(9,   shape=(), dtype=int64)
1value: tf.Tensor(10,  shape=(), dtype=int64)

2value: tf.Tensor(1,   shape=(), dtype=int64)
2value: tf.Tensor(2,   shape=(), dtype=int64)
2value: tf.Tensor(3,   shape=(), dtype=int64)
2value: tf.Tensor(4,   shape=(), dtype=int64)
2value: tf.Tensor(5,   shape=(), dtype=int64)
2value: tf.Tensor(6,   shape=(), dtype=int64)
2value: tf.Tensor(7,   shape=(), dtype=int64)
2value: tf.Tensor(8,   shape=(), dtype=int64)
2value: tf.Tensor(9,   shape=(), dtype=int64)
2value: tf.Tensor(10,  shape=(), dtype=int64)
```

The next section contains a code sample that illustrates how to concatenate two TF 2 Datasets.

## Concatenating TF 2 `tf.Data.Datasets`

Listing C.3.3 shows the content of `tf2_concatenate.py`, which illustrates how to concatenate two TF 2 Datasets.

### LISTING C.3.3: tf2_concatenate.py

```
import tensorflow as tf
import numpy as np

x1 = np.array([1,2,3,4,5])
x2 = np.array([6,7,8,9,10])

ds1 = tf.data.Dataset.from_tensor_slices(x1)
ds2 = tf.data.Dataset.from_tensor_slices(x2)
ds3 = ds1.concatenate(ds2)

try:
  for value in ds3.take(20):
    print("value:",value)
except tf.errors.OutOfRangeError:
  pass
```

Listing C.3.3 contains two NumPy arrays, x1 and x2, followed by the TF 2 Datasets ds1 and ds2 that act as containers for x1 and x2, respectively. Next, the dataset ds3 is defined as the concatenation of ds1 and ds2.

The next portion of Listing C.3.3 is a try/except block that contains a for loop to display the contents of ds3. The output from launching the code in Listing C.3.4 is here:

```
ds3 value: tf.Tensor(1, shape=(), dtype=int64)
ds3 value: tf.Tensor(2, shape=(), dtype=int64)
ds3 value: tf.Tensor(3, shape=(), dtype=int64)
ds3 value: tf.Tensor(4, shape=(), dtype=int64)
ds3 value: tf.Tensor(5, shape=(), dtype=int64)
ds3 value: tf.Tensor(6, shape=(), dtype=int64)
ds3 value: tf.Tensor(7, shape=(), dtype=int64)
ds3 value: tf.Tensor(8, shape=(), dtype=int64)
ds3 value: tf.Tensor(9, shape=(), dtype=int64)
ds3 value: tf.Tensor(10, shape=(), dtype=int64)
```

One other point to keep in mind: different structures *cannot* be concatenated. For example, consider the variables y1 and y2:

```
# y1 = { (8, 9), (10, 11), (12, 13) }
# y2 = { 14.0, 15.0, 16.0 }
```

If you create a TF 2 Dataset from y1 and y2, the resulting datasets cannot be concatenated to ds1.

# The TF 2 reduce() Operator

The TF 2 reduce() operator performs a reduction on its input until a single value is produced. For example, you can use the reduce() operator to add all the numbers in an array. Listing C.3.4 shows the content of tf2_reduce.py, which illustrates how to use the reduce() API in TF 2.

### LISTING C.3.4: tf2_reduce.py

```
import tensorflow as tf
import numpy as np

x1 = tf.data.Dataset.range(8).reduce(np.int64(0),lambda x,
_: x + 1)
x2 = tf.data.Dataset.range(8).reduce(np.int64(0),lambda x,
y: x + y)
```

```
print("x1:",x1)
print("x2:",x2)
```

Listing C.3.4 defines the variables x1 and x1 as instances of tf.data. Dataset, which in turn is based on the digits from 0 to 7, inclusive. Notice that x1 and x1 specify different lambda expressions. The lambda expression for x1 returns its input value incremented by one. Since the largest number in the input set of values is 7, the last output value is 8.

On the other hand, x2 defines a lambda expression that returns the sum of two consecutive input values. The initial sum is 0, so the final output equals the sum of the numbers 1, 2, . . ., and 7, which equals 28. The output from launching the code in Listing C.3.4 is here:

```
x1: tf.Tensor(8,  shape=(), dtype=int64)
x2: tf.Tensor(28, shape=(), dtype=int64)
```

## Working with Generators in TF 2

Earlier in the appendix, you were introduced to TF 2 *generators*, which are Python functions (for our code samples, let's just name this function gener()) that work somewhat like a "pipe." For example, you read a single value each time that the gener() function is invoked. You can also think of a TF 2 generator as a function that emits one value when the function is invoked. [If you are familiar with the Go programming language, this is essentially the same as a channel.]

After emitting the last available value, the pipe no longer returns any values. Contrary to what you might expect, no error message is displayed when the pipe is empty.

Now that you understand the underlying behavior of a generator in TF 2, let's look at the following code snippet (which you've seen already) that shows you how to define a TF 2 tf.data.Dataset that involves a generator:

```
ds = tf.data.Dataset.from_generator(gener, (tf.int64))
```

If you read the previous code snippet in English, it would be as follows: "the Dataset ds obtains its values from the Python function gener() that emits a value of type tf.int64." If you iterate through the values of ds via a for loop, the gener() function is invoked and yields a single value. Hence, the number of times your code iterates through the values of ds equals the number of times that the gener() function is invoked.

Listing C.3.5 shows the content of `tf2_generator1.py`, which illustrates how to define a generator in TF 2 that yields a value that is three times its input value.

### LISTING C.3.5: tf2_generator1.py

```
import tensorflow as tf
import numpy as np

x = np.arange(0, 10)

def gener():
  for i in x:
    yield (3*i)

ds = tf.data.Dataset.from_generator(gener, (tf.int64))

for value in ds.take(len(x)):
  print("value:",value)

for value in ds.take(2*len(x)):
  print("value:",value)
```

Listing C.3.5 contains the NumPy variable x, which contains the digits from 0 to 9, inclusive. The next portion of Listing C.3.4 defines the Python function gener(), which contains a for loop that iterates through the values in x. Notice that it's not necessary to specify a @tf.function decorator because the definition of ds specifies the Python function gener() as a generator.

However, recall that the yield keyword performs a parsimonious operation: it yields only a single value. In this example, the variable i ranges from 0 to 9, but the first invocation of gener() returns only the value 3*0 because i equals 0.

The next invocation of gener() returns the value 3*1 because i equals 1. Each subsequent invocation of gener() returns the sequence of values 3*2, 3*3, . . . , 3*9. In a sense, the for loop in the gener() function is a stateful loop because it "remembers" the current value of i during subsequent invocations of the gener() function.

The output from launching the code in Listing C.3.5 is here:

```
value: tf.Tensor(0,  shape=(), dtype=int64)
value: tf.Tensor(3,  shape=(), dtype=int64)
value: tf.Tensor(6,  shape=(), dtype=int64)
value: tf.Tensor(9,  shape=(), dtype=int64)
```

```
value: tf.Tensor(12, shape=(), dtype=int64)
value: tf.Tensor(15, shape=(), dtype=int64)
value: tf.Tensor(18, shape=(), dtype=int64)
value: tf.Tensor(21, shape=(), dtype=int64)
value: tf.Tensor(24, shape=(), dtype=int64)
value: tf.Tensor(27, shape=(), dtype=int64)
value: tf.Tensor(0,  shape=(), dtype=int64)
value: tf.Tensor(3,  shape=(), dtype=int64)
value: tf.Tensor(6,  shape=(), dtype=int64)
value: tf.Tensor(9,  shape=(), dtype=int64)
value: tf.Tensor(12, shape=(), dtype=int64)
value: tf.Tensor(15, shape=(), dtype=int64)
value: tf.Tensor(18, shape=(), dtype=int64)
value: tf.Tensor(21, shape=(), dtype=int64)
value: tf.Tensor(24, shape=(), dtype=int64)
value: tf.Tensor(27, shape=(), dtype=int64)
```

## The TF 2 `filter()` Operator (1)

The `filter()` operator uses Boolean logic to filter the elements in an array to determine which elements satisfy the Boolean condition. As an analogy, if you hold a piece of smoked glass in front of your eyes, the glass will filter out a portion of the light spectrum. A filter in TF 2 performs an analogous function: it generally results in a subset of the original set. [A filter that returns every input element is technically possible, but it's also pointless.]

As a simple example, suppose that we have a NumPy array [1,2,3,4] and we want to select only the *even* numbers in this array. The result is [1,2], whose contents are a subset of the original array. Listing C.3.6 shows the content of `tf2_filter.py`, which illustrates how to use the `filter()` operator in TF 2.

### LISTING C.3.6: tf2_filter.py

```
import tensorflow as tf
import numpy as np

#def filter_fn(x):
#   return tf.reshape(tf.not_equal(x % 2, 1), [])

x = np.array([1,2,3,4,5,6,7,8,9,10])
ds = tf.data.Dataset.from_tensor_slices(x)
```

```
ds = ds.filter(lambda x: tf.reshape(tf.not_equal(x%2,1),
[]))
#ds = ds.filter(filter_fn)

for value in ds:
  print("value:",value)
```

Listing C.3.6 initializes the variable x as a NumPy array consisting of the integers from 1 through 10, inclusive. Next, the variable ds is initialized as a TF 2 Dataset that is created from the contents of the variable x. The next code snippet invokes the filter() operator, inside of which a lambda expression returns only even numbers because of this expression:

```
tf.not_equal(x%2,1)
```

The next portion of Listing C.3.6 is a for loop that iterates through the elements of the dataset ds. The output from launching the code in Listing C.3.6 is here:

```
value: tf.Tensor(2,  shape=(), dtype=int64)
value: tf.Tensor(4,  shape=(), dtype=int64)
value: tf.Tensor(6,  shape=(), dtype=int64)
value: tf.Tensor(8,  shape=(), dtype=int64)
value: tf.Tensor(10, shape=(), dtype=int64)
```

## The TF 2 filter() Operator (2)

Listing C.3.7 shows the content of tf2_filter2.py, which illustrates another example of the filter() operator in TF 2.

### LISTING C.3.7: tf2_filter2.py

```
import tensorflow as tf
import numpy as np

ds = tf.data.Dataset.from_tensor_slices([1,2,3,4,5])
ds = ds.filter(lambda x: x < 4) # [1,2,3]

print("First iteration:")
for value in ds:
  print("value:",value)

# "tf.math.equal(x, y)" is required for equality comparison
def filter_fn(x):
  return tf.math.equal(x, 1)
```

```
ds = ds.filter(filter_fn)

print("Second iteration:")
for value in ds:
  print("value:",value)
```

Listing C.3.7 defines the variable ds as a TF 2 Dataset that is created from the array [1,2,3,4,5]. The next code snippet invokes the fil-ter() operator, inside of which a lambda expression returns numbers that are less than 4. The for loop prints the numbers in the ds variable, which consists of the filtered list of digits 1, 2, and 3.

The next portion of Listing C.3.7 is the decorated Python function filter_fn() that is specified as part of the new definition of ds, as shown here:

```
ds = ds.filter(filter_fn)
```

The preceding code snippet executes the decorated Python function filter_fn() in the *second* for loop in Listing C.3.7. The output from launching the code in Listing C.3.7 is here:

```
First iteration:
value: tf.Tensor(1, shape=(), dtype=int32)
value: tf.Tensor(2, shape=(), dtype=int32)
value: tf.Tensor(3, shape=(), dtype=int32)
Second iteration:
value: tf.Tensor(1, shape=(), dtype=int32)
```

# The TF 2 batch() Operator (1)

The batch(n) operator processes a batch of n elements during each iter-ation. Listing C.3.8 shows the content of tf2_batch1.py, which illus-trates how to use the batch() operator in TF 2.

### LISTING C.3.8: tf2_batch1.py

```
import tensorflow as tf
import numpy as np

x = np.arange(0, 34)
ds = tf.data.Dataset.from_tensor_slices(x).batch(3)

for value in ds:
  print("value:",value)
```

Listing C.3.8 initializes the variable x as a NumPy array consisting of the integers from 0 through 33, inclusive (note that this array contains 34 numbers). Next, the variable ds is initialized as a TF 2 Dataset that is a container for the contents of the variable x. Notice that the definition of x involves method chaining by "tacking on" the batch(3) operator as part of the definition of ds.

The final portion of Listing C.3.8 contains a loop that iterates through the elements of the dataset ds. Now launch the code in Listing C.3.8 to see the output in its entirety, as shown here:

```
tf.Tensor([0 1 2],     shape=(3,), dtype=int64)
tf.Tensor([3 4 5],     shape=(3,), dtype=int64)
tf.Tensor([6 7 8],     shape=(3,), dtype=int64)
tf.Tensor([ 9 10 11],  shape=(3,), dtype=int64)
tf.Tensor([12 13 14],  shape=(3,), dtype=int64)
tf.Tensor([15 16 17],  shape=(3,), dtype=int64)
tf.Tensor([18 19 20],  shape=(3,), dtype=int64)
tf.Tensor([21 22 23],  shape=(3,), dtype=int64)
tf.Tensor([24 25 26],  shape=(3,), dtype=int64)
tf.Tensor([27 28 29],  shape=(3,), dtype=int64)
tf.Tensor([30 31 32],  shape=(3,), dtype=int64)
tf.Tensor([33],        shape=(1,), dtype=int64)
```

## The TF 2 `batch()` Operator (2)

Listing C.3.9 shows the content of tf2_generator2.py, which illustrates how to use a generator function to display batches of numbers.

### LISTING C.3.9: tf2_generator2.py

```
import tensorflow as tf
import numpy as np

x = np.arange(0, 12)

def gener():
  i = 0
  while(i < len(x/3)):
    yield (i, i+1, i+2)
    i += 3

ds = tf.data.Dataset.from_generator(gener,
(tf.int64,tf.int64,tf.int64))
```

```
third = int(len(x)/3)
for value in ds.take(third):
    print("value:",value)
```

Listing C.3.9 initializes the variable x as a NumPy array consisting of the integers from 0 through 12, inclusive. The Python function gener() return a triple of three consecutive numbers from the NumPy array x. Since the next code snippet invokes the from_generator() API with the gener() function, the latter is treated as a generator (you saw an example of this behavior earlier in this appendix).

The final portion of Listing C.3.9 contains a for loop that iterates through the elements of ds, printing three consecutive values during in each print() statement. The output from launching the code in Listing C.3.9 is here:

```
value: (<tf.Tensor: id=34, shape=(), dtype=int64, numpy=0>,
<tf.Tensor: id=35, shape=(), dtype=int64, numpy=1>, <tf.
Tensor: id=36, shape=(), dtype=int64, numpy=2>)
value: (<tf.Tensor: id=40, shape=(), dtype=int64, numpy=3>,
<tf.Tensor: id=41, shape=(), dtype=int64, numpy=4>, <tf.
Tensor: id=42, shape=(), dtype=int64, numpy=5>)
value: (<tf.Tensor: id=46, shape=(), dtype=int64, numpy=6>,
<tf.Tensor: id=47, shape=(), dtype=int64, numpy=7>, <tf.
Tensor: id=48, shape=(), dtype=int64, numpy=8>)
value: (<tf.Tensor: id=52, shape=(), dtype=int64, numpy=9>,
<tf.Tensor: id=53, shape=(), dtype=int64, numpy=10>, <tf.
Tensor: id=54, shape=(), dtype=int64, numpy=11>)
```

The companion files contains tf2_generator1.py and tf2_generator3.py, which illustrate variations of the preceding code sample. Experiment with the code by changing the hard-coded values and then see if you can correctly predict the output.

# The TF 2 map() Operator (1)

The map() operator is often defined as a projection, and while this is technically correct, the actual behavior might not be clear. Here's the basic idea: when you provide a list or an array of values as input for the map() operator, this operator applies a lambda expression to each input element.

For example, the lambda expression lambda x: x*2 returns twice its input value x, whereas the lambda expression lambda x: x/2 returns half its input value x. In both lambda expressions, the input list and the output list have the same number of elements. In many cases, the size of these two lists is the same, but there are many exceptions. For example, the lambda expression lambda x: x%2 returns the value 0 for even numbers and the value 1 for odd numbers, so the output consists of, at most, two numbers, whereas the input list can be arbitrarily large. Listing C.3.10 shows the content of tf2_map.py, which illustrates a complete example of the map() operator in TF 2.

### LISTING C.3.10: tf2_map.py

```
import tensorflow as tf
import numpy as np

x = np.array([[1],[2],[3],[4]])
ds = tf.data.Dataset.from_tensor_slices(x)
ds = ds.map(lambda x: x*2)

for value in ds:
  print("value:",value)
```

Listing C.3.10 initializes the variable x as a NumPy array consisting of four elements, where each element is a 1x1 array consisting of the numbers 1, 2, 3, and 4. Next, the variable ds is initialized as a TF 2 Dataset that is created from the contents of the variable x. Notice how ds.map() then defines a lambda expression that doubles each input value (which takes the value of each integer from 1 to 4) in this example.

The final portion of Listing C.3.10 contains a for loop that iterates through the element of ds and displays their values. The output from launching the code in Listing C.3.10 is here:

```
value: tf.Tensor([2], shape=(1,), dtype=int64)
value: tf.Tensor([4], shape=(1,), dtype=int64)
value: tf.Tensor([6], shape=(1,), dtype=int64)
value: tf.Tensor([8], shape=(1,), dtype=int64)
```

## The TF 2 map() Operator (2)

Listing C.3.11 shows the content of tf2_map2.py, which illustrates two techniques for defining a dataset, as well as how to invoke multiple occurrences of the map() operator in TF 2.

### *LISTING C.3.11: tf2_map2.py*

```
import tensorflow as tf
import numpy as np

# a simple NumPy array
x = np.array([[1],[2],[3],[4]])

# make a dataset from a NumPy array
dataset = tf.data.Dataset.from_tensor_slices(x)

# METHOD #1: THE LONG WAY
# a lambda expression to double each value
#dataset = dataset.map(lambda x: x*2)
# a lambda expression to add one to each value
#dataset = dataset.map(lambda x: x+1)
# a lambda expression to cube each value
#dataset = dataset.map(lambda x: x**3)

# METHOD #2: A SHORTER WAY
dataset = dataset.map(lambda x: x*2).map(lambda x: x+1).
map(lambda x: x**3)

for value in ds:
  print("value:",value)
```

Listing C.3.11 initializes the variable x as a NumPy array consisting of four elements, where each element is a 1x1 array consisting of the numbers 1, 2, 3, and 4. Next, the variable dataset is initialized as a TF 2 Dataset that is created from the contents of the variable x.

The next portion of Listing C.3.11 is a commented out code block that consists of three lambda expressions, followed by a code snippet (shown in bold) that uses method chaining in order to produce a more compact way of invoking the same three lambda expressions:

```
dataset = dataset.map(lambda x: x*2).map(lambda x: x+1).
map(lambda x: x**3)
```

The preceding code snippet transforms each input value by first doubling the value, then adding one to the output from the first lambda expression, and then cubing the output from the second lambda expression.

Although method chaining is a concise way to combine operators, invoking many lazy operators in a single (very long) line of code can also become difficult to understand, whereas writing code using the longer way would be easier to debug.

A suggestion: start with each lazy operator in a separate line of code, and after you are satisfied that the individual results are correct, *then* use method chaining to combine the operators in a single line of code (perhaps up to a maximum of four or five lazy operators).

The final portion of Listing C.3.11 contains a `for` loop that iterates through the transformed values and displays their values. The output from launching the code in Listing C.3.11 is here:

```
value: tf.Tensor([27],  shape=(1,), dtype=int64)
value: tf.Tensor([125], shape=(1,), dtype=int64)
value: tf.Tensor([343], shape=(1,), dtype=int64)
value: tf.Tensor([729], shape=(1,), dtype=int64)
```

# The TF 2 `flatmap()` Operator (1)

In addition to the TF 2 `map()` operator, TF 2 also supports the TF 2 `flat_map()` operator. However, the TF 2 `map()` and TF 2 `flat_map()` operators expect functions with different signatures. Specifically, `map()` takes a function that maps a single element of the input dataset to a single new element, whereas `flat_map()` takes a function that maps a single element of the input dataset to a `Dataset` of elements.

Listing C.3.12 shows the content of `tf2_flatmap1.py`, which illustrates how to use the `flatmap()` operator in TF 2.

### LISTING C.3.12: tf2_flatmap1.py

```
import tensorflow as tf
import numpy as np

x = np.array([[1,2,3], [4,5,6], [7,8,9]])

ds = tf.data.Dataset.from_tensor_slices(x)
ds.flat_map(lambda x: tf.data.Dataset.
from_tensor_slices(x))

for value in ds.take(3):
  print("value:",value)
```

Listing C.3.12 initializes the variable x as a NumPy array consisting of three elements, where each element is a 1x3 array of numbers. Next, the variable ds is initialized as a TF 2 Dataset that is a container for the contents of the variable x.

The final portion of Listing C.3.12 contains a `for` loop that iterates through the element of `dataset` and displays their values. Once again, note that the `try/except` block is unnecessary, even if the `take()` method specifies a number that is greater than the number of elements in `ds`. The output from launching the code in Listing C.3.12 is here:

```
value: tf.Tensor([1 2 3], shape=(3,), dtype=int64)
value: tf.Tensor([4 5 6], shape=(3,), dtype=int64)
value: tf.Tensor([7 8 9], shape=(3,), dtype=int64)
```

## The TF 2 `flatmap()` Operator (2)

The code in the previous section works fine, but there is a hard-coded value 3 in the code block that displays the elements of the dataset. The code sample in this section removes the hard-coded value.

Listing C.3.13 shows the content of `tf2_flatmap2.py`, which illustrates how to use the `flatmap()` operator in TF 2, and then iterate through the elements of the dataset.

### LISTING C.3.13: tf2_flatmap2.py

```python
import tensorflow as tf
import numpy as np

x = np.array([[1,2,3], [4,5,6], [7,8,9]])

ds = tf.data.Dataset.from_tensor_slices(x)
ds.flat_map(lambda x: tf.data.Dataset.
from_tensor_slices(x))

for value in ds:
  print("value:",value)
```

Listing C.3.13 initializes the variable x as a NumPy array consisting of three elements, where each element is a 1x3 array of numbers. Next, the variable ds is initialized as a TF 2 Dataset that is created from the contents of the variable x.

The final portion of Listing C.3.13 iterates through the element of ds and displays their values. The `for` loop iterates through the elements of ds. The output from launching the code in Listing C.3.13 is the same as the output from Listing C.3.12:

```
value: tf.Tensor([1 2 3], shape=(3,), dtype=int64)
value: tf.Tensor([4 5 6], shape=(3,), dtype=int64)
value: tf.Tensor([7 8 9], shape=(3,), dtype=int64)
```

## The TF 2 `flat_map()` and `filter()` Operators

Listing C.3.14 shows the content of `comments.txt` and Listing C.3.15 shows the content of `tf2_flatmap_filter.py`, which illustrate how to use the `filter()` operator in TF 2.

***LISTING C.3.14: comments.txt***

```
#this is file line #1
#this is file line #2
this is file line #3
this is file line #4
#this is file line #5
```

***LISTING C.3.15: tf2_flatmap_filter.py***

```
import tensorflow as tf

filenames = ["comments.txt"]

ds = tf.data.Dataset.from_tensor_slices(filenames)

# 1) Use Dataset.flat_map() to transform each file
#    as a separate nested ds, then concatenate their
#    contents sequentially into a single "flat" ds
# 2) Skip the first line (header row)
# 3) Filter out lines beginning with "#" (comments)

ds = ds.flat_map(
    lambda filename: (
      tf.data.TextLineDataset(filename)
      .skip(1)
          .filter(lambda line: tf.not_equal(tf.strings.
substr(line,0,1),"#"))))

for value in ds.take(2):
  print("value:",value)
```

Listing C.3.15 defines the variable `filenames` as an array of text file-names, which consists of just one text file named `comments.txt` (whose contents are shown in Listing C.3.14). Next, the variable `dataset` is initialized as a TF 2 `Dataset` that contains the contents of `comments.txt`.

The next section of Listing C.3.15 is a comment block that explains the purpose of the subsequent code block that defines the variable ds. As you can see, ds involves a small set of operations that are executed via method chaining in order to perform various transformation on the contents of the variable ds.

Specifically, the flat_map() operator flattens whatever is returned by the nested lambda expression, which involves several transformations. The first transformation involves passing each input filename, one at a time, to the tf.data.TextLineDataset class. The second transformation skips the first line of text from the current input file. The third transformation invokes a filter() operator that specifies another lambda expression with conditional logic, as shown here:

```
tf.not_equal(tf.strings.substr(line,0,1),"#"))
```

The preceding code snippet returns the current line of text (from the currently processed text file) if, and only if, the character in the first position of the line of text is not the character #; otherwise, nothing is returned (i.e., the line of text is skipped). These transformations can be summarized as follows: "for each input file, skip the first line, and print any subsequent lines that do not start with the character #."

The final portion of Listing C.3.15 prints two lines of output, which might seem anti-climatic after defining such a fancy set of transformations! Launch the code in Listing C.3.15 to see the following output:

```
value: tf.Tensor(b'this is file line #3 ', shape=(),
dtype=string)
value: tf.Tensor(b'this is file line #4 ', shape=(),
dtype=string)
```

## The TF 2 repeat() Operator

The repeat(n) operator simply repeats its input values n times. Listing C.3.16 shows the content of tf2_repeat.py, which illustrates how to use the repeat() operator in TF 2.

### LISTING C.3.16: tf2_repeat.py

```
import tensorflow as tf

ds = tf.data.Dataset.from_tensor_slices(tf.range(4))
ds = ds.repeat(2)

for value in ds.take(20):
  print("value:",value)
```

Listing C.3.16 initializes the variable ds1 as a TF 2 Dataset that is created from the integers between 0 and 3 inclusive. The next code snippet attaches the repeat() operator to ds, which has the effect of appending the contents of ds to itself. Hence, ds contains 8 numbers: the numbers from 0 through 3, inclusive, and again the numbers 0 through 3, inclusive.

The final portion of Listing C.3.16 contains a for loop that iterates through the elements of the dataset ds. Although the take() method specifies the number 20, the loop is only executed twice because the repeat() operator specifies the value 2. The output from launching the code in Listing C.3.16 is here:

```
value: tf.Tensor(0, shape=(), dtype=int32)
value: tf.Tensor(1, shape=(), dtype=int32)
value: tf.Tensor(2, shape=(), dtype=int32)
value: tf.Tensor(3, shape=(), dtype=int32)
value: tf.Tensor(0, shape=(), dtype=int32)
value: tf.Tensor(1, shape=(), dtype=int32)
value: tf.Tensor(2, shape=(), dtype=int32)
value: tf.Tensor(3, shape=(), dtype=int32)
```

## The TF 2 take() Operator

The take(n) operator takes n input values. Listing C.3.17 shows the content of tf2_take.py, which illustrates another example of the take() operator in TF 2.

### LISTING C.3.17: tf2_take.py

```
import tensorflow as tf

ds = tf.data.Dataset.from_tensor_slices(tf.range(8))
ds = ds.take(5)

for value in ds.take(20):
  print("value:",value)
```

Listing C.3.17 initializes the variable ds1 as a TF 2 Dataset that is created from the integers between 0 and 7, inclusive. The next code snippet attaches the take() operator to ds, which has the effect of limiting the output to the first five integers.

The final portion of Listing C.3.17 contains a for loop that iterates through the elements of the dataset ds. See the code in the preceding section for an explanation of the how the output is generated. The output from launching the code in Listing C.3.17 is here:

```
value: tf.Tensor(0, shape=(), dtype=int32)
value: tf.Tensor(1, shape=(), dtype=int32)
value: tf.Tensor(2, shape=(), dtype=int32)
value: tf.Tensor(3, shape=(), dtype=int32)
value: tf.Tensor(4, shape=(), dtype=int32)
```

## Combining the TF 2 `map()` and `take()` Operators

Listing C.3.18 shows the content of `tf2_map_take.py`, which illustrates how to use method chaining to invoke the `map()` operator three times, using three different lambda expressions, followed by the `take()` operator in TF 2.

*LISTING C.3.18: tf2_map_take.py*

```
import tensorflow as tf
import numpy as np

x = np.array([[1],[2],[3],[4]])

# make a ds from a numpy array
ds = tf.data.Dataset.from_tensor_slices(x)
ds = ds.map(lambda x: x*2).map(lambda x: x+1).map(lambda
x: x**3)

for value in ds.take(4):
  print("value:",value)
```

Listing C.3.18 initializes the variable x as a NumPy array consisting of four elements, where each element is a 1x1 array consisting of the numbers 1, 2, 3, and 4. Next, the variable dataset is initialized as a TF 2 Dataset that is created from the contents of the variable x. The next portion of Listing C.3.18 involves three lambda expressions that are shown in bold and reproduced here:

**ds = ds.map(lambda x: x\*2).map(lambda x: x+1).map(lambda x: x\*\*3)**

The preceding code snippet transforms each input value by first doubling the value, then adding one to the first result, and then cubing the second result.

The final portion of Listing C.3.18 takes the first four elements from the variable dataset and displays their contents, as shown here:

```
value: tf.Tensor([27],  shape=(1,),  dtype=int64)
value: tf.Tensor([125], shape=(1,),  dtype=int64)
value: tf.Tensor([343], shape=(1,),  dtype=int64)
value: tf.Tensor([729], shape=(1,),  dtype=int64)
```

## Combining the TF 2 `zip()` and `batch()` Operators

Listing C.3.19 shows the content of `tf2_zip_batch.py`, which illustrates how to combine the `zip()` and `batch()` operators in TF 2.

### LISTING C.3.19: tf2_zip_batch.py

```
import tensorflow as tf

ds1 = tf.data.Dataset.range(100)
ds2 = tf.data.Dataset.range(0, -100, -1)
ds3 = tf.data.Dataset.zip((ds1, ds2))
ds4 = ds3.batch(4)

for value in ds.take(10):
    print("value:",value)
```

Listing C.3.19 initializes the variables ds1, ds2, ds3, and ds4 as TF 2 Datasets that are created successively, starting from ds1 that contains the integers between 0 and 99 inclusive. The variable ds2 is initialized via the range() operator that starts from 0 and decreased to -99, and the variable ds3 is initialized via the zip() operator that processes two elements at a time, in a pairwise fashion. Next, the variable ds3 is initialized by invoking the batch() operator on the variable ds3. The final portion of Listing C.3.19 prints three lines of batched output, as shown here:

```
value: (<tf.Tensor: id=20, shape=(4,), dtype=int64, numpy-
=array([0,  1,  2,  3])>,  <tf.Tensor:  id=21,  shape=(4,),
dtype=int64, numpy=array([ 0, -1, -2, -3])>)
value: (<tf.Tensor: id=24, shape=(4,), dtype=int64, numpy-
=array([4,  5,  6,  7])>,  <tf.Tensor:  id=25,  shape=(4,),
dtype=int64, numpy=array([-4, -5, -6, -7])>)
value: (<tf.Tensor: id=28, shape=(4,), dtype=int64, numpy-
=array([ 8,  9, 10, 11])>, <tf.Tensor: id=29, shape=(4,),
dtype=int64, numpy=array([ -8,  -9, -10, -11])>)
```

```
value: (<tf.Tensor: id=32, shape=(4,), dtype=int64, numpy-
=array([12, 13, 14, 15])>, <tf.Tensor: id=33, shape=(4,),
dtype=int64, numpy=array([-12, -13, -14, -15])>)
value: (<tf.Tensor: id=36, shape=(4,), dtype=int64, numpy-
=array([16, 17, 18, 19])>, <tf.Tensor: id=37, shape=(4,),
dtype=int64, numpy=array([-16, -17, -18, -19])>)
value: (<tf.Tensor: id=40, shape=(4,), dtype=int64, numpy-
=array([20, 21, 22, 23])>, <tf.Tensor: id=41, shape=(4,),
dtype=int64, numpy=array([-20, -21, -22, -23])>)
value: (<tf.Tensor: id=44, shape=(4,), dtype=int64, numpy-
=array([24, 25, 26, 27])>, <tf.Tensor: id=45, shape=(4,),
dtype=int64, numpy=array([-24, -25, -26, -27])>)
value: (<tf.Tensor: id=48, shape=(4,), dtype=int64, numpy-
=array([28, 29, 30, 31])>, <tf.Tensor: id=49, shape=(4,),
dtype=int64, numpy=array([-28, -29, -30, -31])>)
value: (<tf.Tensor: id=52, shape=(4,), dtype=int64, numpy-
=array([32, 33, 34, 35])>, <tf.Tensor: id=53, shape=(4,),
dtype=int64, numpy=array([-32, -33, -34, -35])>)
value: (<tf.Tensor: id=56, shape=(4,), dtype=int64, numpy-
=array([36, 37, 38, 39])>, <tf.Tensor: id=57, shape=(4,),
dtype=int64, numpy=array([-36, -37, -38, -39])>)
```

For your convenience, here is a slightly more condensed and clearer version of the output from Listing 3.19:

```
[ 0,  1,  2,  3],    [ 0,  -1,  -2,  -3]
[ 4,  5,  6,  7],    [-4,  -5,  -6,  -7]
[ 8,  9, 10, 11], [ -8,  -9, -10, -11]
[12, 13, 14, 15], [-12, -13, -14, -15]
[16, 17, 18, 19], [-16, -17, -18, -19]
[20, 21, 22, 23], [-20, -21, -22, -23]
[24, 25, 26, 27], [-24, -25, -26, -27]
[28, 29, 30, 31], [-28, -29, -30, -31]
[32, 33, 34, 35], [-32, -33, -34, -35]
[36, 37, 38, 39], [-36, -37, -38, -39]
[40, 41, 42, 43], [-40, -41, -42, -43]
[44, 45, 46, 47], [-44, -45, -46, -47]
. . . .
[96, 97, 98, 99], [-96, -97, -98, -99]
```

## Combining the TF 2 `zip()` and `take()` Operators

The `zip()` operator processes two elements at a time, in a pairwise fashion. Think of two lines of people waiting at the entrance to a movie theatre with double doors. After opening the doors, a pair of people – one from each line – enters the theater.

Listing C.3.20 shows the content of `tf2_zip_take.py`, which illustrates how to combine the `zip()` and `take()` operators in TF 2.

### LISTING C.3.20: tf2_zip_take.py

```
import tensorflow as tf
import numpy as np

x = np.arange(0, 10)
y = np.arange(1, 11)

# create dataset objects from the arrays
dx = tf.data.Dataset.from_tensor_slices(x)
dy = tf.data.Dataset.from_tensor_slices(y)

# zip the two datasets together
d2 = tf.data.Dataset.zip((dx, dy)).batch(3)

for value in d2.take(8):
  print("value:",value)
```

Listing C.3.20 initializes the variables x and y as a range of integers from 0 to 9 and from 1 to 10, respectively. Next, the variables dx and dy are initialized as TF 2 Datasets that are created from the contents of the variables x and y, respectively.

The next code snippet defines the variable d2 as a TF 2 Dataset that combines the elements from dx and dy in a pairwise fashion via the `zip()` operator, as shown here:

```
d2 = tf.data.Dataset.zip((dx, dy)).batch(3)
```

Notice how method chaining is performed by "tacking on" the `batch(3)` operator as part of the definition of dcomb.

The final portion of Listing C.3.20 contains a loop that executes 15 times, and during each iteration, the loop prints the current contents of the variable iterator. Each line of output consists of two blocks of numbers, where a block consists of three consecutive integers. The output from launching the code in Listing C.3.20 is here:

```
value:   (<tf.Tensor:   id=16,   shape=(3,),   dtype=int64,
numpy=array([0,  1,  2])>,  <tf.Tensor:  id=17,  shape=(3,),
dtype=int64, numpy=array([1, 2, 3])>)
value:   (<tf.Tensor:   id=20,   shape=(3,),   dtype=int64,
numpy=array([3,  4,  5])>,  <tf.Tensor:  id=21,  shape=(3,),
dtype=int64, numpy=array([4, 5, 6])>)
value:   (<tf.Tensor:   id=24,   shape=(3,),   dtype=int64,
numpy=array([6,  7,  8])>,  <tf.Tensor:  id=25,  shape=(3,),
dtype=int64, numpy=array([7, 8, 9])>)
value: (<tf.Tensor: id=28, shape=(1,), dtype=int64, numpy-
=array([9])>, <tf.Tensor: id=29, shape=(1,), dtype=int64,
numpy=array([10])>)
```

## TF 2 tf.data.Datasets and Random Numbers

Listing C.3.21 shows the content of tf2_generator3.py, which illustrates how to create a TF 2 Dataset with random numbers.

*LISTING C.3.21: tf2_generator3.py*

```
import tensorflow as tf
import numpy as np

x = np.random.sample((8,2))
size = x.shape[0]

def gener():
  for i in range(0,size):
    yield (x[i][0], x[i][1])

ds = tf.data.Dataset.from_generator(gener, (tf.float64,tf.
float64))

for value in ds:
  print("value:",value)
```

Listing C.3.21 initializes the variable x as a NumPy array consisting of 100 rows and 2 columns of randomly generated numbers. Next, the variable ds is initialized as a TF 2 Dataset that is created from the contents of the variable x.

The next portion of Listing C.3.21 defines the Python function gener(), that is, a generator, for the same reason that has been discussed in previous code samples. The final portion of Listing C.3.21 prints the first line of transformed data, as shown here:

```
value:   (<tf.Tensor:   id=32,   shape=(),   dtype=float64,
numpy=0.20591749665857995>, <tf.Tensor: id=33, shape=(),
dtype=float64, numpy=0.5990477322965386>)
value:   (<tf.Tensor:   id=36,   shape=(),   dtype=float64,
numpy=0.4384201871832957>, <tf.Tensor: id=37, shape=(),
dtype=float64, numpy=0.5169209418998256>)
value:   (<tf.Tensor:   id=40,   shape=(),   dtype=float64,
numpy=0.587374875326609>, <tf.Tensor: id=41, shape=(),
dtype=float64, numpy=0.8141864916735249>)
value:   (<tf.Tensor:   id=44,   shape=(),   dtype=float64,
numpy=0.05471699195088109>, <tf.Tensor: id=45, shape=(),
dtype=float64, numpy=0.806596986559444>)
value:   (<tf.Tensor:   id=48,   shape=(),   dtype=float64,
numpy=0.8878379222956106>, <tf.Tensor: id=49, shape=(),
dtype=float64, numpy=0.9533861033011681>)
value:   (<tf.Tensor:   id=52,   shape=(),   dtype=float64,
numpy=0.4504035573049521>, <tf.Tensor: id=53, shape=(),
dtype=float64, numpy=0.6303139480618501>)
value:   (<tf.Tensor:   id=56,   shape=(),   dtype=float64,
numpy=0.84588294357816>, <tf.Tensor: id=57, shape=(),
dtype=float64, numpy=0.916291642540712>)
value:   (<tf.Tensor:   id=60,   shape=(),   dtype=float64,
numpy=0.8851826544276614>, <tf.Tensor: id=61, shape=(),
dtype=float64, numpy=0.6337544549532578>)
```

## TF 2, MNIST, and tf.data.Dataset

In addition to creating a dataset from NumPy arrays of data or from Pandas Dataframes, you can create a dataset from existing datasets. For example, Listing C.3.22 shows the content of tf2_mnist.py, which illustrates how to create a tf.data.Dataset from the MNIST dataset.

*LISTING C.3.22: tf2_mnist.py*

```
tensorflow as tf

train, test = tf.keras.datasets.mnist.load_data()
mnist_x, mnist_y = train

print("mnist_x.shape:",mnist_x.shape)
print("mnist_y.shape:",mnist_y.shape)

mnist_ds = tf.data.Dataset.from_tensor_slices(mnist_x)
```

```
#print(mnist_ds)

for value in mnist_ds:
  print("value:",value)
```

Listing C.3.22 initializes the variables train and test from the MNIST dataset, and then initializes the variables mnist_x and mnist_y from the train variable. The next code snippet initializes the mnist_ds variable as a tf.data.Dataset that is created from the mnist_x variable. The next portion of Listing C.3.22 contains a for loop that iterates through the elements in mnist_ds.

The complete output from launching the code in Listing C.3.22 is very lengthy, and you can see the full output by launching this code sample from the command line.

The next block shows you the shape of mnist_x and mnist_y, followed by a portion of the data (i.e., the pixel values) in the first image contained in the MNIST dataset.

```
mnist_x.shape: (60000, 28, 28)
mnist_y.shape: (60000,)

value: tf.Tensor(
[[ 0    0    0    0    0    0    0    0    0    0    0    0    0
 0    0    0    0
   0    0    0    0    0    0    0    0    0    0]
 [ 0    0    0    0    0    0    0    0    0    0    0    0    0    0
 0    0    0    0
   0    0    0    0    0    0    0    0    0    0]
 [ 0    0    0    0    0    0    0    0    0    0    0    0    0    0
 0    0    0    0
   0    0    0    0    0    0    0    0    0    0]
 [ 0    0    0    0    0    0    0    0    0    0    0    0    0    0
 0    0    0    0
   0    0    0    0    0    0    0    0    0    0]
 [ 0    0    0    0    0    0    0    0    0    0    0    0    0    0
 0    0    0    0
   0    0    0    0    0    0    0    0    0    0]
 [ 0    0    0    0    0    0    0    0    0    0    0    0    3    18
 18   18  126  136
   175   26  166  255  247  127    0    0    0    0]
 [ 0    0    0    0    0    0    0    0   30   36   94  154  170  253
 253  253  253  253
```

```
      225 172 253 242 195  64   0   0   0   0]
// output omitted for brevity
[   0   0   0   0  55 172 226 253 253 253 253 244 133  11
  0   0   0   0
      0   0   0   0   0   0   0   0   0   0]
[   0   0   0   0 136 253 253 253 212 135 132  16   0   0
  0   0   0   0
      0   0   0   0   0   0   0   0   0   0]
[   0   0   0   0   0   0   0   0   0   0   0   0   0   0
  0   0   0   0
      0   0   0   0   0   0   0   0   0   0]
[   0   0   0   0   0   0   0   0   0   0   0   0   0   0
  0   0   0   0
      0   0   0   0   0   0   0   0   0   0]
[   0   0   0   0   0   0   0   0   0   0   0   0   0   0
  0   0   0   0
      0   0   0   0   0   0   0   0   0   0]], shape=(28,
28), dtype=uint8)
```

If you launch the code in Listing C.3.22 from the command line, you will see the complete set of 784 (=28 x 28) pixel values.

## Working with the TFDS Package in TF 2

The tensorflow_datasets package (tfds) contains utilities for loading pre-defined datasets. Keep in mind that these are datasets that contain data, and should not confused with tf.data.Dataset. Listing C.3.23 shows the content of tfds.py, which illustrates how to display the list of available built-in datasets in TF 2 by means of the tfds package.

*LISTING C.3.23: tfds.py*

```
import tensorflow as tf
import tensorflow_datasets as tfds

# See available datasets
print(tfds.list_builders())

# Construct a tf.data.Dataset
ds = tfds.load(name="mnist", split=tfds.Split.TRAIN)

# Build your input pipeline
ds = ds.shuffle(1024).batch(32).prefetch(tf.data.experi-
mental.AUTOTUNE)
```

```
for features in ds.take(1):
  image, label = features["image"], features["label"]
```

Listing C.3.23 contains a print() statement that displays the complete list of built-in datasets in TF 2. The variable ds is initialized as the training-related data in the MNIST dataset. The next code snippet uses method chaining to invoke three operators: first the shuffle() operator (to shuffle the input data), then the batch() operator to specify 32 row per batch, and then the prefetch() method to select the first batch of data. The final code block is a for loop that takes only the first row of data from ds. The output from launching the code in Listing C.3.23 is here:

```
['bair_robot_pushing_small',  'cats_vs_dogs',  'celeb_a',
'celeb_a_hq', 'cifar10', 'cifar100', 'coco2014', 'diabetic_
retinopathy_detection',  'dummy_dataset_shared_generator',
'dummy_mnist',    'fashion_mnist',    'image_label_folder',
'imagenet2012',  'imdb_reviews',  'lm1b',  'lsun',  'mnist',
'moving_mnist',    'nsynth',    'omniglot',    'open_images_
v4',    'quickdraw_bitmap',    'squad',    'starcraft_video',
'svhn_cropped',    'tf_flowers',    'wmt_translate_ende',
'wmt_translate_enfr']
```

As you can see, the previous output contains some well-known datasets, including CIFAR10, CIFAR100, MNIST, and FASHION_MNIST (among others).

## The CIFAR10 Dataset and TFDS in TF 2

Listing C.3.24 shows the content of tfds-cifar10.py, which illustrates how to perform some processing on the CIFAR10 dataset and use lambda expressions and the map() operator to train the datasets.

### LISTING C.3.24: tfds-cifar10.py

```
import tensorflow as tf
import tensorflow_datasets as tfds

loader = tfds.load("cifar10", as_supervised=True)
train, test = loader["train"], loader["test"]

train = train.map(
    lambda image, label: (tf.image.convert_image_dtype(im-
age, tf.float32), label)
).cache().map(
  lambda image, label: (tf.image.random_flip_left_right(im-
age), label)
```

```
).map(
    lambda image, label: (tf.image.random_contrast(image,
lower=0.0, upper=1.0), label)
).shuffle(100).batch(64).repeat()
```

The code in this section is from the following *stackoverflow* post (which contains additional details):

*https://stackoverflow.com/questions/55141076/how-to-apply-data-augmentation-in-tensorflow-2-0-after-tfds-load*

## Summary

This appendix introduced you to TF 2 Datasets that are well-suited for processing the contents of normally-sized datasets as well datasets that are too large to fit in memory. You saw how to define a lambda expression and use that expression in a TF 2 Dataset.

Next, you learned about various lazy operators, including batch(), filter(), flatmap(), map(), take(), and zip(), and how to use them to define a subset of the data in a TF 2 Dataset. You also learned how to use TF 2 generators to iterate through the elements of a TF 2 Datasets.

Next, you learned how to create a TF 2 Dataset from a CSV file and then display its contents. Then you got a brief introduction to the tf.estimator namespace, which contains an assortment of classes that implement various algorithms, such as boosted trees, DNN classifiers DNN regressors, linear classifiers, and linear regressors.

Finally, you learned about various other important aspects of TF 2, such as the tf.keras.layers namespace, which contains an assortment of classes for DNNs (Dense Neural Networks) and CNNs (Convolutional Neural Networks).

# INDEX